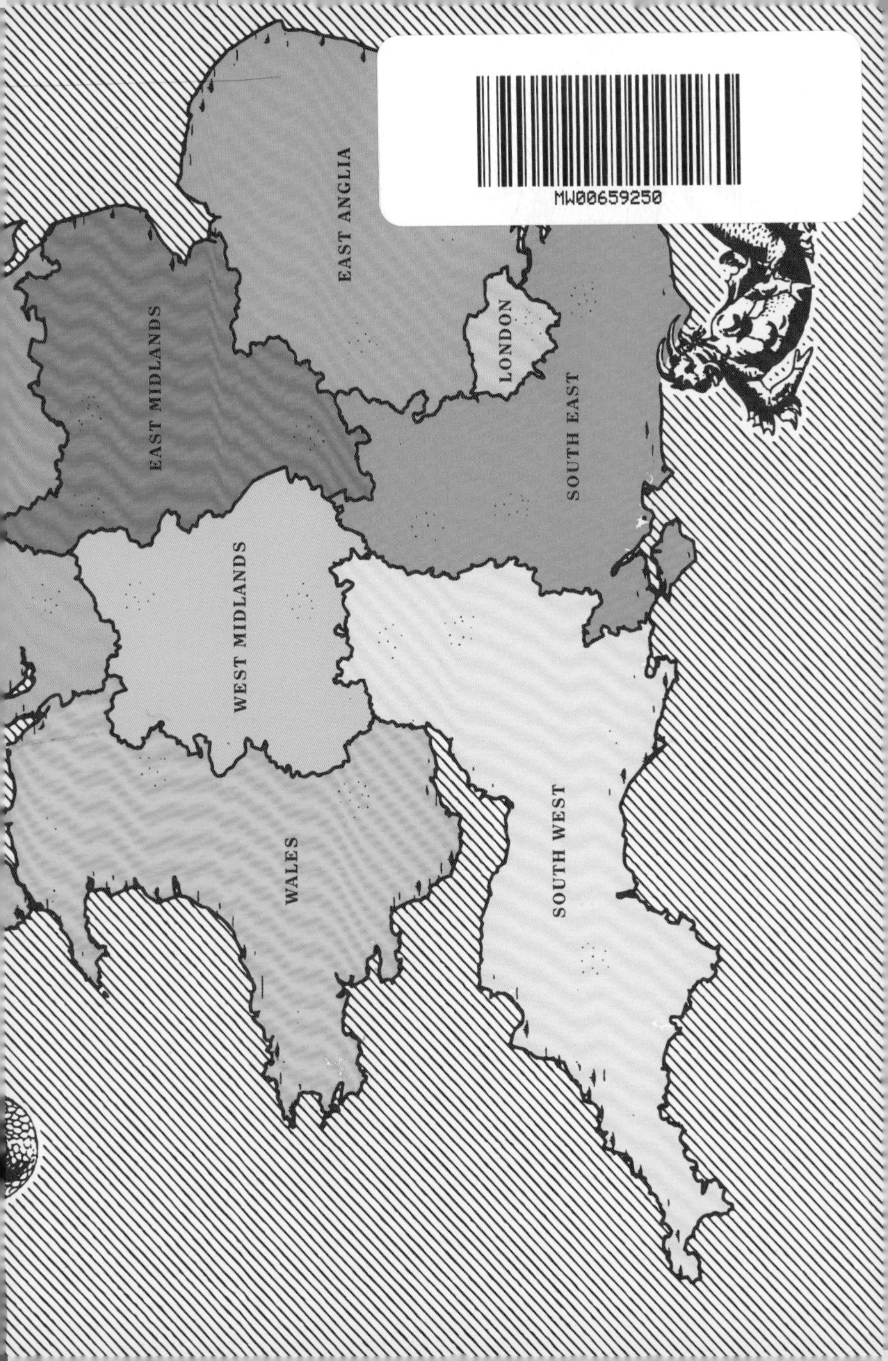
EAST ANGLIA
LONDON
SOUTH EAST
EAST MIDLANDS
WEST MIDLANDS
WALES
SOUTH WEST

THE HELLEBORE GUIDE TO OCCULT BRITAIN AND NORTHERN IRELAND

The Hellebore Guide to OCCULT BRITAIN and Northern Ireland

HELLEBORE BOOKS
ENGLAND, 2021

THE HELLEBORE GUIDE TO OCCULT BRITAIN
AND NORTHERN IRELAND
First published in December 2021

EDITOR:
Maria J. Pérez Cuervo

ART DIRECTOR:
Nathaniel Hébert

MAP EDITOR:
Chris Esson

ICONS AND MAP DESIGN:
Janina Reinhardt

CONTRIBUTORS:
Reggie Chamberlain-King (Northern Ireland)
Elizabeth Dearnley (Scotland)
Verity Holloway (South East, East Anglia, London)
Maria J. Pérez Cuervo (South West, Wales, Film
and TV locations, Literary locations)
John Reppion (North East, North West)
Katy Soar (East Midlands, West Midlands)

Special thanks to Catherine Winter for her support.

ISBN 978 – 1 – 3999 – 0696 – 8
www.helleborebooks.com

Contents

PREFACE, 11

1. THE SOUTH WEST
Cornwall, 16
Devon, 26
Dorset, 33
Somerset, 38
Gloucestershire, 43
Wiltshire, 48

2. THE SOUTH EAST
Hampshire, 58
Berkshire, 62
Buckinghamshire, 64
Oxfordshire, 66
Isle of Wight, 70
Surrey, 72
Sussex, 74
Kent, 76

3. LONDON, 80

4. EAST ANGLIA
Essex, 102
Bedfordshire, 105
Hertfordshire, 106
Cambridgeshire, 108
Suffolk, 110
Norfolk, 117

5. WEST MIDLANDS
Herefordshire, 122
Worcestershire, 124
Warwickshire, 128
Staffordshire, 132
Shropshire, 138

6. EAST MIDLANDS
Northamptonshire, 146
Leicestershire and Rutland, 148
Lincolnshire, 151
Nottinghamshire, 155
Derbyshire, 159

7. NORTH WEST
Cheshire, 166
Greater Manchester, 170
Merseyside, 173
Lancashire, 178
Cumbria, 182
Isle Of Man, 188

8. NORTH EAST
Yorkshire, 194
County Durham, 204
Tyne And Wear, 206
Northumberland, 208

9. WALES
Gwent, 216
Glamorgan, 220
Dyfed, 224
Powys, 226
Gwynedd, 228
Clywd, 236

10. SCOTLAND
Lowlands, 242
Highlands, 258
Islands, 264

11. NORTHERN IRELAND
Fermanagh, 274
Armagh, 278
Down, 282
Tyrone, 284
Derry, 286
Antrim, 288

IMAGE CREDITS, 296
FILM, TV, AND
LITERARY REFERENCES, 304
INDEX, 306

Preface

THIS BOOK is not meant to be an exhaustive guide to British folklore. There are wonderful books that have covered this ground already—particularly, the legendary Reader's Digest volume *Folklore, Myths and Legends of Britain* and the splendid *The Lore of the Land*, by Jennifer Westwood and Jacqueline Simpson. What we've attempted to create here is a travel guide for folk horror and occult fans, to help them plan their next trip according to their personal interests. It is designed to be read in the comfort of your living room, but also to be carried in your bag on a day out as you experience the spirits of place and conjure the scenes that captivated you from the screen or from the pages of a book.

Every corner of these isles is steeped in myth and legend. Focusing on the darker side, we've selected places that we believe are worth visiting, that give a sense of the occult richness of this land, and that have inspired the books, films and television programmes we love. We hope it leads to many wonderful journeys.

Maria J. Pérez Cuervo
November 2021

I. The South West

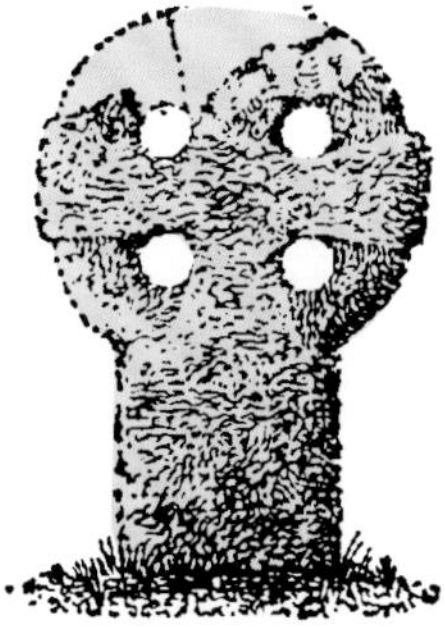

Fig. 70.

Cornwall, 16
Devon, 26
Dorset, 33
Somerset, 38
Gloucestershire, 43
Wiltshire, 48

I. THE SOUTHWEST - CORNWALL

SNOWSHILL MANOR
BELAS KNAP
LONG BARROW
GLOUCESTERSHIRE
PAINSWICK
LYDNEY PARK
THE DEVIL'S PULPIT
ROYAL CRESCENT
& THE CIRCUS
AVEBURY
ROMAN BATHS
STANTON DREW
WILTSHIRE
WOOKEY HOLE CAVES
STONEHENGE
GLASTONBURY
SOMERSET
CHILTON CANTELO
KNOWLTON CHURCH
AND EARTHWORKS
ST MARY'S
CHURCH
BADBURY RINGS
DEVON
PILSDON PEN
CERNE ABBAS
HIGHCLIFFE-
ON-SEA
DORSET
DORSET COUNTY MUSEUM
THE SINGING BARROWS
DARTMOOR

Cornwall

BODMIN MOOR

This remote granite moorland is one of Cornwall's Areas of Outstanding Beauty, and every corner of it is steeped in legend. Dark, bleak, and desolate, punctuated by ruins of the Cornish mining industry, its archaeological remains hint at its importance during the Bronze Age.

The Ritual Landscape

The Hurlers: SX258714, **Rillaton Barrow:** SX260719, **Trethevy Quoit:** SX259688

The concentration of late Neolithic and Bronze Age monuments on the south-eastern edge of Bodmin Moor suggests they formed a ritual landscape, perhaps marking a processional route across the moors.

The Pipers, to the west of The Hurlers, are a pair of outlying upright stones standing close together, said to be the petrified remains of two men who played music on a Sunday.

The Hurlers are three adjacent stone circles, said to be the remains of men petrified for playing the ancient game of hurling on a Sunday. As is often the case with stone circles in Britain, the stones are said to be uncountable.

Rillaton Barrow, to the north west of The Hurlers, is the largest barrow in Cornwall, probably the burial place of a Bronze Age tribal chief. The site was said to be haunted by the ghost of a druidic priest who offered passers-by a drink from a golden cup which could never be emptied. In 1837, stone workers discovered a human skeleton and some grave goods. Among these was a beautiful gold cup, now kept at the British Museum but, by all accounts, empty.

On the southern edge of the moor stands **Trethevy Quoit**, a Neolithic portal dolmen that may have also served as a place of worship.

The Legend of Jan Tregeagle

BODMIN MOOR is said to be haunted by the demonic ghost of Jan Tregeagle, whose greed in life made him commit the wickedest sins. Rumoured to have sold his soul to the Devil, this folk villain—Cornwall's own Faust or Wandering Jew—was in reality a 17th century magistrate who lived in the area of Bodmin.

When Tregeagle died he was buried in an unmarked grave in St Breock's churchyard. To avoid hell, his spirit was tasked with emptying the waters of Dozmary Pool with a limpet shell which had a hole in it. After four years of incessant work, when he dared to rest for a moment the Devil and his hounds descended upon him. Tregeagle fled, looking for sanctuary in the chapel of Roche Rock. Narrowly escaping, he carried on performing impossible tasks in several places in Cornwall, but it is Bodmin Moor that is haunted by his howling ghost, and by the Devil and his hell hounds, chasing him for all eternity.

Dozmary Pool
SX194744
Aside from being linked to the legend of Jan Tregeagle, Dozmary Pool is known as the place from where the Lady of the Lake emerged to King Arthur the sword Excalibur, and where Sir Bedivere returned it after Arthur's death in the Battle of Camlann.

Roche Rock
SW991596
This black granite plateau was associated with witches and demons long before Jan Tregeagle. In the 15th century, a chapel consecrated to St Michael the archangel, who defeated the Devil, was built on it.

MÊN-AN-TOL

Mên-An-Tol: Penzance, TR20 8NU · SW426349
Lanyon Quoit: SW429336
Men Scryfa: SW426352
Nine Maidens of Boskednan: SW434351

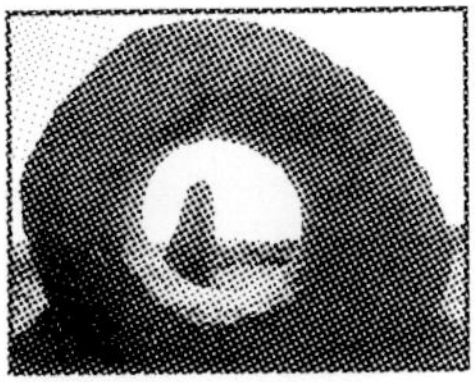

A view through the Mên-An-Tol holed stone

This group of standing stones may have been part of a Neolithic or early Bronze Age circle. "The Stone With the Hole", also known as The Devil's Eye, or The Crick Stone, has been the focus of rituals since ancient times. Placing two brass pins on top of the stones to interpret their movements was a way of foretelling the future. Women who wanted to become pregnant were told to pass through the stone seven times backwards on a full moon. Children with rickets would be cured if they passed nine times through the hole, naked. The stones were said to cure ague and the King's Evil, or scrofula, traditionally curable only by touch of the reigning monarch.

Within a mile or so are a few sites worth exploring: Lanyon Quoit, built around 2500 BCE; the inscribed standing stone of Men Scryfa; the Nine Maidens of Boskednan; and the rocky summit of Carn Galva, the natural feature around which this ceremonial landscape was likely arranged.

The Merry Maidens

THE MERRY MAIDENS OF BOLEIGH

Penzance, TR19 6BQ · SW432245

This late Neolithic stone circle is said to be the petrified remains of nineteen maidens who dared to dance on a Sunday and were turned to stone as a punishment. The two musicians who were playing for the Merry Maidens ran away, but weren't fast enough. They were turned into the two stones now known as The Pipers.

The central stone of Boscawen-Un

BOSCAWEN-UN

Penzance, TR19 6EJ · SW412273

This Bronze Age ceremonial site is unusual in that it has a central stone (slightly southwest of the true centre). This central stone is believed to have been used for ritualistic purposes in the Neolithic era, thus predating the circle of nineteen stones—a number often associated with the cycle of the moon.

For the 1978 *Doctor Who* story "The Stones of Blood", Boscawen-Un became The Nine Travellers, a stone circle located in the fictional Boscombe Moor where a druidic sect perform their blood sacrifices. The goddess they worship, the Cailleach, is later revealed to be a bloodthirsty alien criminal able to command the stones at will.

Tregeseal East stone circle.

TREGESEAL STONE CIRCLE

Tregeseal: St Just, Penzance, TR20 8PU · SW386323
Carn Kenidjack: SW387329

The late Neolithic stone circle of Tregeseal is associated with the fairy folk, and the nearby Carn Kenidjack, a natural outcrop with a distinctive shape, is known as the site of the Devil's wrestling match. The story goes that two miners saw the cairn glowing as they were returning home, and found a group of demon wrestlers in a match presided over by the Devil.

BOLEIGH FOUGOU

Rosemerryn, Lamorna, Penzance, TR19 6BN · SW436252

The grounds of Rosemerryn house hide a mysterious underground tunnel that can be visited if requested. Lined with stone walls and roofed with stone slabs, it has a main passage which is over 10m long, as well as a side chamber. Books mention a shallow carving known as the "god of the fogou" on the left-hand side: a figure with its right arm raised up, now almost completely faded.

These kinds of structures, named fogous (pronounced foo-goos), appear in Iron Age settlements in Cornwall and Scotland, but their original purpose is still unknown. During the English Civil War, Boleigh Fougou was used as a hiding place for Royalists, and legend has it that it was a meeting place for witches, used for ceremonies by the inhabitants of the house.

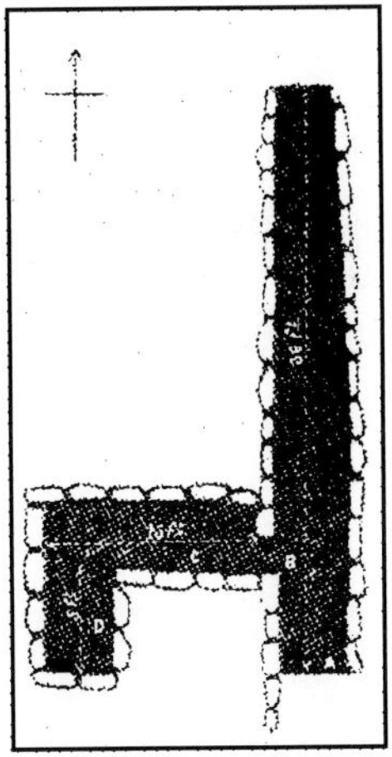

Boleigh Fougou

The Stones of Lamorna

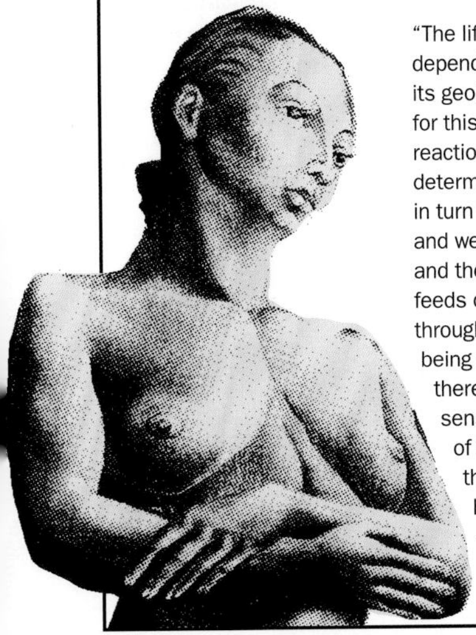

Head 1931 (Self Portrait)

"The life of a region depends ultimately upon its geological substratum, for this sets up a chain reaction which passes, determining their character, in turn through its streams and wells, its vegetation and the animal life that feeds on this, and finally through the type of human being attracted to live there. In a profound sense also the structure of its rocks gives life to the psychic life of the land."
— Ithell Colquhoun, *The Living Stones*, 1957.

BRITISH surrealist painting, writer, and occultist Ithell Colquhoun (1906–1988) spent the latter part of her life in Cornwall, first in Vow Cave, a now demolished hut near Lamorna Gate, then in the village of Paul. In *The Living Stones* she painted a portrait of a land built on layers of myth and magic, from her arrival in 1949 to her visits to Padstow, Harlyn or Tintagel. For Colquhoun, Lamorna's numinous quality emanates from the land itself.

Museum of Witchcraft and Magic

MUSEUM OF WITCHCRAFT AND MAGIC

The Harbour, Boscastle, PL35 0HD / £

From its origins in Castleton on the Isle of Man, where it was originally founded by Cecil Williamson in 1951, with Gerald Gardner as its resident witch, the Museum of Witchcraft and Magic has moved between different locations before settling in Boscastle in 1960.

Dedicated to European witchcraft and magic, it contains objects linked with folk magic, ceremonial magic, Freemasonry, and Wicca.

Porthcurno Cove

PORTHCURNO COVE

TR19 6JX · SW397220

The treacherous coastline near Porthcurno Cove was said to be frequented by witches. They would gather near the Logan Rock, a naturally balancing stone near Treen, invoking storms that would make ships crash against the rocks, so they could steal their cargoes.

There are also tales of a ghostly ship gliding over the sea and the sand before vanishing like smoke. Some have linked the hauntings to a strange sailor who used to live in the area, and whose servant was said to be the Devil himself.

MERLIN'S CAVE

Atlantic Rd, Tintagel, PL34 0DS · SX051890

This 330-foot long cave formed by marine erosion is said to have been the abode of the wizard Merlin of Arthurian legends. Not far from it are the ruins of Tintagel Castle, the rumoured birth place of King Arthur himself.

ISLES OF SCILLY

Bants Carn Burial Chamber: SV909123
Abbey Gardens, Tresco: TR24 0QQ · SV892141 / £

This cluster of islands is associated with the mythical land of Lyonesse, swallowed by the sea in a single night, and said to be the home of the Arthurian hero Tristan. The abundance of megalithic chambered cairns explains why they were thought to be Isles of the Dead, where the remains of people from elsewhere were brought to be buried. Particularly worth seeing are the Bants Carn Burial Chamber and, below it, the Iron Age village of Halangy Down and its cemetery, both on St Mary's Island.

In the old Abbey Gardens at Tresco there stands a four-feet-long holed stone. Couples would pass their hands through the holes and join them to become engaged. It was also used as a wishing-stone, or, according to J.C. Tonkins, to break spells, where "a ring would be passed through the holes with some incantations".

Bants Carn Burial Chamber

Lanyon Cromlech

Star Castle, St. Marys

The Great Beast In Cornwall

"Shortly before the war, the man whom the sensational press is still calling 'the wickedest man in the world' paid a visit to Mousehole. This was a gift to gossip... The accusations range widely in seriousness; some merely assert he was a bad influence in the district; others, that he and his followers danced naked round the stone circle at Tregaseal; yet others that he performed rites on the rocks above Trevelloe; that he revived Druidic cults involving human sacrifice and that his disciples in the locality still resort to this practice, kidnapping women for the purpose... Not a word of factual evidence is brought forward in substantiation."
— Ithell Colquhoun , *The Living Stones*, 1957.

Carn Cottage
Private land, Zennor, TR26.
Hidden amongst the bracken, not far from the B3306, stands an abandoned cottage known as Aleister Crowley's house. The cottage, now situated on private land, acquired a sinister reputation after the mysterious death of Katherine Laird Cox in 1938.

Ka Cox, as she was known, was a member of the Neo-Pagans and a friend of the Bloomsbury Group who became the first woman magistrate in Cornwall. After the war, she settled at Eagle's Nest, below Carn Cottage, which was then rented by a couple, Gerald and Ellaline Vaughan. The Vaughans welcomed a child in 1937, after which Ellaline's mental health rapidly deteriorated.

On May 21st 1938, the couple invited Ka Cox to their cottage. Whatever happened that evening, by the end of it Cox was dead. It was rumoured that the Vaughans had befriended Aleister Crowley, who had dragged them into a web of black magic, and that, as a local magistrate, Cox intended to help them. There were also rumours that the locals, who didn't want the couple nearby, were gaslighting them by moving piles of stones and casting strange shadows. Some people say that Crowley had summoned a demon at the cottage, and that it was fear that killed Ka Cox and drove Gerald mad, eventually sending him into Bodmin Asylum.

That Crowley's diary entries don't place him anywhere near Cornwall at the time seems irrelevant—he was, however, in the area of Penzance a few months later, in August, visiting his son Ataturk and staying in The Lobster Pot in Mousehole.

Gerald Vaughan was never interned in Bodmin Asylum.

As for Ka Cox, her death certificate states she died of a brain haemorrhage. Nevertheless, Crowley's enduring notoriety seems fused with this little cottage, whose isolated location—among the ancient megaliths of the moorland, in an area brimming with witchcraft folklore—guarantees that it will continue to inspire lurid tales.

The nearby **Zennor Quoit** (TR26 3BU · SW468380) is a megalithic burial chamber said to possess mystical powers and a certain sentience: any stones removed from the structure would mysteriously find their way back in the middle of the night.

Devon

DARTMOOR

With its treacherous bogs, dramatic rock formations, prehistoric remains, and the merciless River Dart, said to claim one life every year, Dartmoor remains one of Britain's most haunted landscapes in the popular imagination.

Church Of St Pancras

Widecombe-in-the-moor, TQ13 7TA · SX718768

On October 21st, 1638, the so-called Cathedral of the Moor was hit by a terrible thunderstorm while the congregation was listening to the parson's sermon. The debris killed at least four parishioners and injured sixty. Set into the floor are grave slabs of Roger Hill and his wife, two of the victims.

Legend has it that the thunderstorm was caused by the Devil when he rode a black horse to the church to collect the soul of a young gambler who had made a pact with him and fell asleep during the service. After snatching him away, they rode into the storm, and, as they were reaching Birch Tor, the four aces from the young man's pack of cards fell to the ground. It is said that four of the ancient field enclosures that can be seen from Warren House Inn are shaped like the symbols from a pack of cards: clubs, diamonds, hearts, and spades.

Before reaching the church, the Devil had stopped at Tavistock Inn, in nearby Poundsgate, where the parishioners noticed his cloven feet. He ordered a mug of ale, which hissed as it went down his throat. His mug left a mark on the counter, and when he left, the coins he'd used to pay turned to dried leaves.

The Lych Way

From Bellever Forest (Yelverton, PL20 6TW · SX656771) to St Petroc's Church, Lydford (EX20 4BH · SX509847), **Coffin Stone:** SX677733

This twelve-mile ancient pathway was followed by the farmers who lived on the northern fringe of the moor to go to the church in Lydford. It was also a corpse road, trod by those who carried their dead to be buried in consecrated ground, so it is also known as the Way of the Dead or the Corpse Way, along which ghostly processions and spectral monks are still seen.

On Dartmeet Hill stands the Coffin Stone, with initials and crosses carved in. It was used as a resting place for the coffin while the bearers stopped to have a refreshment before continuing their journey to the church, and it is said that the Devil hit it with a shaft of lightning when a man of ill repute was rested on it.

Vixen Tor

Private land, SX542742

The highest free-standing rock on Dartmoor stands on private land, but it can be seen from the distance. It is associated with the legend of the witch Vixana, who lived in a cave at the foot of the tor. Vixana had the power to conjure up mist, so any unwary travellers who passed the bog nearby would meet their end. But a handsome young man of the moor who had the power to see through the mist and to make himself invisible pushed her to her death—according to one version, she crashed on the rocks below the tor, while others say she drowned in the bog.

The Footprints of a Gigantic Hound

SIR ARTHUR CONAN DOYLE (1859–1930) captured the eerie wilderness of Dartmoor in Sherlock Holmes' most gothic adventure, *The Hound of the Baskervilles*, incorporating local legends with supernatural elements that somehow hit harder when contrasted with the detective's rationalist methods.

WISTMAN'S WOOD

PL20 6SR · SX612774

With the branches of gnarled trees forming a sinister canopy and the large, moss-carpeted boulders making it hard to traverse, this high-altitude oak wood has long been a setting for supernatural occurrences. Its very name derives from "wisht", meaning "eerie" or "pixie-led".

The wood is believed to have been a sacred grove of the druids, where they held their rituals, near the so-called Druids' Stone. But it is also supposed to be the dwelling place of the demonic Wisht Hounds, who hunt across the moors at night, searching for unwary travellers to drag them to the Otherworld. Some say their leader is the Devil, others that it is Woden, Old Crockern (the spirit of the moor who lived at Crockern Tor), or the diabolical squire from Buckfastleigh, Sir Richard Cabell.

FOX TOR MIRES

Fox Tor: SX626698

About one kilometre north-east of Fox Tor lies Fox Tor Mires, the swampy land—a peat bog—that became Grimpen Mire in *The Hound of the Baskervilles*. Do not venture into it, it's extremely treacherous.

IPPLEPEN

St Andrew's Church:
TQ12 5RZ
2 Wesley Terrace:
TQ12 5SX

Park Hill House is the former home of journalist Fletcher Robinson (1870–1907), who told all these Dartmoor legends to his friend Arthur Conan Doyle. Robinson died of enteric fever and peritonitis at 36, which Conan Doyle and others attributed to a mummy's curse. His grave is in St Andrew's churchyard, where also lies Reverend Robert Duins Cooke, who assisted Robinson in his location scouting for the Scottish author.

The house on 2 Wesley Terrace was the residence of Conan Doyle's chauffeur on Dartmoor, Henry Baskerville, whose surname he borrowed for the novel. The men went drinking at the nearby 13th-century Old Church House Inn, reputedly extremely haunted.

HOLY TRINITY CHURCH

Church Hill, Buckfastleigh,
TQ11 0EZ

Known locally as The Sepulchre, the pagoda-like building on the south side of the church in Buckfastleigh's churchyard contains the body of the wicked local squire Sir Richard Cabell, the inspiration for Conan Doyle's Sir Hugo Baskerville, rumoured to have sold his soul to Satan. The squire's hounds are said to howl outside his grave in stormy nights; and demons often linger outside the mausoleum, trying to retrieve his soul.

If you run around his tomb seven times and place your finger through the bars of the mausoleum (or your little finger into the keyhole of the wooden door), Cabell will come out of his grave and gnaw at it.

Lewtrenchard Manor

LEWTRENCHARD

Lewtrenchard Manor and Church of St Peter: Okehampton, EX20 4PN

Lewtrenchard Manor, now an exclusive hotel, was the former home of Sabine Baring-Gould (1834–1924), the Anglican priest-scholar who studied werewolves, ghosts and superstitions, penning classics such as *A Book of Ghosts* and *The Book of Were-Wolves*. Many of the bench ends at the Parish Church of St Peter were restored by him. He's buried in the churchyard, next to his wife.

THE DEVIL'S STONE, SHEBBEAR

Shebbear, EX21 5RU

Each year, at 8pm on November the 5th, the bellringers of Shebbear turn over a rock in the village square to avoid a calamity falling on the village. Legend has it that the Devil himself is trapped under the one-tonne rock. To trap him again for another year, the stone needs to be flipped over.

SAUNTON SANDS

Saunton Sands: EX33 1LQ

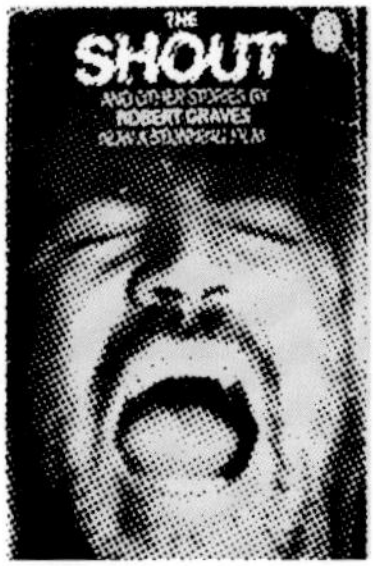

The dunes of Saunton Sands and the adjacent Braunton Burrows on the North Devon coast become a mythical landscape in Jerzy Skolimowski's *The Shout* (1978), based on a story by Robert Graves. In real life, Saunton Sands is a paradise for surfers, but it is hard not to hear the echoes of Crossley's death shout when it's not crowded.

The Shout (1978)

Drake and the Devil

KNOWN to posterity as the naval hero who defeated the Spanish Armada, Tavistock-born Sir Francis Drake (1540–1596) was also a slave trader and a privateer who circumnavigated the globe. Perhaps due to his preternatural prowess at sea, he remains associated with tales of witchcraft and pacts with the Devil.

DEVIL'S POINT

Admiralty Rd, Stonehouse, Plymouth, PL1

Legend has it that Drake met the Devon witches at this headland to cast storms against the Spanish Armada—eventually defeating it. Echoes of their incantation are supposedly heard on windy nights at Devil's Point.

BUCKLAND ABBEY

Yelverton, PL20 6EY/ £

The architect of Drake's home was said to be none other than the Devil himself, to whom the seafarer sold his soul in exchange for his extraordinary skills.

Posterity turned Drake into one of the Sleeping Heroes of English folklore. On his deathbed, aboard his ship off the coasts of Panama, he asked his drum to be sent back to Buckland Abbey, with the idea that if anyone beat on it, he would return to lead his country. Drake's drum was kept at Buckland Abbey for many years, and it is now in The Box, Plymouth. It's supposed to beat of its own accord whenever the country is in danger—and apparently did so in 1914, at the beginning of World War I.

Dorset

THE SINGING BARROWS

Weymouth, DT3 5PU · SY689847

These six Bronze Age burial mounds are said to emit sounds reminiscent of an eerie singing. If you place your ear close to the apex at noon, you'll hear an otherworldly music coming from the ground. The singing has been attributed to the fairy folk.

John Pinney, Azariah's great-great nephew.

BETTISCOMBE

Pilsdon Pen: DT6 5NX · ST412012

Dorset's most famous screaming resident is the alleged skull of one of Azariah Pinney's slaves. Pinney was one of the Monmouth rebels, who escaped from the noose in exchange for a ransom and was shipped in 1685 to the island of Nevis in the West Indies. He made his fortune there by enslaving Africans in sugar plantations.

The screaming skull was believed to belong to one of his slaves, an 18th-century man who was buried away from his native land against his wish. The site of his grave was haunted by his shrieks, which only stopped when his skull was taken to Bettiscombe Manor. Any attempts to remove it were said to bring calamity upon the house's occupants.

Bettiscombe Manor isn't far from Kennetmead Coppice and it is now a private home. The skull was reportedly examined in 1963, when it was revealed to be that of a European woman who died 3,000 to 4,000 years ago. The skull could have come from the well at the foot of the nearby Iron Age fort on Pilsdon Pen, where it might have been placed with ritual purposes—as an offering to water spirits.

The screaming skull of Bettiscombe Manor

The Church of St Mary the Virgin in Batcombe

ST MARY'S CHURCH, BATCOMBE

Batcombe, Dorchester, DT2 7BG

St Mary's Church is associated with the legend of John Minterne, or Conjuring Minterne, a 16th century squire who lived in nearby Newlands Manor. One day, he was riding his horse near the village when he remembered he'd left his grimoire of black arts open on his desk. Fearing his secrets would be revealed, he spurred his horse to take a shortcut crossing over the church. The horse's hooves knocked off a stone pinnacle on the tower and the Conjuror landed at the so-called Pitching Plot near the church. This spot is said to bear the imprint of the horse's hooves. The pinnacle was left untouched for many years, and it stands crooked to this day.

KNOWLTON CHURCH AND RINGS

Knowlton, Wimborne, BH21 5AE

"There lingers in the air some flavour of the sinister and macabre."
– Archaeologist Jacquetta Hawkes (1910–1996)

FEW sites convey the transition from the old religion to Christianity as starkly as this ruined 12th-century church standing at the centre of an ancient ritual henge earthwork, part of one of the most important Neolithic and Bronze Age ceremonial complexes in the south of England.

Aside from the Church Circle, there are three more earthworks on the site, largely destroyed by ploughing: the North Circle, the Southern Circle (the largest), and the so-called Old Churchyard, which, in spite of its name, is also prehistoric. The tree-covered mound to the east of the Church Circle is the Great Barrow, the largest round barrow in Dorset.

The church was in use until the 17th century. A 19th-century legend says it was abandoned after its bell was stolen by the Devil, who threw it into the river Allen, from where it's never been retrieved. Naturally, there are also tales of hauntings: a horse and its rider gallop through the

Before his death, Minterne requested that his body should lie "neither in the church nor out of it". His stone sepulchre was built into the wall of the family chapel, but the chapel was demolished during 19th-century restorations. Inside the church are two plaques commemorating him.

HIGHCLIFFE-ON-SEA

Southridge: 3 Highland Avenue, Highcliffe-on-Sea, BH23 5LN
Mill House: 14 Mill Lane, Highcliffe-on-Sea, BH23 5LA

Between 1938–1945, Gerald Gardner (1884–1964) and his wife, Dorothea, lived in a house named Southridge in the small town of Highcliffe-on-Sea. It was during his time here that he was initiated in the secrets of witchcraft by a woman he referred to as "Old Dorothy"—a crucial event in his

earthwork before they pass through the church walls and disappear; a face peers out of the upper window in the church tower; and a weeping woman has been seen kneeling down outside the church.

To the north west of Knowlton Church and Rings is the **Dorset Cursus**, formed by twin banks of chalk that stretch for over six miles. This is where ritual processions would run in ancient times, possibly towards the ceremonial centre of Hambledon Hill.

About 20 miles from Knowlton is the site of **Badbury Rings (ST963030)**, next to which was a Romano-Celtic temple. The Iron Age hill fort is supposedly haunted by the ghostly cavalcade formed by King Arthur and his knights and by a wounded Roman warrior who likes to press his face against car windows.

Badbury Rings

Chewton Mill House

life, since he would later be regarded as the father of Modern Witchcraft. Historian Philip Heselton argues Gardner's initiation might have taken place in Chewton Mill House, then home to a wealthy woman named Dorothy Clutterbuck, possibly the Old Dorothy from Gardner's writings.

CERNE ABBAS

DT2 7AL

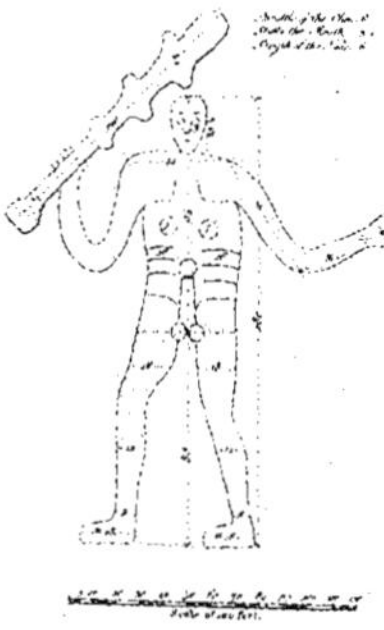

The carved figure which dominates the slope above the town of Cerne Abbas with his conspicuously erect 30ft penis was long thought to be an ancient pagan deity. The first written reference to it dates from 1694, and recent tests on the soil suggest it dates from Medieval times or later. Joseph Bettey argued it was probably carved in the 1650s to satirise Oliver Cromwell, whose admirers compared to Hercules—Hercules is traditionally depicted with a club in his hand and an animal skin, both of which the giant originally had.

The giant's phallus

Even if its origins aren't as ancient as previously thought, the figure has been the centre of fertility rituals through the centuries: infertile couples were encouraged to have sex within its outline to be able to conceive. It is said that on May Day the sun rises on the hill in line with his erection. A maypole would be raised just above its head, in a small Iron Age enclosure known as The Trendle.

The viewpoint on A352, just north of Cerne Abbey, gives the best views of the giant—and, while you're there, the ruins of the abbey are also worth a visit.

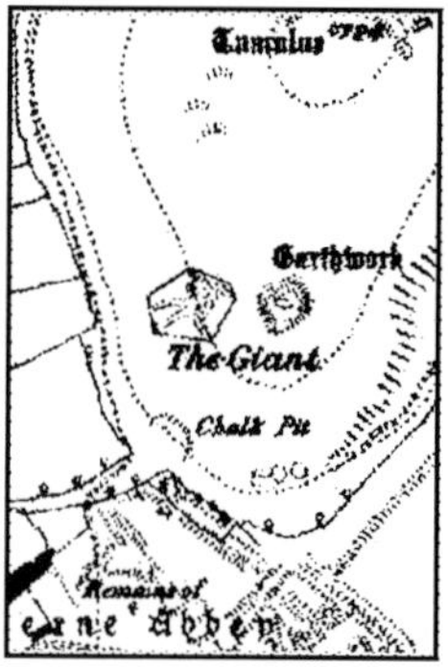

Ordnance Survey, 1891

THE DORSET OOSER

Dorset County Museum: DT1 1XA

This fearsome-looking hollow wooden head was probably a mask used to humiliate those whose behaviour strayed from the norm. In the 19th century it was under the ownership of the Cave family, of Holt Farm in Melbury Osmond. The original mask has disappeared, but a replica is kept at the Dorset County Museum.

Ooser replica at the Dorset County Museum

A photograph of the original Dorset Ooser

Bligh Bond's Psychic Archaeology

In 1908, Glastonbury Abbey was excavated by Frederick Bligh Bond (1864–1945), an architect and antiquarian who, along with his friend Captain John Allan Bartlett, used automatic writing to uncover its missing features in what is considered the first documented instance of psychic archaeology.

Bligh Bond also designed the cover of the Chalice Well, where the two interlocking circles forming the esoteric symbol *Vesica Piscis* are surrounded by the Glastonbury Thorn. The latter—a form of common hawthorn found in the area—is said to have grown from where Joseph of Arimathea thrust his staff when he visited Glastonbury, bringing with him the Holy Grail.

Somerset

GLASTONBURY

Glastonbury Abbey: Magdalen Street, BA6 9EL
St John the Baptist Church: High Street, BA6 9DR
Chalice Well Gardens: Chilkwell Street, BA6 8DD
Glastonbury Tor: ST512386

AT THE core of this small Somerset town lie the ruins of a once great monastery that claimed to hold the grave of King Arthur. Dominating the landscape for miles is Glastonbury Tor, the conical hill crowned by the tower of St Michael's church, once an island surrounded by marshy land. It is associated with the isle of Avalon, and thought to be the doorway to the Celtic otherworld, guarded by Gwyn ap Nudd, King of the Fairies and leader of the Wild Hunt. The Tor has been a site of pilgrimage since Medieval times, and the seven levels of terraces around it are used as a ritual maze to climb to the top.

An abbot of Glastonbury

At the foot of the Tor are the Chalice Well Gardens, whose red spring, rich in ferrous oxide, is said to flow from the place where Joseph of Arimathea left the Holy Grail. The Victorian pump house nearby harbours the so-called White Spring, rich in calcium, and also said to have healing properties.

Dion Fortune's Avalon

Occultist Violet Firth, best known as Dion Fortune (1890-1946), was one of the most influential ceremonial magicians in the twentieth century. Born in North Wales and brought up in the West Country, she established a base for her occult group in Glastonbury. In 1924, they bought an old orchard at the foot of Glastonbury Tor and built a veranda and a series of huts. Their so-called Chalice Orchard is now occupied by a house built by a Welsh architect who named it Berachah, which means "place of special spiritual blessing". It is currently a guest house that overlooks the Chalice Well Gardens. Fortune was buried in the churchyard of St John's Church.

Limestone caves at Wookey Hole

WOOKEY HOLE CAVES

The Mill, High St, Wookey Hole, Wells, BA5 1BB / £

The limestone caves at Wookey Hole, used for around 45,000 years, are one of the main tourist attractions in Somerset. The legendary witch of Wookey Hole is supposed to have been a woman who lived in the cave and who, having been spurned by her lover, acquired the habit of cursing young couples. One of her victims later became a monk in Glastonbury Abbey. Seeking revenge, he entered the caves and blessed the underground water, splashing the witch with it. As a result, she turned into the stalagmite known as the Witch of Wookey.

The section called The Witch's Chimney contains a large number of apotropaic marks, which would have been carved to offer ritual protection against evil, probably dating from 1550-1750.

A view at Stanton Drew, 1723

The Great Cicle at Stanton Drew

STANTON DREW

BS39 4EW · ST600633

Lesser known than Stonehenge and Avebury, Stanton Drew is now thought to be a much more important ritual site than previously imagined. The three stone circles that form it were built during the late Neolithic period, around 2500BCE.

- The Great Circle is one of the largest stone circles in the country, with 26 surviving upright stones surrounded by a deep circular ditch. Inside the circle were nine concentric rings of wooden posts.
- The north-east circle is the smallest of the three circles. Within it were four timber posts standing in a square.
- The three large stones in the garden of the village pub are known as The Cove.

As recorded by John Aubrey in 1664, locals called the stones "The Wedding", believing they were the petrified guests of a wedding party celebrated on a Saturday night. The fiddler stopped playing at midnight, respecting the rule of not dancing on a Sunday, but a handsome fiddler—the Devil in disguise—carried on playing, faster and faster, until the wedding guests collapsed and turned into stone. The three stones from The Cove are said to be the parson, bride, and bridegroom. At midnight on the sixth day after a full moon, the stones are said to come alive and walk down to the river Chew to have a drink.

Counting the stones is supposed to be an impossible task that will bring calamity or death. After John Wood did so in 1749, a violent storm shook the village. It is said that a baker once placed a loaf of bread on each stone to help him count them, but the bread disappeared every time he turned his back.

John Aubrey

Druidical Fancies

The Circus: Bath, BA1 2ET
Royal Crescent: Bath, BA1 2LX

IN HIS survey of Stanton Drew, antiquarian and architect John Wood the Elder (1704-1754) argued that the three stone circles that form it corresponded to the solar, lunar, and Earth cycles, and that the complex had been used as a university for the druids. Inspired by these conclusions and those he drew from his survey of Stonehenge, Wood designed one of the most famous buildings in Bath, The Circus, where each house was decorated with a pagan or occult motif. The Circus, whose diameter matches the circumference of the stone circle at Stonehenge, is said to represent the sun, and the Royal Crescent, also designed by Wood, is said to represent the moon. Brock Street, which links the two, is supposed to follow an ancient ley line. When seen from above, the layout of The Circus, Brock Street, and Queen Square forms the shape of a key—a recurring motif in Wood's work, and a symbol of occult secrets.

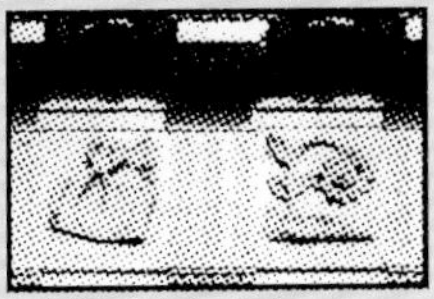

Occult motifs at The Circus

Roman Baths and Abbey

Gorgon's head, a symbol of Sulis MInerva.

ROMAN BATHS, BATH

Abbey Churchyard, Bath, BA1 1LZ/ £

This sacred spring supplied water for a Roman Bath House that attracted visitors from across the Empire. Between 60–70CE, a temple was built next to it. The Roman Baths are one of the main tourist attractions in modern day Britain, with the waters still emanating an ancient sacredness. A suspended walkway above the temple courtyard allows visitors to see the space consecrated to the goddess Sulis Minerva, where sacrifices were performed.

The museum contains an intriguing stone found in 1965, set up by L. Marcius Memor, a haruspex—a priest with the power of divination who was consulted before important decisions. Many objects have been retrieved from the sacred spring: coins, votives, or offering to the goddess, and even curses inscribed on sheets of lead or pewter.

Higher Farm, Chilton Cantelo.

ST JAMES'S CHURCH AND HIGHER FARM, CHILTON CANTELO

Yeovil, BA22 8BE

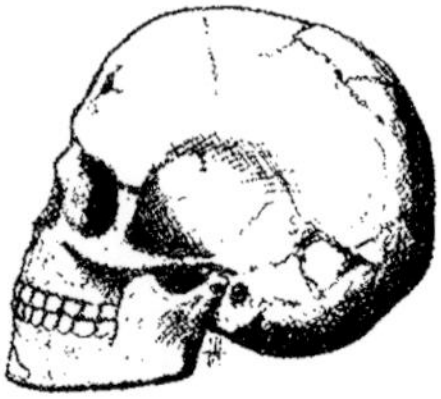

Opposite St James' church in Chilton Cantelo is a farm that remains associated with a screaming skull, supposedly the skull of Theophilus Broome, a repentant Royalist who, horrified by the acts committed by these troops, defected to the Roundheads. Broome died in 1670. His body lies in a tomb within St James's Church, but his skull, as he instructed, remains in the farmhouse. As in other screaming skull legends, any attempts to bury it would result in endless shrieking. The skull can only be seen by written appointment.

Gloucestershire

PAINSWICK

Rococo Gardens: Gloucester Rd, Painswick, GL6 6TH / £
Church: 3 New St, Painswick, GL6 6XH
Beacon House: New Street, Painswick, GL6 6UN

The town of Painswick in the Cotswolds was the centre of one the most notable examples of Pan worship in Britain. In the 18th century, this cult was presided over by Benjamin Hyett of Painswick House. Reverend John Wiltshire mentions a spring procession that ran from the church to the woods near Hyett's house—a procession that might have involved ritual dressing up, drinking, and debauchery, all in honour of the half-goat god.

Pan's Lodge, the Pan-inspired pavilion Hyett built about a mile away from his house, near Bull's cross, was sadly demolished some time before 1824, but a compelling statue of Pan by Jan Van Nost still welcomes the visitors to Hyett's Rococo Gardens. The cult of Pan also inspired some architectural details in Beacon House, built by church-warden John Garden in 1757-59, now privately owned. Its Rococo plasterwork was a revelry of Pagan motifs and depictions of the god—unfortunately, most of it was shipped off to America in the 1920s.

The procession died out in the 1830s, but was revived five decades later by the vicar W. H. Seddon, a folklore enthusiast who incorporated it to the clipping ceremony that was still celebrated each September. Seddon had a statue of Pan installed in the churchyard, which became the meeting point for the procession. In 1950 a more conservative vicar decided to end it all, burying the statue at an unknown location in the church's graveyard.

The Great God Pan, Arthur Machen, 1894

LYDNEY PARK ESTATE, LYDNEY

Lydney, GL15 6BT/ £

This 17th century estate, occupied by the Bathurst family since 1719, contains the ruins of a Roman temple dedicated to Nodens, a Romano-Celtic deity associated with healing and the sea, whom Arthur Machen and H.P. Lovecraft incorporated to their works.

At the healing shrine in Lydney, visitors would follow a ritual that involved bathing at the thermae and making offerings to Nodens through a funnel in his temple before the incubation, or sacred sleep, where supplicants received a visit from the god revealing a cure for their ailments, often presented in a cryptical manner. A mosaic found at the site suggests these visions were once interpreted by a priest named Victorinus.

The Roman Temple

The Cursed Ring

LYDNEY PARK was riddled with tunnels, the vestige of Roman mining activities. Locals referred to the site as Dwarf's Hill, believing it inhabited by the Little People. In the 1920s, it was excavated by Mortimer and Tessa Verney Wheeler, who enlisted the help of a young Anglo-Saxon scholar from Oxford to investigate Nodens. The scholar's name was J. R. R. Tolkien (1892–1973).

The landscape and its legends might have influenced Tolkien's Middle Earth, but perhaps even more so did a curious find that had been unveiled in the 19th century excavations—a tablet bearing this inscription: "To the God Nodens. Silvanus has lost a ring. He has [vowed] half its value to Nodens. Amongst all who bear the name of Senicianus, refuse thou to grant health to exist, until he bring back the ring to the Temple of Nodens." Curiously, the ring had already been found—not at Lydney, but a hundred miles away, in a ploughed field at Silchester, in 1785, identified by the inscription "Senicianus, may you live in God". Believed to have inspired Tolkien's epic fantasy, the ring is now kept at the Vyne Museum at Basingtoke.

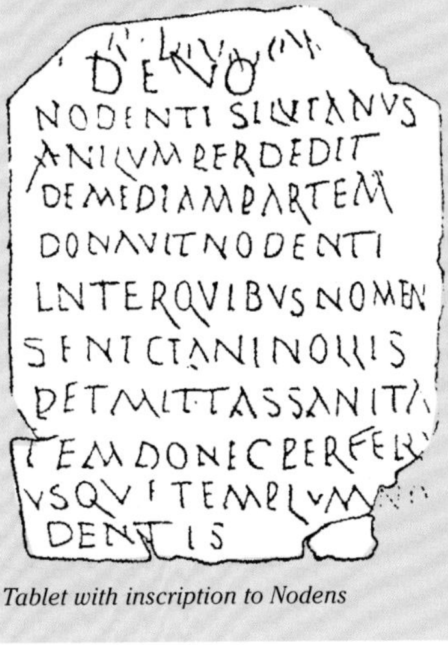

Tablet with inscription to Nodens

J.R.R Tolkien

Belas Knap burial chamber

BELAS KNAP LONG BARROW

Winchcombe, Cheltenham, GL54 5AL · SP020254

This impressive Neolithic long barrow was built around 3000 BCE and used for successive burials over a long period of time. 19th-century excavations uncovered the remains of 31 people in its chambers.

The burial chambers are entered from the sides of the barrow. Its false entrance may have worked as a "spirit door", so the dead would be able to access the offerings brought to the tomb by their descendants.

Exterior of Snowshill Manor

SNOWSHILL MANOR

Snowshill, Broadway, WR12 7JU / £

This 16th-century manor house was acquired by architect and collector Charles Paget Wade in 1919. While he stayed at the garden's Priest's House, he restored the main building to house his collection of curios, containing over twenty suits of Samurai armour, ancient musical instruments, clocks, and other unusual objects.

Wade's interest in astrology is patent in the name of the southernmost and northernmost rooms, Zenith and Nadir, and in the zodiacal motifs that can be seen around the property and in the garden. But the house's most intriguing feature is a room that cannot be visited: at the top of the house, accessible after climbing up onto a small minstrel's gallery, is the secret room he named The Witches' Garrett.

When Wade moved to the Caribbean he donated the house and its contents to the National Trust. They found a room decorated with magic circles and astrological and alchemical symbols, and a collection of objects used in ritual practice: cauldrons, animal skulls, the mummified left hand of an Egyptian, and the so-called Wondrous Candle, which had the power to reveal hidden treasures.

The National Trust donated Wade's ritual objects to Cecil Williamson, whose Museum of Witchcraft was then in the nearby town of Bourton-on-the-Water. Most of them are now in the museum's current location at Boscastle, though some were damaged in the 2004 flood.

Charles Paget Wade

THE DEVIL'S PULPIT

Tidenham, Chepstow, NP16 J7R · ST542995

This rocky viewpoint overlooks Tintern Abbey and the village of Tintern, on the Welsh bank of the river Wye. It is said that the Devil created the pulpit to preach to the monks and lure them to his side.

View from Devil's Pulpit

Wiltshire

AVEBURY

SN8 1RF

Developed over a thousand years, this Neolithic complex likely served as a stage for rituals and processions. The relationship between the community and the landscape evolved during this time, which suggests that the purpose and function of the complex may have changed too.

Avebury Stone Circles

THE LARGEST stone circle in Europe—and the only one with a village within—dates back to 2600 BCE and contains two smaller circles inside. At the centre of the inner southern circle are the remains of the Cove, said to be the most sacred space—it's been speculated that it was reserved for supernatural beings, deities or ancestor spirits.

During the Middle Ages, many stones were toppled and buried by the locals, who associated the site with the Devil. Some of these associations persist today: the largest stone by the south entrance is known as the Devil's Chair, said to expel black smoke from its top when the Devil is in residence. Running around the stone a hundred times widdershins (anticlockwise) will summon him.

The Diamond Stone near the north-western entrance is said to cross over to the other side of the road when the clock strikes midnight.

For *Children of the Stones* (1977, bottom right), Avebury became Milbury, a seemingly idyllic village surrounded by a Neolithic stone circle. With its ideas of cosmic horror, psychic control, petrification, and Gothic repetition, and with its haunting, atonal music score, the series still holds its reputation as one of the scariest children TV programmes ever made.

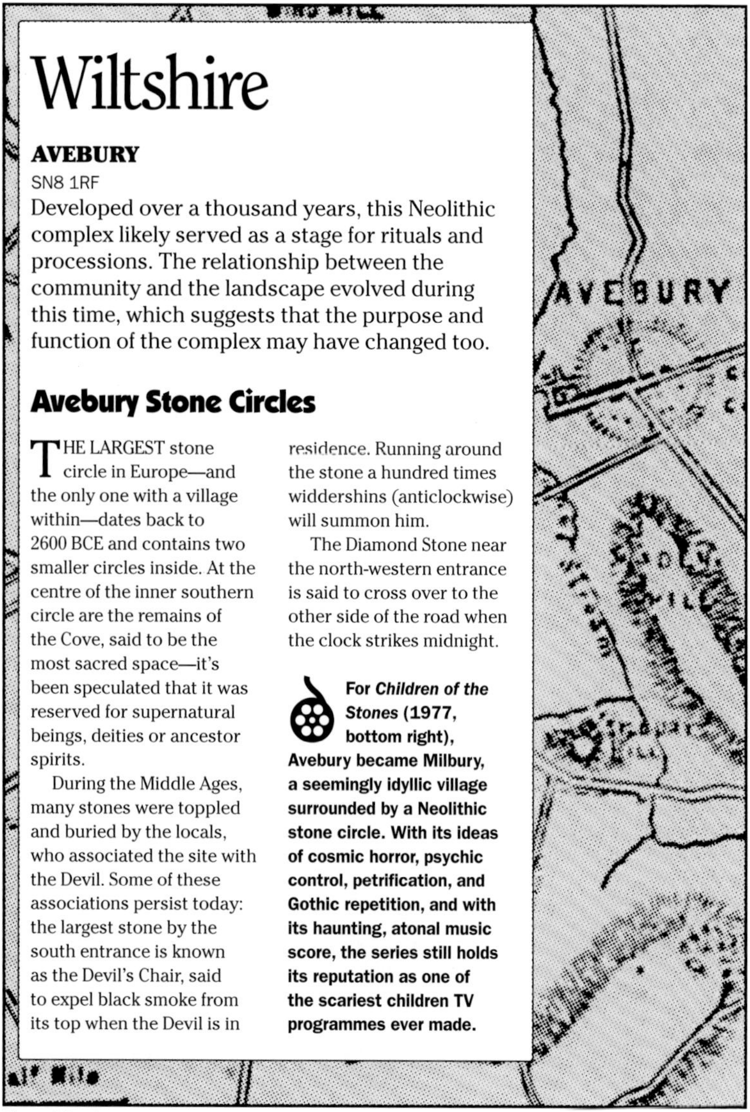

Map of Avebury

The Serpent Temple

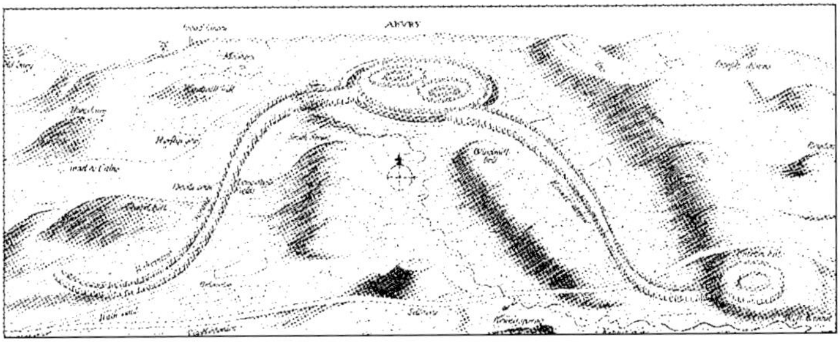

IN THE 18th century, antiquarian William Stukeley (1687–1765) interpreted Avebury as a serpent temple built by the Druids. The Sanctuary was the head of the serpent, whose body ran from the West Kennet stone avenue to the main stone circle before re-emerging again. Stukeley believed this "winged-globe and serpent" represented the cycle of death and rebirth.

Avebury's Ritual Landscape

The Sanctuary

SN8 1EY · SU118680

The purpose of this complex of concentric timber and stone settings, now represented by concrete posts, is unknown. Large quantities of human bones have been found here, which suggests it might have been used in death rituals.

West Kennet Avenue

SN8 1RD · SU105695

This avenue would have marked the route between the stone circles and The Sanctuary, around 2.5km away. Almost each tall, narrow stone is paired up with a triangular one opposite, probably representing the masculine and the feminine. Human bones have been found at the foot of the stones—likely either the remains of important people or sacrificial offerings.

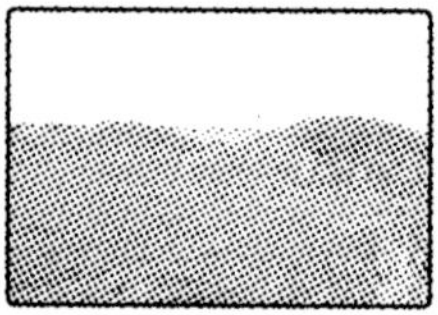

The Seven Barrows

SN8 1QG · SU118681

The name Seven Barrows is deceiving: there are at least twelve on Overton Hill, near The Sanctuary. Excavations in this Bronze Age barrow cemetery have uncovered bronze daggers, ceramics, and bone implements.

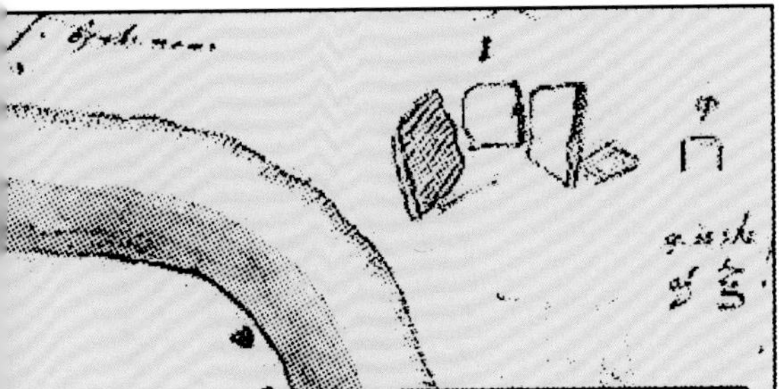

Silbury Hill
SN8 1QH · SU100685
Built between 2470-2350 BCE, Silbury Hill is the largest artificial prehistoric mound in Europe. Imposing and totemic, it's all the more intriguing because we don't know its purpose or the meaning it had for the people who built it. Half a million tonnes of material were used in its construction, and the scale of it gave way to the myth that it was built by the Devil. Traditionally, it was thought to be the resting place of a King Sil or Zel, who was buried on horseback—his ghost is said to ride across the landscape at night, wearing a golden armour.

West Kennet Long Barrow
SN8 1QH · SU104678
This Neolithic chambered tomb was used to bury nearly fifty people before its chambers were blocked. It might have been constructed in several phases, possibly evolving from small shrines to appease local spirits.

Bowing to Pan

Archaeologist Alexander Keiller (1899–1955), the heir of a marmalade emporium, bought Avebury in the late 1930s to return it to its Neolithic glory. He cleared away many of the more modern buildings and self-funded an excavation that uncovered and re-erected stones previously thought lost.
Although Keiller was fascinated by witchcraft and the occult, he was dismissive of Margaret Murray's Witch-Cult hypothesis and of Stukeley's view of Avebury as a Serpent Temple. But while he was living in Avebury Manor he seemed to have been interested in the great god Pan. An anecdote told in his biography by Linda Murray says that one Hallowe'en night he brought some friends to the garden of the manor house, which used to have a statue of Pan. Carrying a phallic symbol, the group bowed three times before the goat-footed god, chanting witch-like incantations.

STONEHENGE

Salisbury, SP4 7DE / £

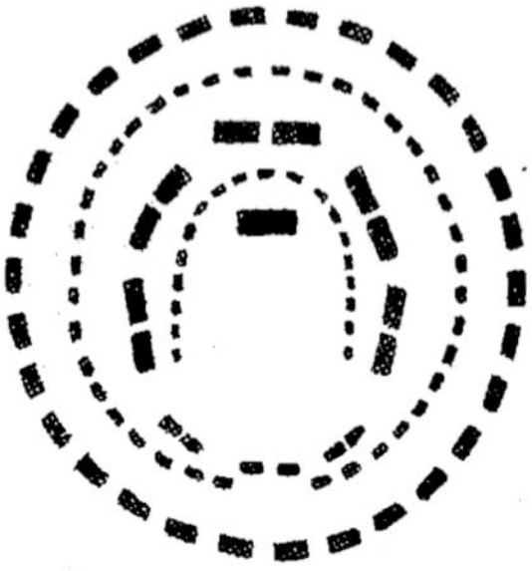

GROUND PLAN.

The only surviving lintelled stone circle in the world—and the most architecturally sophisticated, according to UNESCO—was built in several stages. The early henge monument dates from 5,000 years ago, and the stone circle was erected in about 2,500 BCE. Two types of stones were used: the sarsens, which form the inner horseshoe and the outer circle, came from Marlborough Downs; the bluestones—the smallest ones—came from the Preseli Hills in Wales. Curiously, folklore says Merlin built the circle with stones transported magically from Ireland.

Ideas about Stonehenge's function have changed through the centuries. 17th and 18th-century antiquaries believed it to be a temple of druids, and some thought that blood sacrifices were performed within it. Nowadays, however, it is generally accepted that Stonehenge was a prehistoric temple aligned with the movements of the sun, as well as one of the largest cremation cemeteries known in Britain.

A large recumbent stone outside the central monument is known as the Slaughter Stone. Rainwater accumulates on the shallow depressions on its surface, turning a rusty red due to the iron content of the stone reacting with a type of algae. This might have fuelled legends of blood staining its surface—supposedly the blood of sacrificial victims.

View of Stonehenge

Stonehenge (restored), from Cassell's Illustrated History of England.

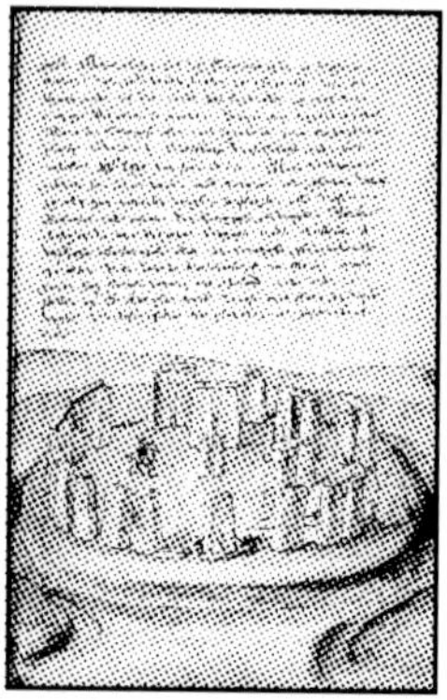

Drawing of Stonehenge, Netherlands, circa 1574

The Stonehenge Landscape

THE landscape around the stones is peppered with ancient burial mounds and earthworks. Many believe that The Avenue—over 2.5km long and predating the stone circle—might have been the original entrance to Stonehenge, and that the Cursus—the 5,000-year-old rectangular enclosure that extends for nearly two miles—was used for processions.

Most of these monuments and earthworks are aligned with the movements of the sun. Two miles away from Stonehenge, to the north-east, is the site of Woodhenge, once formed by six concentric ovals of standing posts and built to align with the midsummer. The Southern Circle, another timber monument nearby, is also aligned with the midwinter sunrise.

Approach to Stonehenge from the east.

II. The South East

Hampshire, 58
Berkshire, 62
Buckinghamshire, 64
Oxfordshire, 66
Isle of Wight, 70
Surrey, 72
Sussex, 74
Kent, 76

II. THE SOUTH EAST

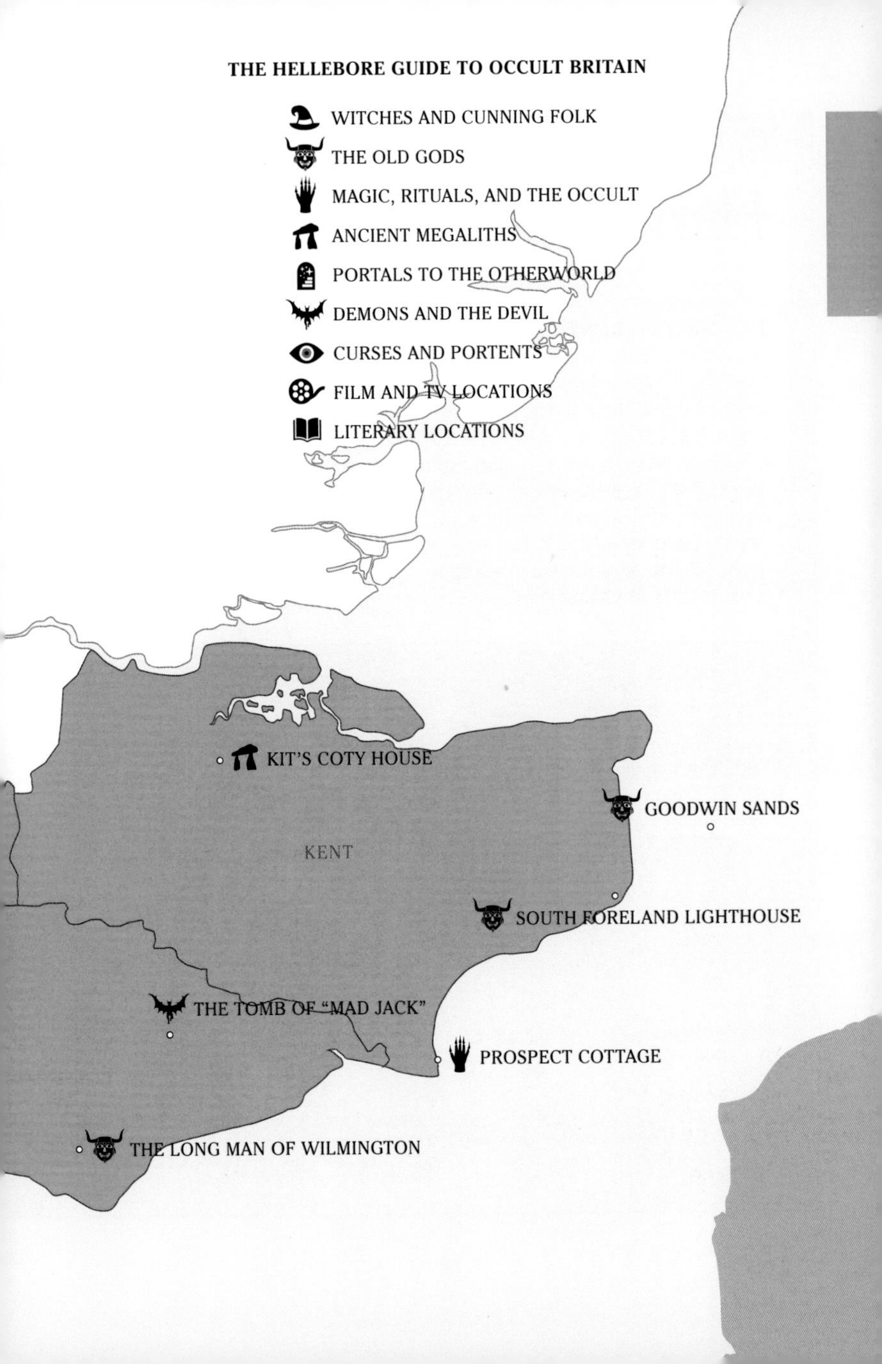
THE HELLEBORE GUIDE TO OCCULT BRITAIN
WITCHES AND CUNNING FOLK
THE OLD GODS
MAGIC, RITUALS, AND THE OCCULT
ANCIENT MEGALITHS
PORTALS TO THE OTHERWORLD
DEMONS AND THE DEVIL
CURSES AND PORTENTS
FILM AND TV LOCATIONS
LITERARY LOCATIONS
KIT'S COTY HOUSE
GOODWIN SANDS
KENT
SOUTH FORELAND LIGHTHOUSE
THE TOMB OF "MAD JACK"
PROSPECT COTTAGE
THE LONG MAN OF WILMINGTON

Hampshire

THE NEW FOREST

Covering an area of 219 square miles, the New Forest is known as the site where King William II was fatally wounded with an arrow in 1100, a spot now marked with the iron-clad Rufus Stone. But these woodlands also have many occult ties, particularly with Gerald Gardner's New Forest coven and with the paranormal investigations of Arthur Conan Doyle.

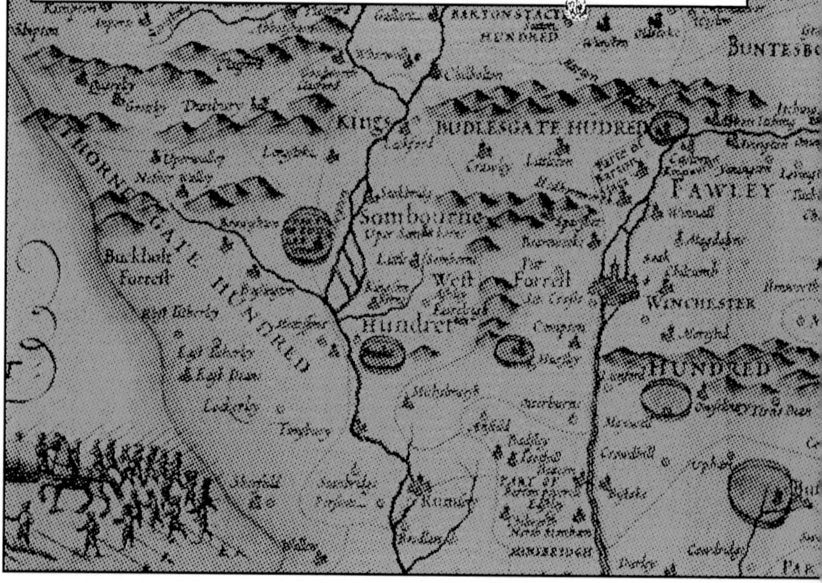

GLASSHAYES HOUSE

78 High St, Lyndhurst, SO43 7NL

Built in the early 19th century as a country retreat, Glasshayes House later became the abode of the 1st Duc de Stacpoole, an Anglo-French Catholic aristocrat who operated a local smuggling ring. After his death, Glasshayes passed through several hands before being turned into a hotel in the early 20th century. By then, the house was so haunted it captured the attention of Sir Arthur Conan Doyle, who visited it often and held séances in the octagonal tower under the auspices of the manageress. In 1912, the Sherlock Holmes author redesigned the building's façade so its features would represent the journey to the afterlife: life, death, afterlife, spirits in harmony, and higher spiritual place. The seven Devil Squares over the entrance signal each of the ghost sightings that took place during the construction work. Glasshayes has recently been under threat from developers, though Conan Doyle's involvement and the unusual concept behind its redesign might protect the historic features of the house. Developers should also fear the ghost of the Duc de Stacpoole, who has previously directed his wrath towards builders. He is said to celebrate an annual ball for the dead on the 7th of July, when otherworldly music can be heard in some of the rooms.

BROCKENHURST

St Nicholas' churchyard: Church Lane, SO42 7UB

A marble headstone in St Nicholas' churchyard commemorates the life of the New Forest Snakecatcher, Brusher Mills (1840–1903), born in Emery Down. The eccentric Mills made a living by trapping snakes with a forked stick and a sack, selling them to London Zoo, where they would be used as fodder for other animals. Victorian tourists saw him as a local attraction and purchased his snake ointments and snake skeletons as souvenirs.

BEAULIEU

Palace House: John Montagu Building, SO42 7ZN / £

The magnificent Cistercian Abbey that gave Beaulieu its name was largely destroyed during the Dissolution, but its gatehouse became the core of the Palace House, an imposing Gothic mansion regarded as one of the Treasure Houses of England. Sir Arthur Conan Doyle famously held a séance here, enthralled by tales of ghostly monks haunting the abbey ruins, and by visions of a Lady in Blue. Visitors have reported hearing Gregorian chants and smelling incense in one of the rooms of the house. Both events are regarded as bad omens. Beaulieu is also associated with two wise women. 18th-century Mary Dore was thought to have the ability to shapeshift into a hare, a bird, or a cat. After her death, the Duke of Montagu, who had a soft spot for her, paid for her gravestone, but the locals defaced and destroyed it, and her exact place of burial is now lost. In the 19th century, lovesick villagers would call on Witchy White, a charwoman at Palace House who specialised in love spells.

Arthur Conan Doyle was so enamoured with the New Forest he bought a country home on the edge of Bignell Wood. He is buried next to his second wife in the graveyard of All Saint's Church, Minstead.

Operation Cone of Power

"You cannot cross the sea.
You cannot cross the sea.
Not able to come.
Not able to come."
(Incantation used in Operation Cone of Power)

Brockenhurst: SO42
The Naked Man: BH24 4HY · SU245017
Ferny Knapp: SU255033

ON LAMMAS EVE of 1940, founding members of Gerald Gardner's New Forest coven instituted Operation Cone of Power to magically prevent the German High Command invading Britain. According to historian Philip Heselton, the group met near Brockenhurst in the New Forest, by an ancient gallows tree known as The Naked Man. They walked to Ferny Knapp Inclosure, where they performed the ritual, dancing naked around a magic circle. Gardner claimed two of the seventeen witches involved died of pneumonia shortly afterwards.

The Witch of Burley

Burley: BH24

PARADING the town in a black cloak with her pet jackdaw on her shoulder, Sybil Leek (1917–82) was once dubbed "Britain's most famous witch". The intelligent and flamboyant Leek was a witch, psychic, and antique dealer who came to prominence after witchcraft laws were repealed in 1951. As High Priestess of the Horsa coven in the New Forest, Leek never shied away from publicity and wrote dozens of books on astrology, reincarnation, and herbalism. Nowadays, Burley revels in a kitsch atmosphere, boasting several emporiums of all things cauldrons-and-broomsticks. "I have been called 'a legend'," said Leek, "which seems a rather delightful thing to be."

Berkshire

Wayland's Smithy

WAYLAND'S SMITHY

Ashbury, SN6 8NX

The Saxon god of metalworking is said to have a special connection to this Neolithic long barrow nestled in the green Berkshire countryside. The stone structure is built on an older, simpler burial site dating to around 3590 and 3555 BCE. Fourteen individuals were interred in the original barrow, some of whom appeared to have died violently and been scavenged by animals prior to burial.

The name Wayland's Smithy has been attached to the site since at least the year 955CE, and later stories tell of travellers hitching their tired horses to the stones and finding them carefully reshoed by a generous spirit. Wayland was a figure borrowed from Norse invaders—known as Völundr, he was an Alfar, a spirit or god associated with burial mounds and fallen heroes—and was named in *Beowulf*.

Wayland the Smith, 1893

ALDWORTH

St Mary's Church, Bell Ln, RG8 9SB

The church of the tiny parish of Aldworth houses nine 14th-century effigies, each seven feet tall, commemorating the De La Beche family, said to be giants in stature and deed. As powerful knights, generations of De La Beche men were embroiled in royal intrigue, travelling on crusades and returning with great wealth. Colonel Symonds, the Royalist diarist, wrote of the giants during the English Civil War, noting that four of the effigies were known to locals as John Long, John Strong, John Never Afraid, and John Ever Afraid. John Ever Afraid, lost to time, was set in an alcove in the south wall of the church. In life, the knight was said to have sold his soul to the Devil, who told him he would collect his soul when he was buried inside or outside the church. John Ever Afraid beat the Devil by being buried neither inside nor outside.

St Mary's Church

OAKLEY COURT

Windsor Rd, Water Oakley, Windsor, SL4 5UR

It is likely that this spellbinding Victorian Gothic manor house appears in at least one of your favourite films. Its moody, gargoyle-adorned exteriors can be spotted in folk horror favourites *The Reptile* and *Plague of the Zombies*, and, more famously, in Hammer's *Dracula* and *The Rocky Horror Picture Show*. The mansion is now a hotel whose corridors pay tribute to its cinematic credentials.

Double horror show!

Buckinghamshire

Francis Dashwood, 11th Baron le Despencer

THE HELLFIRE CAVES

Hellfire Caves: HP14 3AH / £

West Wycombe Park: High Wycombe, HP14 3AE / £

This man-made network of caves was first excavated in the mid-1700s on behalf of noted politician and mischief-maker Sir Francis Dashwood, who quickly repurposed them as a meeting place for his notorious Hellfire Club. The caves, stretching for a quarter of a mile underground, begin with a church of Gothic flint and snake downwards past an underground stream named the river Styx into several quasi-ecclesiastical banqueting halls. The Hellfire Club was founded as a joke at the expense of self-important

"secret societies", but soon found a reputation as a blasphemous cult of devil worshippers. In reality, the club's activities were centred around fancy dress and carousing. The caves are open for modern explorers, although the addition of electric light has spoiled some of the atmosphere of this Gothic party venue.

Dashwood embellished his estate at West Wycombe Park with a collection of pagan follies—among them, the scandalous Temple of Venus, reconstructed in the 1980s, whose entrance is said to represent "the entrance by which all come to the world".

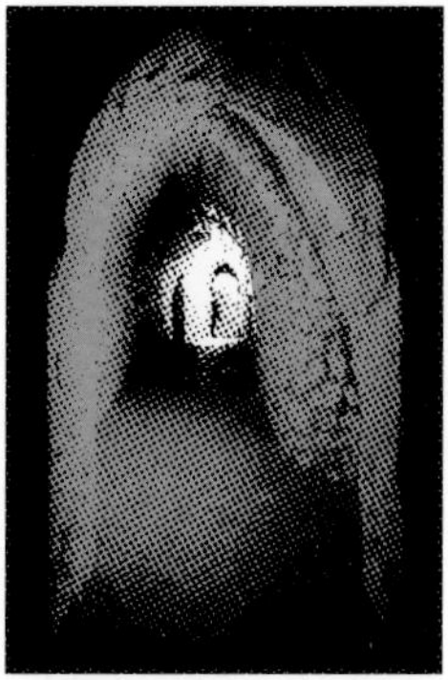

Hellfire Caves

TAPLOW COURT

Cliveden Road, Taplow, SL6 0ER

This mid-19th century house doubled up as Hempnell Medical College in *Night of the Eagle*, where professor Norman Taylor's hardline scepticism turns into sheer terror as he quite literally confronts his demons. Sadly, the stone eagle from the dénouement isn't part of the original building, but the smaller eagles at the gates will still bid you welcome. The house is now the headquarters of a lay Buddhist society, and its grounds are open to the public on certain dates throughout the summer.

Night of the Eagle, 1962

Taplow Court

HAMBLEDEN

RG9 6RP

Hambleden remains virtually unchanged since it stood in for Heddaby, the sleepy village that harbours a sinister secret in the Nigel Kneale-penned folk horror *The Witches* (1967). Eagle-eyed visitors might recognise the houses of the main characters, the post office, the butcher's, and the front of Heddaby school (Hambleden's village hall). The Elizabethan manor house opposite the church—which in real life isn't derelict—became the home of the Baxes.

St Mary the Virgin, Hambleden

Oxfordshire

OXFORD

A seat of learning since the 11th century, the towers and spires of Oxford are no strangers to alchemy, occult philosophy, and esoteric knowledge. Its sandstone walls have inspired some of the best-known fantasy sagas of our time, and they seem to be wrapped in an aura of magic.

Bodleian Library

Broad St, OX1 3BG

The second largest library in Britain and one of the oldest in Europe houses a collection of books and manuscripts of occult interest, such as the 15th-century Rawlinson necromantic manuscript or the Cabbalistic treatise known as the Book of Soyga.

Balliol College

OX1 3BJ

Co-founded by Devorguilla of Galloway, who travelled everywhere with the embalmed heart of her deceased husband, Balliol is one of the oldest colleges in Oxford. In the 16th century, Adam Squire, then its Master, fell from grace after being accused of dealing with the supernatural: he was said to have procured familiar spirits to those who wanted to win at dice games.

Ashmolean Museum

Beaumont St, OX1 2PH

Founded in 1683 from a collection of curiosities gathered by antiquarian, politician, and devoted alchemist Elias Ashmole (1617–1692), the Ashmolean Museum is a treasure trove of archaeological specimens and artworks. Scour its corridors for its engravings of witches and demons and you might find John Dee gazing at you from his 16th-century portrait.

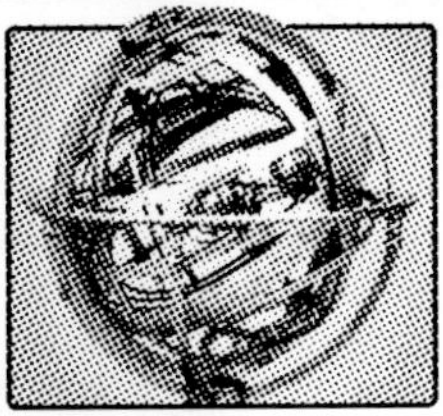

History of Science Museum

Broad St, OX1 3AZ

Amulets, magical sigils, and astrolabes are among the most fascinating items in this museum, which also houses a marble copy of John Dee's Holy Table. The original was made of wood and brightly painted, with carved Enochian characters so angels could convey their messages. The marble copy was produced nearly a century later, and might have belonged to astrologer William Lilly (1602–1681).

Pitt Rivers Museum

S Parks Rd, OX1 3PW

The labyrinthine displays of the Pitt Rivers museum contain a remarkable selection of magical and ritual items from all over the world, from the 19th-century Haida Totem Pole to a witch trapped in a bottle collected by archaeologist and folklorist Margaret Murray (1863–1963).

THE ROLLRIGHT STONES

Rollright Road, Little Rollright, Chipping Norton, OX7 5QB/ £

"As Long Compton thou canst not see,
King of England thou shalt not be,
Rise up stick, stand still stone,
For King of England thou shalt be none.
Thou and thy men hoar stones shall be,
And I myself an eldern tree."
(Traditional rhyme)

SLOWLY erected over a period of two thousand years, the Rollright Stones are a complex of three Neolithic and Bronze Age megalithic monuments. The popular legend of the stones was first recorded in Camden's *Britannia* in 1586, namely that they were once living men enchanted by "a wonderful Metamorphosis". Other versions of the tale specify that they were an invading king and his knights, turned to stone either by a Saxon general or by a witch—sometimes identified with the Tudor soothsayer Mother Shipton.

The stone circle is known as **the King's Men**. Stukeley described its stones as "corroded like worm-eaten wood, by the harsh Jaws of Time". As with most ancient stone monuments in Britain, they are said to be uncountable.

The remains of the burial chamber are known as **the Whispering Knights**, five treacherous officers plotting against their king. Local lore says they come to life at midnight to drink water from a spring down the hill.

The monolith, **The King Stone**, has long been the focus of fertility rituals, where women who wanted to conceive would rub their bare breasts against the stone.

One of the elder bushes growing around the stones is said to embody the witch. Cutting its branches will draw the witch's blood, making the stones shiver and come back to life—but it will also incur her wrath.

ST JAMES' OLD CHURCH, BIX BOTTOM

RG9 6BJ / SU726870

This Norman church was left to ruin in the mid-19th century, and in 1971 it was used as a setting for the folk horror juggernaut *The Blood On Satan's Claw*. Tucked in on the side of a country road, its crumbling walls might appear peaceful, but they were the vessel for the violent Satanic ritual at the heart of the film.

Ruins of St James' church

THE UFFINGTON WHITE HORSE

Dragon Hill Rd, Uffington, Faringdon SN7 7UK / £

Close to the spot where Saint George is said to have slayed the dragon, spilling its poison blood and staining the land white, the Uffington White Horse is the oldest chalk-cut hill figure in Britain. Roughly the size of a football field and thought to be over three thousand years old, it marks the ancient route through Dorset to the Wash in East Anglia. With its short head and sleek limbs, some have speculated the horse is in fact a dragon, but others claim it is more likely a depiction of Epona, the Celtic goddess of healing and death. Without regular maintenance, the horse would vanish beneath the grass, and the community take great pride in contributing to its ongoing survival. Offerings of coins, flowers, and candles frequently appear alongside the figure, which holds special significance to neo-pagans.

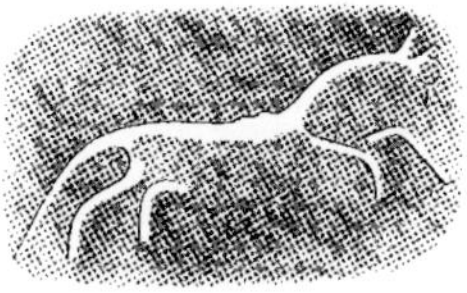

Uffington White Horse

Bas relief of Epona

THE ICKNIELD WAY

From Ivinghoe Beacon (LU7 9DJ) to Knettishall Heath Nature Reserve (IP22 2TQ)

Passing through ancient fenland and chalk ridges, the Icknield Way is a 170-mile trackway, one of the four highways of medieval England given special royal protection by Edward the Confessor. The road spans six counties, but some travellers claim it goes all the way around the world, or even into the next: a man in the 1890s walked the Way until he came to "fiery mountains" with choking smoke and sulphurous fumes. He turned back.

The Icknield Way

Isle of Wight

The Needles

THE NEEDLES

Alum Bay New Rd, Alum Bay, Totland Bay, PO39 0JD

The Druids of the Isle of Wight were purported to hold three sites as sacred. One of these—The Pinnacle of Ur—was a tall, thin spire of chalk, part of the formation known as The Needles on the west coast of the isle, adjacent to the site where the Arch Druids officiated their rituals. The giant Orri, one of the most powerful giants of the island, imbued the pinnacle with his magic. When the island's kings conspired to enslave Orri, he cursed them, prophesising of the day the Pinnacle of Ur would fall into the sea, taking all the magic of the island to The Other Place. Orri left the island, and the kings were subsequently overthrown by the invading Saxons. When the last of the Arch Druids died in the 18th century,

The Other Place

IN THE folklore of the Isle of Wight, The Other Place is a second invisible island where the gods, fairies, and Forever Magic dwelled. This island can be glimpsed by cunning folk during a weather

the Pinnacle of Ur collapsed into the sea, taking the island's magic with it.

MOTTISTONE LONGSTONE

Newport, PO30 4EB / £

"Moot", the Saxon for "meeting place", may hold the key to this 6000-year-old monument's name, but its original purpose was a mystery until 1956, when Jacquetta Hawkes, the first woman to receive a degree in archaeology and anthropology, discovered the four-metre-high stone was the entrance to a long barrow, or tomb, stretching for thirty-one metres. Aligned east-to-west, it is possible the Longstone was originally a place of solar worship as well as burial. Island folklore states the stones were flung into place during a battle between Saint Catherine and the Devil.

Mottistone Longstone

Jacquetta Hawkes

phenomenon known as The Swaailen, a thick, rolling fog that comes in off the sea in the summer months, even on clear days. Stories tell of smugglers on the west of the island sailing into the Swaailen and vanishing,

Isle of Wight smuggler

only to reappear years later with no understanding that time has passed. Precautions against the Swaailen include the laying of "stean" or small pebbles, promising to anchor you to this world even if you wander into The Other Place by mistake.

Surrey

FRENSHAM

MOTHER LUDLAM'S CAVE

Moor Park, Farnham,
GU10 1RJ

Inside a sandstone cliff close to the village of Frensham lies the subterranean home of a 17th-century witch. Mother Ludlam, sometimes referred to as the White Witch of Waverley, was known for granting favours—petitioners would have to stand on a boulder and call into the cave, stating the item they needed. It would then appear on their doorstep, on the condition that it be returned after two days. Other stories tell of Mother Ludlam feeding weary travellers and tending to wounds, suggesting the character was based on a real cunning woman or midwife serving her community.
18th-century illustrations depict the cave's interior as surprisingly salubrious, with paved flooring and numerous benches surrounding a small stream running out of the cave's mouth. Considering the cave was likely created by a natural spring, the site may once have been a holy well laid out for pilgrim visitors hoping for healing or favours. Most of the cave is now inaccessible owing to a collapse in the mid-1970s.

ST MARY THE VIRGIN CHURCH

The St, Frensham,
Farnham, GU10 3EA

Behind the altar at Saint Mary the Virgin Church, under the protective stained-glass gaze of Saint Michael, is a nineteen-inch copper cauldron. Its origin story, first recorded in 1890, tells of a man who borrowed the cauldron from the fairies who lived beneath a long, flat stone on nearby Borough-hill. When he failed to return the cauldron on the agreed date, the cauldron followed him wherever he went until he died at Frensham, seeking sanctuary in the church. The cauldron was then used for brewing beer. Alternative versions of the legend have the cauldron loaned out by Mother Ludlam, although the witch is not otherwise described as the vengeful type.

Mother Ludlam's Cave

HORSLEY TOWERS

Ockham Road South, East Horsley, KT24 6DT

The whimsical walls of this 19th-century country house—now a wedding and conference venue—became a container for residual hauntings in Nigel Kneale's influential *The Stone Tape*, where it was renamed Taskerlands. In real life, Horsley Towers once was the home of Ada Lovelace, Lord Byron's daughter and—like the heroine of *The Stone Tape*—a computer programming pioneer.

The entrance to Horsley Tower

Ada Lovelace, computer programmer

The Stone Tape (Peter Sasdy, 1972)

Horsley Towers from the lake

Sussex

Neolithic dew-ponds and cattle-ways" (1905)

Doreen Valiente

CHANCTONBURY RING

Chanctonbury Hill, Steyning, BN44 3DP

"Care for some soup?"

Commanding the sweeping landscape for miles around, this prehistoric hillfort was once co-opted by the Romans as a temple, most likely dedicated to Mithras, god of soldiers and honour. The beech trees crowning the site were first planted by an 18th-century landowner. Counting them correctly is said to summon Julius Caesar and his ghostly army.

English Wiccan Doreen Valiente believed women seeking to increase their fertility should sleep beneath the trees at the site for one full night, while her contemporary Victor Neuburg composed gory poems about the druidic sacrifices he imagined taking place at the Ring. Both Neuburg and his on-and-off associate, Aleister Crowley, believed the site to be a "place of power". Modern occultists and UFO enthusiasts have reported unpleasant sensations at the site, including electric shocks and difficulty breathing. The Ring is notorious for its association with the Devil: walk three times naked around it and the Devil will appear, offering you a bowl of soup in exchange for your soul.

The Devil in Sussex

THE DEVIL made many appearances in Sussex. As it is unlucky to mention him by his proper name, he crops up in Sussex lore as Old Nick, Poor Man, Old Scratch, Old Harry, Naughty Man, Mister Grim and He, to name just a few of his aliases.

Devil's Dyke

Devil's Dyke Rd, Brighton
BN1 8YJ

Sussex was said to be the final bastion of paganism in England. So furious was the Devil when Sussex converted to Christianity, he tore up chunks of the landscape with the intention of creating a trench deep enough to drown the populace in a flood. When the hermit Cuthman of Steyning discovered the Devil's plans, he proposed a wager. If the Devil could dig his trench in one night, he could have Cuthman's soul. If he failed, he must leave Sussex forever. Cuthman watched the Devil as he worked through the night. As the trench was almost complete, Cuthman lit candles and made a cock crow, fooling the Devil into believing dawn had arrived. The Devil fled, leaving behind the Devil's Dyke, his half-finished trench.

The two humps at the bottom of the dyke are known as the Devil's Graves, under which the Devil and his wife are supposedly buried. Satan can be summoned by running backwards seven times around the mounds.

Mick Mills' Race

St Leonard's Forest,
Horsham, RH12 4TG

When smuggler and renowned braggart Mick Mills claimed he could outrun anyone, the Devil overheard and challenged him to a one-mile race through St Leonard's Forest. Mills won, getting to keep his soul, and in some versions of the tale gaining immortality. You can run the race yourself, but if you attempt it at midnight on horseback, the Devil will squeeze onto the saddle behind you.

The Tomb of "Mad Jack"

St Thomas a Becket Church,
Brightling Rd, TN32 5HH

In 1811 John "Mad Jack" Fuller, politician and eccentric, had an enormous pyramid mausoleum built in preparation for his death. Fuller was rumoured to be entombed sitting at a table laid out with wine and a roast chicken, and it was said he believed he could keep the Devil out of his tomb by sprinkling broken glass on the floor. Modern restoration work showed both these tales to be untrue. However, running backwards around the tomb seven times may raise the spirit of Mad Jack, if not the Devil himself.

Kent

A view of Kit's Coty House and plan, by William Stukeley.

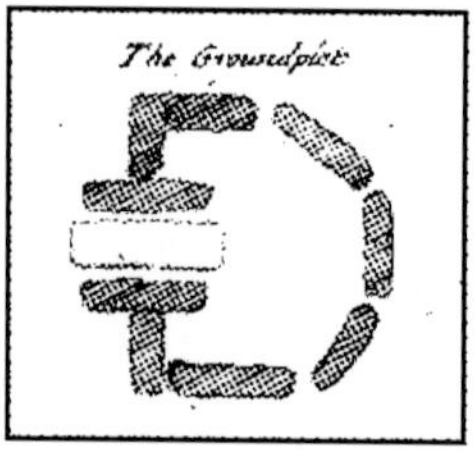

KIT'S COTY HOUSE

Chatham Rd, Blue Bell Hill, ME20 7EZ

Constructed sometime between 4000 and 3000 BC, Kit's Coty is a Neolithic burial chamber topped with a ten-foot high "house" of stone. The Kent landscape would have been heavily forested at the time of the megalith's creation, though now it stands on a windswept hill. In 1722, the antiquarian Hercules Ayleway recorded the local folk belief that the monument was erected to commemorate the deaths of two rival kings of Kent. It is said that if a visitor offers a sacrifice of a precious personal belonging by placing it on top of the stones during a full moon, they will be granted otherworldly powers. Modern pagan groups gather at the site throughout the year, and the local Morris men—who take their name from the monument—annually dance there on May Day morning.

The Long Man of Wilmington

THE LONG MAN OF WILMINGTON

S Downs Way, BN26 5SW / TQ542034

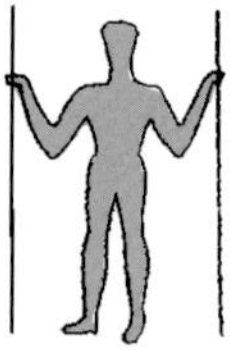

Dominating the South Downs, the naked figure of a male with twin staffs is carved into the chalk hills. Though the figure appears mysteriously ancient, researchers believe it may have been created as late as the 16th or 17th century, although for what purpose, no one can agree. During WW2, the Man was painted green to hide him from German bomber pilots who were using him as a landmark.

DUNGENESS

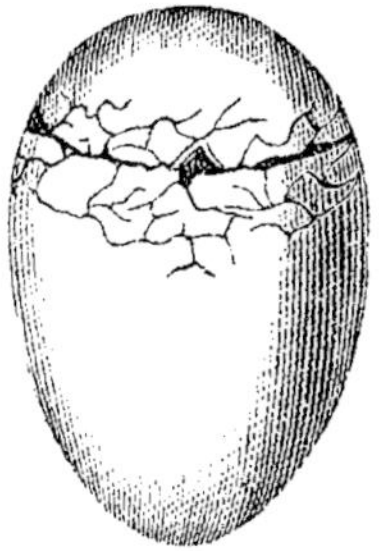

Said to be the closest thing England has to a desert, Dungeness has long had a reputation for danger and otherworldly goings-on. One 16th-century topographer described the area as "evil in winter, grievous in summer, never good", prone to outbreaks of malaria known to locals as "Old Johnny". Its desolation made it a hotspot for smugglers in the 18th and 19th centuries. Witches were said to ride the waves in eggshells, therefore all eggshells in Kent must be thoroughly crushed after breakfast.

Derek Jarman's Prospect Cottage

Dungeness Rd, Dungeness, Romney Marsh, TN29 9NE

IN THE shadow of a nuclear power station on the great shingle expanse of Dungeness beach, this black hut with yellow windows was home to filmmaker and poet Derek Jarman (1942-1994) for eight years, until his death of AIDS-related complications. Jarman could be spotted tending to his garden in a hooded robe, arranging rocks in mystical circles and hanging lucky hagstones on leather garlands. "People thought I was building a garden for magical purposes," he said, "a white witch out to get the nuclear power station."

A strong thread of occultism runs through Jarman's body of work, most strikingly in his 1977 film *Jubilee*, in which court magician John Dee conjures an angel to show Elizabeth I a vision of England's future. The queen is transported to a bloody punk London where law and order have been abolished, ballet dancers twirl for naked pagan idols, and Westminster Cathedral has been converted into a gay club where couples dance to a punk-disco rendition of William Blake's *Jerusalem*.

Jarman was buried in St Clement's churchyard in Old Romney, under a headstone bearing his signature. A crowdfunding campaign secured the future of Prospect Cottage, and plans for regular guided tours and artists' residencies are underway.

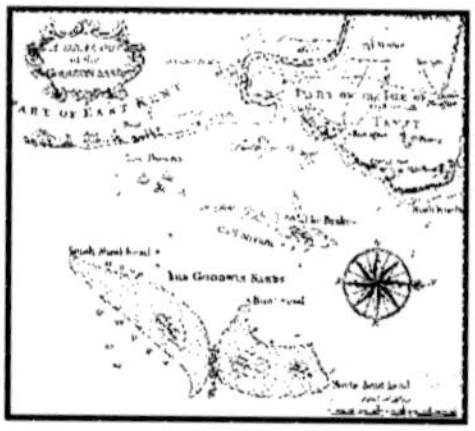

Goodwin Sands

South Foreland Lighthouse

GOODWIN SANDS

From St Margaret's Bay (CT15 6DX) to Ramsgate (CT11 8LU)
South Foreland Lighthouse: St Margaret's Bay, Dover, CT15 5NA

The outline of the treacherous Goodwin Sands is constantly changing due to the effect of the tides ebbing and flowing through the narrow neck of the Dover Straits. Since 1298, over a thousand shipwrecks have been recorded along them, some of which are still visible at low tide today. Warning lights have been positioned on the White Cliffs since the 14th century. The 19th-century South Foreland Lighthouse—the first lighthouse to use an electric light—is open for guided tours.

The Lady Lovibond

A wreck on the Goodwin Sands

WHEN the Lady Lovibond set sail for Portugal in 1748, the wedding party on deck erupted into violence before the ship ran aground on the sucking sands, killing everyone on board. Every fifty years, on the anniversary of the wreck, vessels have claimed to have spotted the three-masted schooner breaking up in the surf and almost suffered catastrophe themselves. Sounds of celebration can be heard from the ghostly wreck. An example of a "stone tape" haunting, or a genius loci reminding us of its destructive power despite the advances in maritime technology?

III. London

pp. 82 – 97

III. LONDON

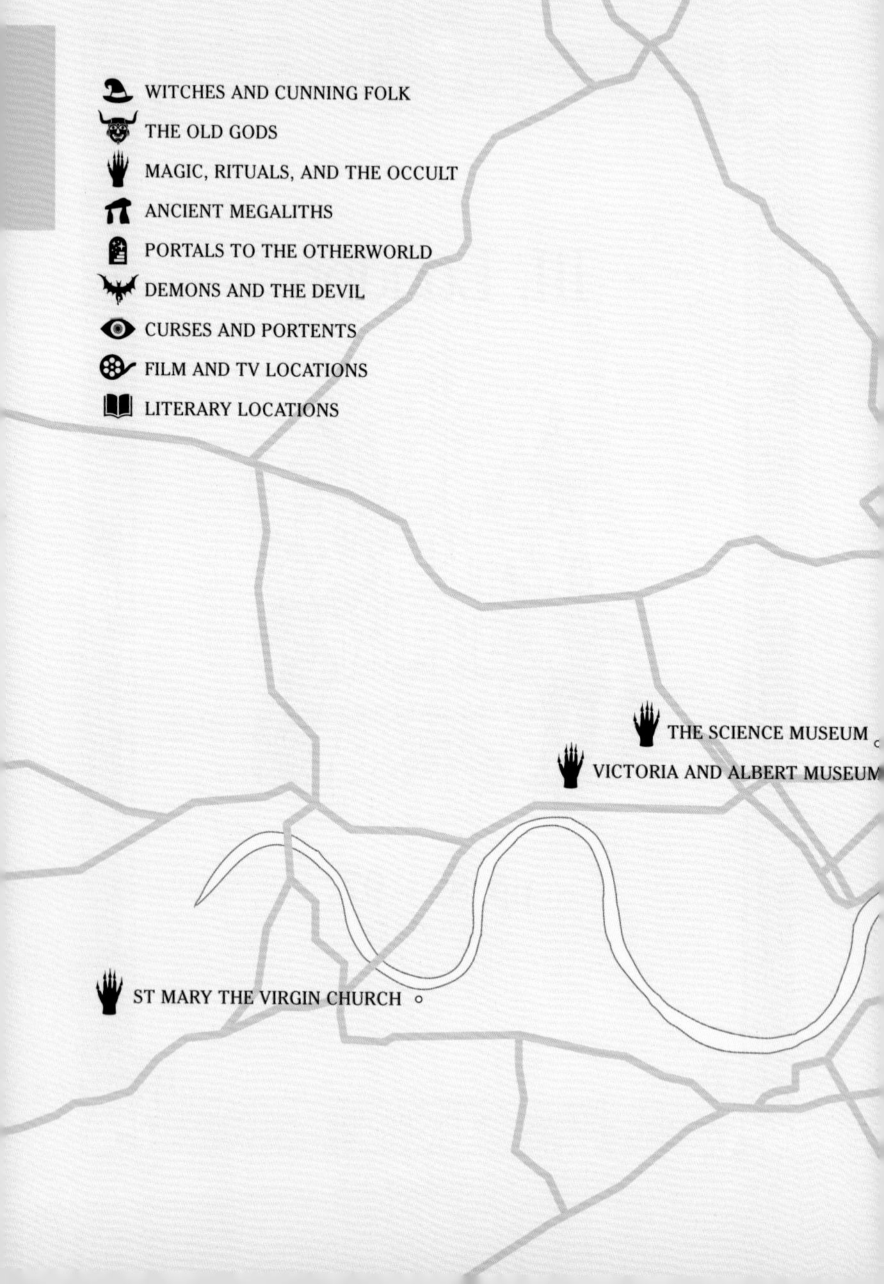
WITCHES AND CUNNING FOLK
THE OLD GODS
MAGIC, RITUALS, AND THE OCCULT
ANCIENT MEGALITHS
PORTALS TO THE OTHERWORLD
DEMONS AND THE DEVIL
CURSES AND PORTENTS
FILM AND TV LOCATIONS
LITERARY LOCATIONS
THE SCIENCE MUSEUM
VICTORIA AND ALBERT MUSEUM
ST MARY THE VIRGIN CHURCH

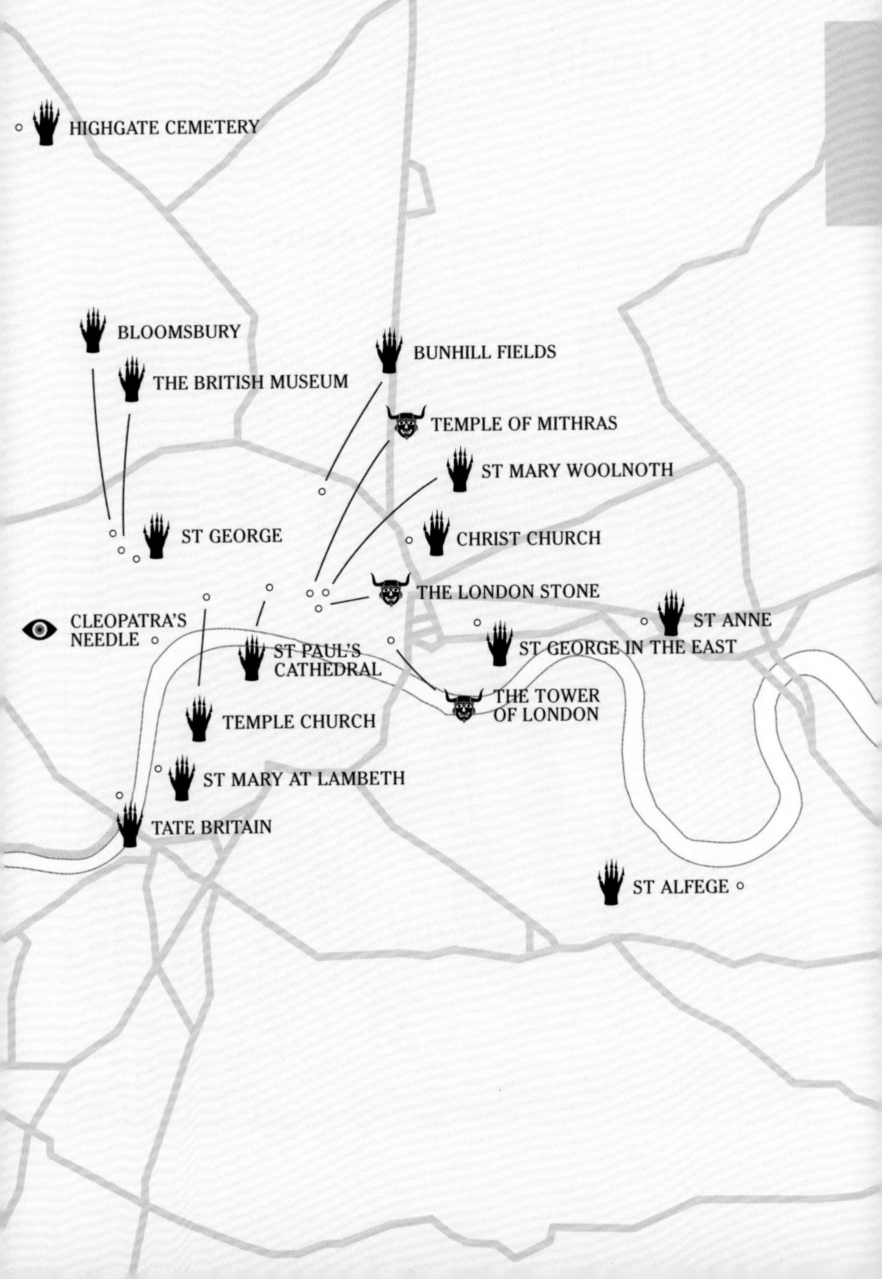
HIGHGATE CEMETERY
BLOOMSBURY
THE BRITISH MUSEUM
BUNHILL FIELDS
TEMPLE OF MITHRAS
ST MARY WOOLNOTH
ST GEORGE
CHRIST CHURCH
THE LONDON STONE
CLEOPATRA'S NEEDLE
ST ANNE
ST PAUL'S CATHEDRAL
ST GEORGE IN THE EAST
THE TOWER OF LONDON
TEMPLE CHURCH
ST MARY AT LAMBETH
TATE BRITAIN
ST ALFEGE

III. London

The Tower of London

THE TOWER OF LONDON

Covent Garden, EC3N 4AB / £

Tower Hill, Tower of London

This Norman castle is one of London's most recognisable landmarks, and has served as royal residence, armoury, prison, place of execution, public record office, home of the Crown Jewels, and tourist attraction, among other things.

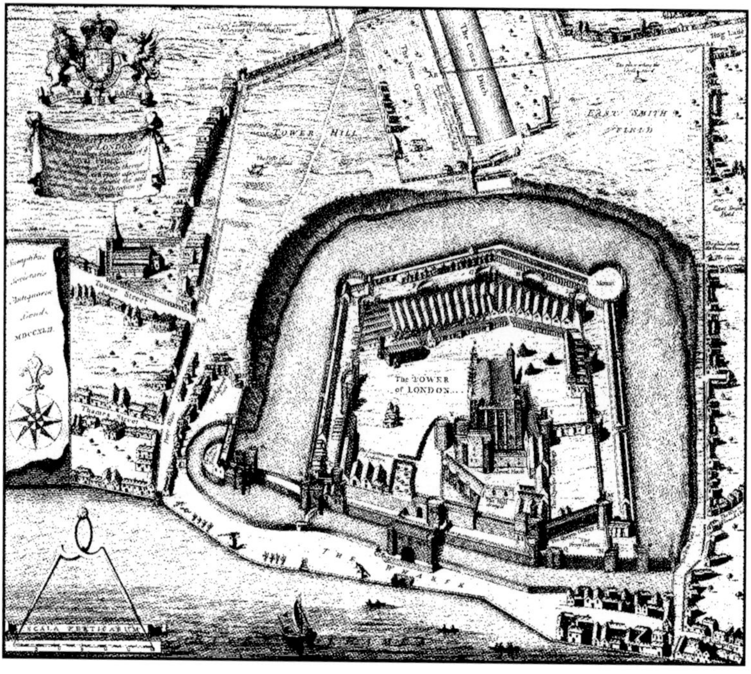

The London Tower boasts a flock of six permanent corvid residents.

Every child in England knows that if the ravens leave the Tower, the nation will fall. This story likely only dates back as far as the 1940s, though the Raven Master of the Tower takes his role very seriously, keeping a flock of six permanent corvid residents. A much earlier folktale tells how Brân The Blessed, the mythical king of the Britons, commanded his followers to cut off his head and bury it under the white hill where the Tower of London now stands. There he could protect the land from invasion for eternity. The name Brân is often translated as crow or raven, and the Celtic raven deity Brân was a god connected to the so-called "cult of the head" in which the human head was seen as the seat of the soul, capable of magic and protection.

THE LONDON STONE

111 Cannon St, EC4N 5AR

Cannon Street

A police constable standing before the London Stone

This unimpressive block of limestone has been a part of the fabric of London since the Roman occupation, and has long been said to be key to the city's wellbeing and prosperity. Variously described as a relic of druidic sacrifice, a Roman milliarium or milestone, and a ley line marker, the stone has captured the imaginations of Londoners for centuries, breeding new legends with each passing age. The stone has attracted attention from such London luminaries as William Shakespeare, William Blake, and Peter Ackroyd.

Block of limestone

Bloomsbury

Russell Square, King's Cross St. Pancras, Euston Square, Goodge Street, Covent Garden

WELL-KNOWN for being a literary hub, in the 19th century Bloomsbury was the beating heart of occult London, hosting the headquarters of the Freemasons, the Order of the Golden Dawn, the Theosophical Society, the Swedenborg Society, and the Society for Psychical Research. The neighbourhood's former residents include Madame Blavatsky, Margaret Murray, W. B. Yeats, Dion Fortune, Aleister Crowley, and Gerald Gardner.

THE BRITISH MUSEUM
Great Russell Street, WC1B 3DG
At the height of the 19th-century occult revival, the ancient artefacts on display at the British Museum inspired many to perform psychic readings in situ. The Reading Room, styled after the Pantheon in Rome, regularly welcomed occult figures—which makes the fictional exchange between Dr Holden and the sinister Karswell in *Night of the Demon* (1957) somewhat plausible. Head to the Enlightenment Gallery to marvel at some of Dr Dee's possessions, and visit the Egyptian galleries for a glimpse of the Unlucky Mummy, a coffin lid blamed for deaths, calamities, and the sinking of the Titanic.

FREEMASONS' HALL
60 Great Queen Street, WC2B 5AZ
This imposing Art Deco building is the third Masonic Hall on this site, a meeting place for the Freemasons since 1775. The Museum of Freemasonry on the first floor is open to visitors, as well as some of its rooms.

THE WARBURG INSTITUTE
Woburn Square, WC1H 4EZ
The library of this research institution holds an important collection of volumes on the history of magic and the largest collection of writings by Aleister Crowley. Entry by appointment.

TREADWELL'S BOOKSHOP
33 Store St, WC1E 7BS
Since its opening in 2003, this bookshop has become an occult institution, with a carefully curated selection of magical volumes and a programme of evening lectures. Don't miss Pamela Colman Smith's fireplace, rescued from her Cornish home.

THE ATLANTIS BOOKSHOP
49A Museum St, WC1A 1LY
Gerald Gardner used to host regular coven meetings in the basement of this family-run bookshop established in 1922. The Gardner Room is now used for workshops and events, art exhibitions and book launches.

ST GEORGE'S CHURCH
Bloomsbury Way,
WC1A 2SA
One of the six London churches designed by architect and Freemason Nicholas Hawksmoor in the 18th century.

SENATE HOUSE
Malet St, WC1E 7HU
Home to the Harry Price Library of Magical Literature, a collection of books, pamphlets, and periodical titles on the supernatural, magic, and the occult compiled by psychical researcher Harry Price.

Cleopatra's Needle

CLEOPATRA'S NEEDLE

WC2N 6PB

Embankment

A stone's throw from Embankment Underground station stands a 3500-year-old Egyptian obelisk. The sixty-nine-foot high "needle" was gifted to Britain by the Egyptian ruler Muhammad Ali Pasha in 1819 to celebrate British victory over the French in Egypt. The obelisk was originally carved on the orders of Pharaoh Thutmose III to stand at the entrance of the Temple of the Sun in Heliopolis, and had lain in the desert since an earthquake in 1303. It would take nearly sixty years to get the obelisk to London, as Parliament could not agree on funding or how to approach the political sensitivity of the gift. Eventually, surgeon and Egyptology enthusiast William

Doctor Dee's London

ELIZABETHAN polymath Dr John Dee (1527– c.1609) was born in London to an Anglo-Welsh family. His extraordinary life took him from Cambridge to the continent, from jail to advising Elizabeth I and lecturing across a series of European castles. In 1582 he met Edward Kelley, who would become his spirit medium. The two of them constructed a magical system of communicating with angels with the aim of healing the rift between God and Man that took place after the Fall. Dee spent his final years at Mortlake, forced to sell off his books to support himself and his daughter, and died in poverty at the venerable age of 81.

THE BRITISH MUSEUM

Great Russell Street, WC1B 3DG

Tottenham Court Road, Holborn, Russell Square, Goodge Street

THE British Museum is in possession of several objects related to Dr Dee. His Mexican obsidian mirror, also known as "the Devil's looking-glass", was used to call forth spirits. The mirror comes in a leather carrycase with a label thought to be inscribed by Gothic revival pioneer Horace Walpole. Three engraved wax discs served

James Erasmus Wilson paid for voyage himself, though the journey was not without incident—the 200-tonne artefact was almost lost at sea during a storm.

In 1917, a German bomb damaged its pedestal and the sphinxes that guard it, but the obelisk remained intact, which some have attributed to magical powers. Victorian ghost hunter Elliott O'Donnell believed the spot where it stands to be haunted, with "unearthly groans and hellish, mocking laughter" rising from the river.

Elliott O'Donnell

WATKINS BOOKS

19-21 Cecil Court, WC2N 4EZ

⊖ Leicester Square

When Madame Blavatsky lamented the absence of occult and esoteric bookshops in London, her

as anchors for the table where Dee performed his divinations. The golden talisman labelled as Dr Dee's Disc is inscribed with a shield-like diagram of one of Edward Kelley's visions of angels.

THE SCIENCE MUSEUM

South Kensington, SW7 2DD

⊖ South Kensington

THE museum houses a purple crystal on a silver chain that once belonged to Dr Dee, allegedly received from Archangel Uriel in 1582. The scrying crystal was later gifted by Dee's son to the physician and alchemist Nicholas Culpeper, who claimed a demonic entity emerged from it in 1651. He never used it again.

A gift from Archangel Uriel

ST MARY THE VIRGIN CHURCH, MORTLAKE

Richmond, SW14 8JA

DEE'S home at Mortlake, where he conducted his experiments and compiled his magical library, once stood opposite the site of St Mary the Virgin Church. The doctor was buried beneath the church's chancel, and is memorialised as "astronomer, geographer, mathematician, and advisor to Queen Elizabeth I" in a plaque that coyly sidesteps his occult reputation.

Watkins Books

Relief of Mithras

Head of Mithras

Temple Church

disciple and friend John M. Watkins decided to set up his own. Since its opening in 1893, Watkins Books has been frequented by the most prominent occult figures, including W.B. Yeats, Arthur Machen, G.R.S. Mead, and Aleister Crowley.

TEMPLE OF MITHRAS

12 Walbrook, EC4N 8AA

Cannon Street, Bank

Discovered in 1954 during the post-Blitz rebuilding of London, this Roman temple was dedicated to the god Mithras and his cult of bull sacrifice. The temple was constructed eighteen feet below the surface of the street to mimic the cave where Mithras slew the bull in his legend. Built on the banks of the River Walbrook, one of London's "lost rivers" which has since been diverted underground, the temple eventually succumbed to natural erosion and was abandoned. Since 1838, over 300 deliberately disarticulated human skulls have been discovered in and around the Walbrook, leading to speculations of human sacrifice, or that a rebellion was crushed on the site. Many of the so-called Walbrook skulls are now on display at the Museum of London, while the Temple of Mithras has been reconstructed on its original site with atmospheric lightning and music, offering visitors a taste of Roman Londinium.

TEMPLE CHURCH

EC4Y 7BB

Temple, Blackfriars

Among an oasis of ancient buildings between the Thames and Fleet Street lies this round, domed church, designed to echo the Church of The Holy Sepulchre in Jerusalem. Once the headquarters of the Knights Templar in Britain, the church was taken over by the Crown when the order was abolished in 1307. It sports plenty of amusing grotesques and several effigies of knights in repose, including Sir William Marshal, known as the greatest knight that ever lived.

ST MARY AT LAMBETH

Garden Museum, Lambeth Palace Road, SE1 7LB / £

Vauxhall, Westminster, Lambeth North

Lambeth has attracted many magicians, alchemists, occultists, and visionaries through the centuries. Some of them are buried in this pretty, garden-like churchyard.

Simon Forman (1552–1611) was an Elizabethan occultist and physician who predicted his own demise. A high-profile murder trial five years after his death cemented his reputation as a black magician: posterity remembers him as the Devil Forman, who supplied magical potions to patients wishing to eliminate their enemies.

Politician Elias Ashmole (1617–1692) was a committed student of alchemy, astrology, and Hermetic magic, as well as a prominent antiquary known for his cabinet of curiosities which led to the foundation of the Ashmolean Museum in Oxford.

The highlight of the churchyard is the 17th-century tomb of the Tradescant family. In life they were botanists and gardeners who amassed a collection of exotic curiosities from far-flung lands. They left behind an extraordinary tomb carved with fantastical beasts, gnarled trees, and apocalyptic ruins. Their collection of curiosities passed into the hands of Ashmole.

Hawksmoor's London

ARCHITECT Nicholas Hawksmoor (c.1661–1736) was commissioned to build six churches across London during the 18th century. A Freemason and man of eccentric interests, Hawksmoor's churches show diverse international and mystical influences, featuring decidedly mysterious obelisks, pyramids, and mock sacrificial altars. These unusual decisions led to modern speculation that the architect was a Satanist, and even that the churches are built on the bodies of child sacrifices: Alan Moore and Eddie Campbell's *From Hell* and Peter Ackroyd's *Hawksmoor* are prime examples of the architect's dark appeal.

St George, Bloomsbury
Bloomsbury Way, WC1A 2SA
Ⓞ Holborn, Tottenham Court Road
Visible in the background of Hogarth's infamous Gin Lane, St George features a portico inspired by the Temple of Bacchus at Baalbek, Lebanon, and a pyramid-style tower that copies the design of the Mausoleum of Halicarnassus—peculiar choices for an Anglican place of worship.

St George in the East, Wapping
14 Cannon St Rd, E1 0BH
Ⓞ Shadwell
Severely damaged in the Blitz, St George in the East still dominates the Wapping skyline with its multiple turrets and windows described by the Grub Street Journal of 1734 as like "that of a prison". Not far from the church, Ensign Street and Grace's Alley were used as filming locations for *Interview with the Vampire* (1994).

Christ Church, Spitalfields
Commercial St, E1 6LY
Ⓞ Liverpool Street, Aldgate East
Looming over the markets of Spitalfields like an obelisk, Christ Church is a dramatic combination of Gothic and Palladian architecture. Described by poet John Betjeman as "a huge, heavy galleon of white Portland stone", it is regarded as one of the finest surviving Baroque churches in England.

St Anne, Limehouse
Colt St, E14 7HA
In the churchyard of this Byzantine church, you will find a pyramid inscribed with a unicorn and the words "the wisdom of Solomon" in English and Hebrew. The purpose of the seven-metre pyramid is a mystery, though in Sax Rohmer's 1930s Fu Manchu novels, it hides the entrance to an opium den. Puzzlingly, the churchyard also features a two-sided gravestone from the 1760s—one side is inscribed normally, while the other is upside down.

St Alfege, Greenwich
Greenwich Church St, SE10 9BJ
Supposedly built upon the spot where Viking raiders killed Alfege, Archbishop of Canterbury, in 1012, this was the first of the six commissioned Hawksmoor churches. Evidence shows the commissioners toned down Hawksmoor's original plans for the building. During the Blitz, four families lived in the crypt, using spare sarcophagi as beds for the children.

St Mary Woolnoth, the City
1 King William St, EC4N 7BJ
⊖ Bank, Cannon Street
Remains of a Roman temple were discovered beneath the foundations of St Mary Woolnoth, the Hawksmoor church near the Bank of England. The interior is based on a Roman atrium, suggesting Hawksmoor was sensitive, if not sympathetic, towards the thousands of years of pagan worship beneath his feet.

The Visions of William Blake

Tate Britain: Millbank, SW1P 4RG, ⊖ Pimlico, Vauxhall, Westminster,
V&A: Cromwell Rd, SW7 2RL ⊖ South Kensington, Gloucester Road,
Bunhill Fields: 38 City Rd, EC1Y 2BG ⊖ Old Street

POET, artist, political radical, and visionary William Blake (1757–1827) was born in Soho and lived in London for most of his life. The England of Blake's imagination was a landscape of angels and factories, chimneysweeps, and divine prophecy. He died in poverty, his poems and engravings unappreciated, but he has since been hailed as one of the most remarkable and influential English artists, inspiring everyone from the Pre-Raphaelite Brotherhood to Iron Maiden. Many of his best-known artworks—often imbued with esoteric and spiritual symbolism—are on display at Tate Britain and the V&A. He was buried in Bunhill Fields, but the exact location of his grave was only ascertained 191 years after his death.

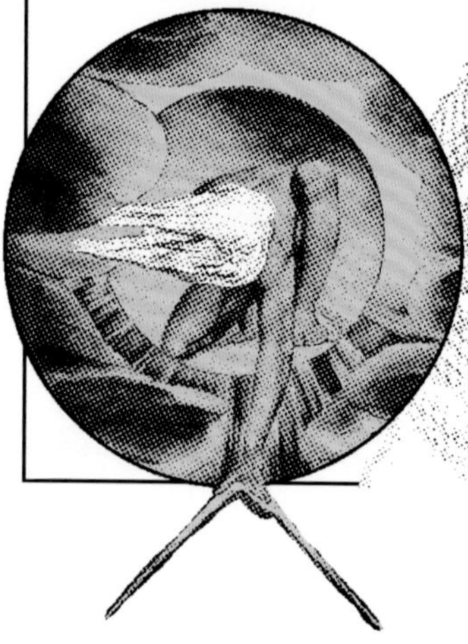

ST PAUL'S CATHEDRAL

St Paul's Churchyard, EC4M 8AD / £

St Paul's, Ludgate, Blackfriars, Mansion House

Out of the ashes of a temple that burnt during the Great Fire of London, architect Sir Christopher Wren (1632–1723) built the beacon of his New Jerusalem. Standing on the top of Ludgate Hill—where Brutus, the legendary founder of London, had erected a temple to Diana—the dome of St Paul's Cathedral miraculously survived the Blitz and remains one of London's most recognisable landmarks.

Wren's links with Freemasonry have been much debated. Whether he was or wasn't a Grand Master, his redevelopment plans for the City, with grid patterns and starbursts, have inspired darker readings. His occult reputation, nevertheless, has been eclipsed by that of his protégé Nicholas Hawksmoor.

St Paul's Cathedral

HIGHGATE CEMETERY

Swain's Ln, N6 6PJ

Archway

Since its opening in 1839, Highgate Cemetery has housed the earthly remains of thousands of Londoners, great and obscure, and is known for its exceptional beauty and aesthetic decay. The western part of the cemetery is a labyrinth of impressive ivy-clad monuments, vaults, and obelisks, its design influenced by the cultural zeitgeist that followed to Napoleon's Egyptian campaigns. In the 1960s, the area around the Egyptian Avenue and the Circle of Lebanon was neglected and overgrown, and became the playground of the infamous Highgate Vampire.

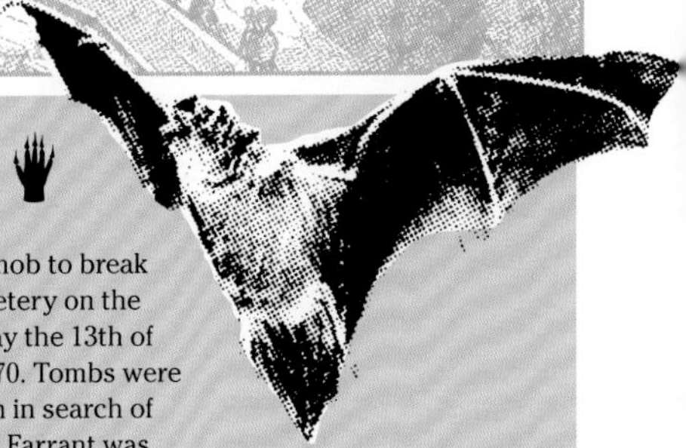

The Highgate Vampire

IN THE LATE 1960s and early 70s, Highgate was the scene of a series of strange apparitions witnessed by local schoolgirls. When the headless body of a woman—approximately one hundred years dead—was discovered some way from her grave, the tabloids blamed occultists. Meanwhile, others attributed the events to a supernatural entity. Rival vampire hunters David Farrant and Sean Manchester gave incendiary media interviews, triggering a mob to break into the cemetery on the night of Friday the 13th of February, 1970. Tombs were cracked open in search of the fiend and Farrant was charged with desecration. The pair continued to argue about the exact nature of the Highgate vampire—disembodied spirit or undead blood-drinker—until Farrant's death in 2019.

Man, a cross, a stake—and a vampire

IV. East Anglia

Essex, 102
Bedfordshire, 105
Hertfordshire, 106
Cambridgeshire, 108
Suffolk, 110
Norfolk, 117

IV. EAST ANGLIA

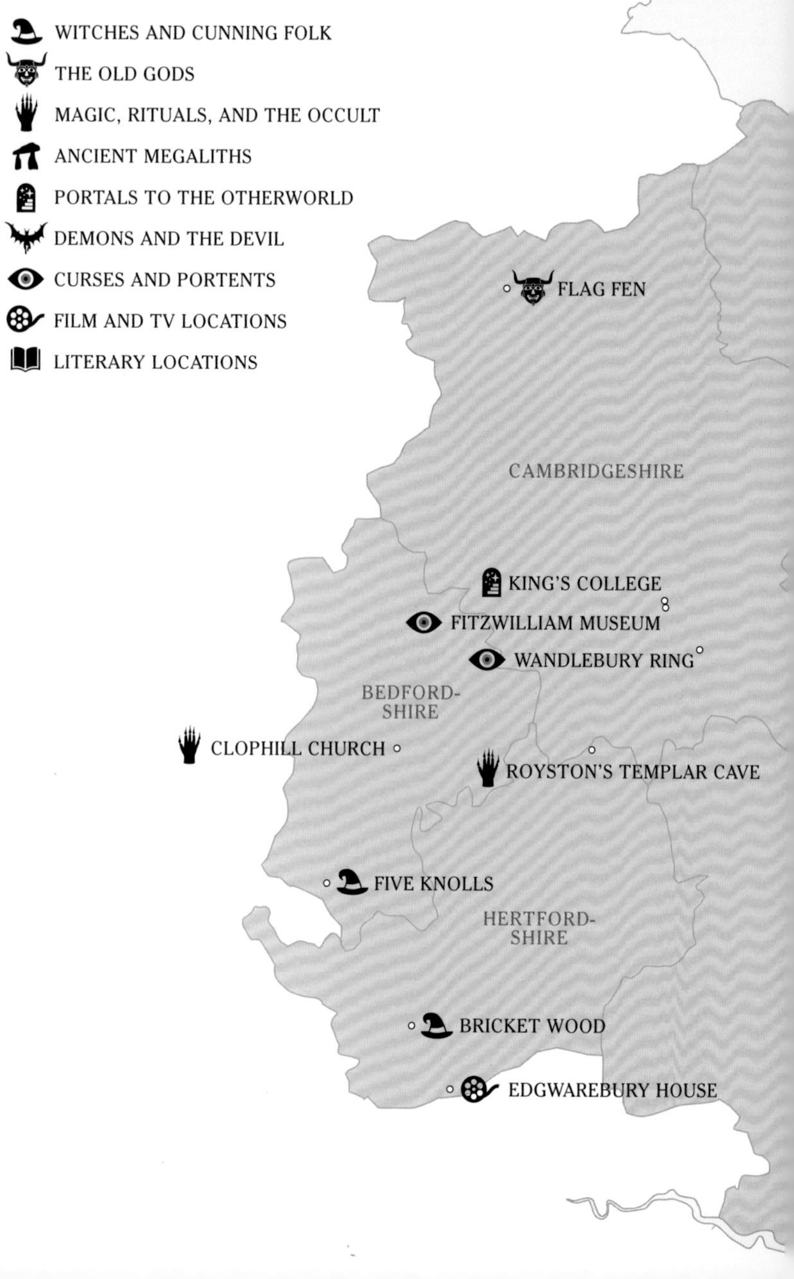

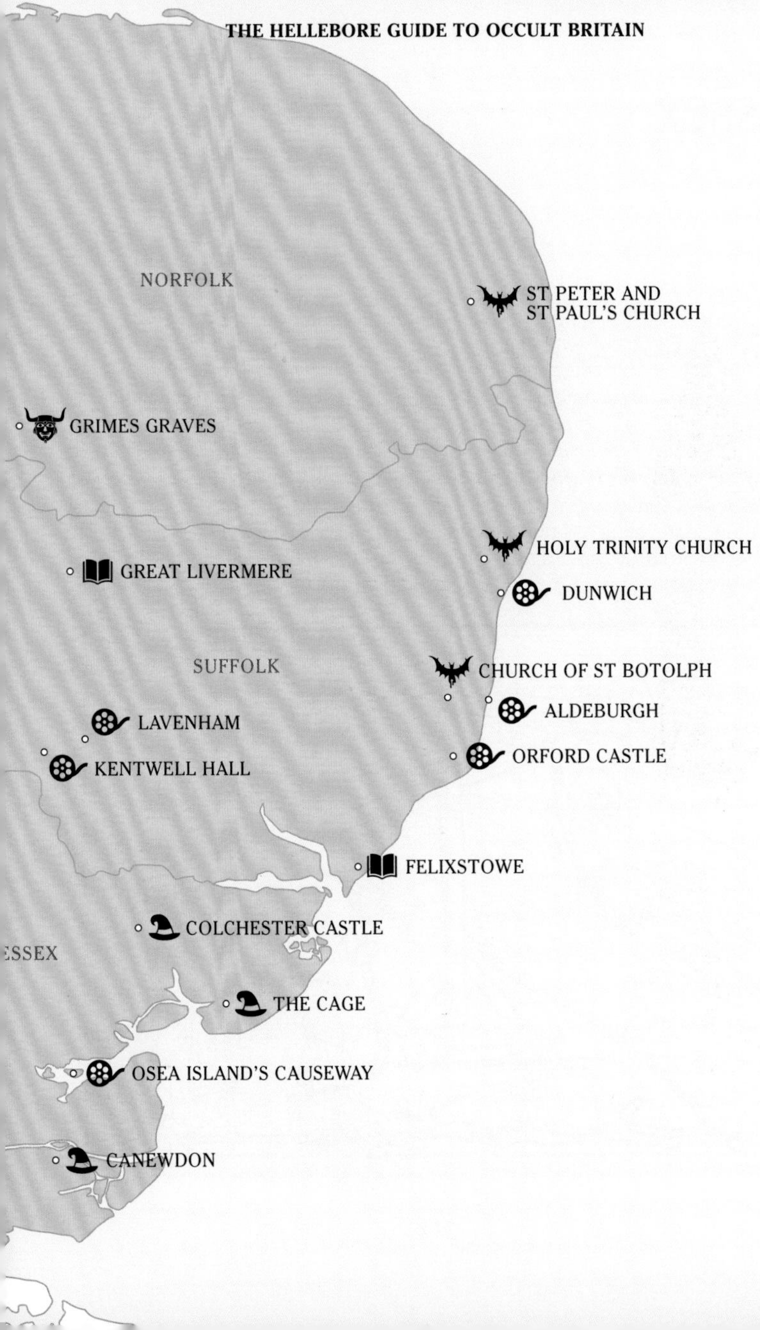
NORFOLK
ST PETER AND
ST PAUL'S CHURCH
GRIMES GRAVES
HOLY TRINITY CHURCH
GREAT LIVERMERE
DUNWICH
SUFFOLK
CHURCH OF ST BOTOLPH
ALDEBURGH
LAVENHAM
ORFORD CASTLE
KENTWELL HALL
FELIXSTOWE
COLCHESTER CASTLE
ESSEX
THE CAGE
OSEA ISLAND'S CAUSEWAY
CANEWDON

Essex

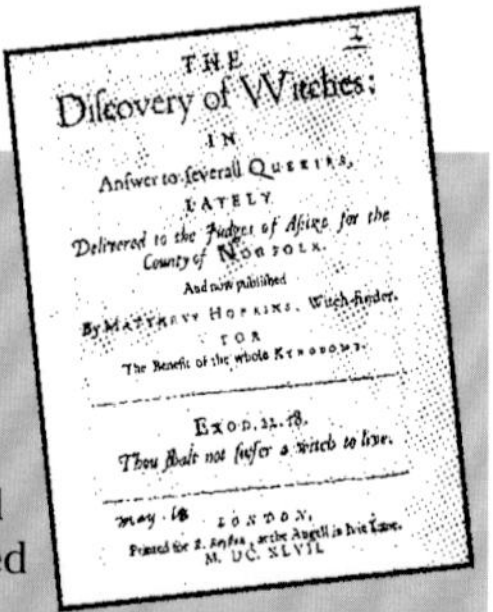
THE
Discovery of Witches:
IN
Answer to severall QUERIES,
LATELY
Delivered to the Judges of Assize for the County of NORFOLK.
And now published
By MATTHEW HOPKINS, Witch-finder.
FOR
The Benefit of the whole KINGDOME.

EXOD. 22. 18.
Thou shalt not suffer a witch to live.

LONDON,
Printed for R. Royston, at the Angell in Ivie Lane.
M. DC. XLVII.

Witch County

ESSEX was the epicentre of the witch trials of the mid-1600s. Fuelled by Matthew Hopkins' *The Discovery of Witches*, a manual on the detection of "maleficium", the witch trials saw accused witches—usually social outcasts, such as disabled people or the elderly—denounced, tested, and executed. In total, the English witch hunts lasted approximately 200 years, resulting in around 700 recorded deaths.

CANEWDON

SS4 3QE

The isolated village of Canewdon on the edge of the Thames Estuary teems with stories of witches and cunning men, yet the community remained strangely unscathed during the reign of Matthew Hopkins. Indeed, the Witchfinder General never visited, leading to a belief that the witches of Canewdon were simply too formidable for him. During the previous century, several villagers were indicted for witchcraft, and although one was found guilty, her life was spared, though excommunication damned her soul. Local characters were professing supernatural powers as late as the 1880s, most notably local cunning man George Pickingill, who was rumoured to control nine covens across the Southern counties.

The tower of the 12th-century church of St Nicholas has become a totem of local folklore. Walking around it will summon the Devil or a ghost, or open up a portal to the past—the outcome will be determined by the direction and number of steps taken. Novice witches would walk around the church tower twelve times at midnight to summon the Devil, so he could initiate them into the local coven.

English cunning man George Pickingill

OSEA ISLAND'S CAUSEWAY

Osea Rd, CM9 4SA

The eeriness of this tidal road—an ancient Roman causeway—was put to good use in both the TV adaptation and the 2012 film adaptation of *The Woman in Black*, as well as in the HBO folk horror series *The Third Day*. The island, named after St Osyth, has been farmed since the Neolithic era, and later became a sacred burial ground for the Vikings. It is now privately owned.

Witch and familiar, 1619 engraving

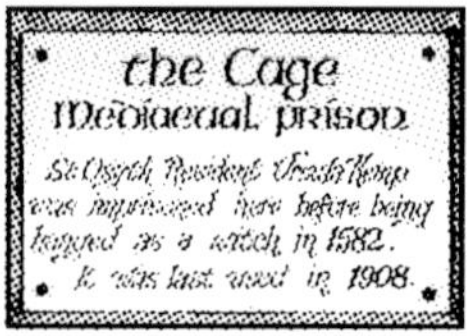

Plaque at the Cage, St.Osyth

THE CAGE, ST OSYTH

Colchester Rd, CO16 8HA

In 1582, the testimony of Ursula Kemp's eight-year-old son led her to the gallows on the charge of causing death by means of sorcery. Kemp confessed to communing with two male spirits and two females, who brought about death and sickness respectively. Before being taken to Chelmsford for trial, Kemp was imprisoned in the tiny "cage" house, which is now a private residence popular with ghost-hunting parties.

COLCHESTER CASTLE

CO1 1TJ / £

The largest witch jail in England. The castle—an unusual Roman design—has extensive underground chambers that were used to house the accused and act as interrogation rooms during the reign of Matthew Hopkins. The jail is subject to "replay"-style hauntings, most notably visions of Roman feet marching across the floor. A plaque dedicated to the 200 people held at the castle on suspicion of witchcraft can be seen at the gates of Castle Park.

Bedfordshire

FIVE KNOLLS

Dunstable, LU6 2NT

The Neolithic burial mounds of the windswept Dunstable Downs have long been connected to witchcraft in the local consciousness. Used as a gallows site and a burial ground for the condemned throughout the medieval period, covens of witches were said to convene upon the mounds. During the Dunstable witch trials of 1667, one Elizabeth Pratt confessed to meeting with three other women there, where the Devil—in the guise of a man, a woman, and a cat—commanded them to bewitch two children to death. The Devil promised to make Pratt the finest woman in the town, but she "found him to be a liar". Pratt died in Bedford gaol, awaiting trial.

Neolithic burial mounds

CLOPHILL CHURCH

Old St Mary the Virgin, Old Church Path, Bedford, MK45 4BJ

Vandals lay siege to this four-hundred-year-old church throughout the 1960s and 70s. Gravestones were desecrated with occult graffiti, a "satanic" altar erected, and the skull of one Jenny Humberstone who died in 1770 was mounted on a stake. The alarm was raised when local children were noticed playing in the street with human remains. Humberstone's grave was ransacked a further two times, and the severed heads of six cows and a horse were discovered in a nearby wood, igniting fears of ritual sacrifice. Luton librarians experienced a subsequent spike in demand for witchcraft literature. To avoid further vandalism, all headstones were removed from the site at the height of the disturbances. They have since been turned into a path through a garden of remembrance on the site.

Ruins of Old St Mary the Virgin Church and its gravestones

Hertfordshire

The Devil Rides Out (1968)

EDGWAREBURY HOUSE, ELSTREE

Barnet Ln, WD6 3RE

Converted into a private country club in the 1930s and then into a hotel, this Tudor mansion served as Richard and Marie's abode in *The Devil Rides Out* (1968), where Mocata carried out his psychic attack after announcing "I shall not be back. But something will". Those seeking to spend the night in a magic circle with the Duke De Richleau will be sad to learn that neither the circle nor Richleau remain here.

Sigils on the cottage door

BRICKET WOOD

Five Acres: 10 Five Acres Ave, AL2 3PY

The father of modern Witchcraft, Gerald Gardner, moved to Bricket Wood after the war and purchased a plot in Fouracres, a naturist colony that would later be renamed Five Acres. On his new grounds he installed a 16th-century single-storey cottage that had initially been erected near Ledbury, in Herefordshire, and later transported to Abbey Folk Park, an open-air museum near London then owned by Gardner's friend J S M Ward, where he exhibited it as a witch's cottage. From 1946 onwards, the transplanted cottage, decorated with magical sigils on the inside, hosted the coven of Gerald Gardner, initially with Dafo as the High Priestess. The Bricket Wood Coven continues to exist today, though the cottage is no longer their base. The naturist club still stands.

ROYSTON'S TEMPLAR CAVE

Melbourn St, SG8 7BZ / £

Accidentally discovered by workmen in 1742, no one knows for certain the origin or purpose of Royston's chalk cave and its strange carvings. Theories range from an early Freemason lodge to the lonely dwelling of an anchorite. The most popular theory is that some of the eerie carvings show Templar knights and their horses, suggesting a secret meeting place. However, Templars predate the full plate armour depicted. Other carvings include Saint Catherine and the wheel of her martyrdom, the naked Sheela-Na-Gig, multiple swords, and elaborate geometric patterns.

Staircase into the cave

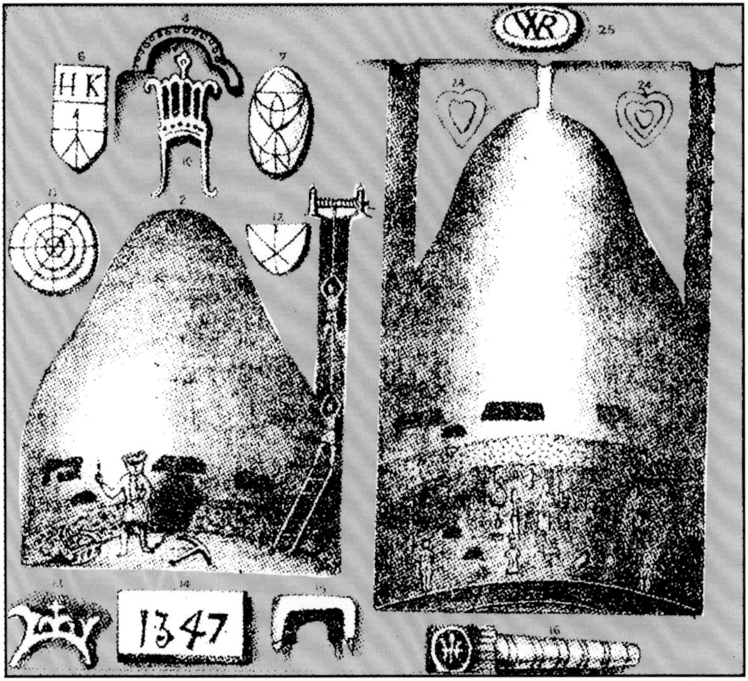

Joseph Beldam, The Origins and Use of the Royston Cave, 1884

Cambridgeshire

The wooden effigy of Gogmagog at Guildhall, London, carved by Captain Richard Saunders in 1709.

WANDLEBURY RING

Wandlebury Ring, Gog Magog Hills, CB22 3AE

Known locally as "The Gogs", the hills of Gog Magog are a series of low-lying chalk hills stretching for several miles across the otherwise flat Cambridgeshire countryside. Geoffrey of Monmouth's *Historia Regum Britanniae* identifies the hills as the final resting place of Gogmagog, the last surviving giant of Albion. The "detestable monster" was thrown off a cliff during a wrestling match by the legendary warrior Corineus.

Wandlebury Ring is all that remains of an Iron Age hillfort at the crest of the hills, and it is said to offer visitors the chance to fight a spectral knight. Hopefuls may enter the fort by moonlight and call out "Knight, tonight come forth!" A knight on horseback may then appear, prepared to joust. Be warned, the ghostly champion is said to deal real wounds which will reopen annually on the anniversary of the battle. The legend was first recorded eight centuries ago by the cleric Gervase of Tilbury, who claimed a knight named Osbert Fitz Hugh once bested the spectre.

King's College, Cambridge, ca. 1890–1900

KING'S COLLEGE, CAMBRIDGE

King's Parade, CB2 1ST / £

Writer and scholar M. R. James produced some of his best ghost stories during his residence at King's College. Many of his personal papers, as well as the original illustrations by James McBryde, are kept at the archives.

King's College Chapel has an interesting

legend attached: a subterranean tunnel is said to communicate it with the 15th-century manor house at Grantchester, three miles away. It has been surmised that the tunnel offered scholars an escape route in times of plague, but a more fanciful theory is that it leads directly to hell. At Granchester, local legend states that a travelling musician once set out to explore the tunnels, playing the fiddle so his friends at the entrance could keep track of him. The tune faded as the man ventured deeper, never to be seen again.

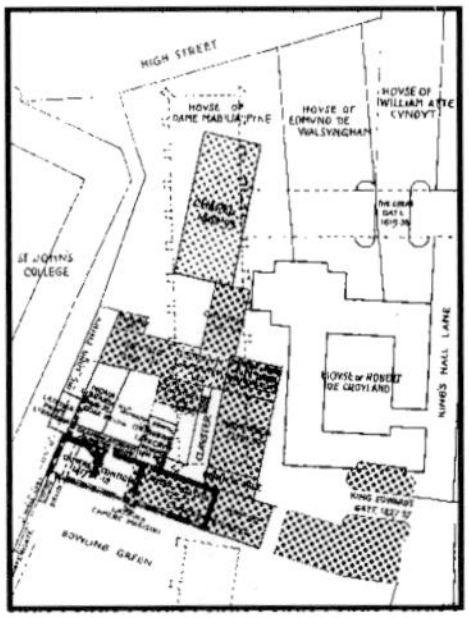

Plan of King's Hall before 1557

FLAG FEN

The Droveway, Northey Road, Peterborough, PE6 7QJ

Now an open-air archaeology park with reconstructed Bronze Age roundhouses, Flag Fen was the site of an ancient causeway from where votive offerings were thrown into the waters below. Archaeological excavations revealed a wooden platform built between 1350 and 950BCE and stretching for nearly a kilometre across the fen, remarkably preserved due to the natural conditions of the environment. Daggers, jewellery, and other high-status goods have also been found, as well as pebbles that weren't from the local area, which suggests that people travelled from afar to leave their offerings to the water gods.

Inside the roundhouse at Flag Fen

FITZWILLIAM MUSEUM, CAMBRIDGE

Trumpington St, CB2 1RB

THE LIONS that guard Fitzwilliam Museum are said to leave their posts on the stroke of midnight to either drink from the gutters a few meters away or visit the museum exhibits.

Suffolk

The Hauntings of M.R. James

MONTAGUE RHODES JAMES (1862–1936) was an antiquarian scholar, theologian, Vice-Chancellor of Cambridge University, and author of ghost stories now considered masterpieces of the genre. His tales often follow a socially awkward scholar, and typically feature the discovery of an ancient artefact protected by a vengeful supernatural entity which threatens the protagonist's rational worldview. The stories draw on James' experience as an academic as well as his youth in the rural parishes and coastal towns of Suffolk, with their atmospheric landscapes and rich archaeological sites.

ALDEBURGH, **Martello Tower:** IP15 5NA, **White Lion:** Market Cross Pl, IP15 5BJ

The lonely seaside town of Seaburgh in *A Warning To The Curious* (1925) is based on the Victorian holiday resort of Aldeburgh. James knew the town well and frequently visited his grandmother there. The Martello tower—an imposing 19th-century fortification—and the White Lion pub both feature in this tale of lingering spirits and violent deaths. In 1646, the burgesses of Aldeburgh paid for the services of Witchfinder General Matthew Hopkins, resulting in the execution of seven local women.

GREAT LIVERMERE, St Peter's Church: IP31 1JR

James' father was a clergyman, and the family lived at the rectory in Great Livermere, Suffolk, from 1865 to 1909. Now known as Livermere Hall, it is a private house. *A Vignette* (1936), the last ghost story James would write, is based on an encounter the young author had with a shrouded figure in the woods surrounding the rectory. James also borrowed names from the neighbouring churchyard, most notably *The Ash Tree*'s Mrs Mothersole and *The Mezzotint's* Mr Gaudy. A memorial plaque in St Peter's Church proclaims James "No longer a sojourner, but a fellow citizen with the saints, and of the household of God".

FELIXSTOWE, IP11 7BE

The shingle beaches of Felixstowe held special significance to James, who often spent the Christmas holidays of the 1880s and 90s there at the red-brick lodge of his friend, Felix Cobbold. In the house overlooking the North Sea, Cobbold would host parties for fellow academics. Tragedy struck in 1886 when James Kenneth Stephen, cousin of Virginia Woolf and a well-liked figure among the group, was thrown from his horse during one of these Christmas gatherings. The resulting brain damage turned Stephen violent, and he died in an asylum. The unfairness of the accident—a gentleman scholar struck down during an innocent activity—and the accident's apparent cause, a sudden whistle from a train, is thought to have influenced James' story, *Oh, Whistle, and I'll Come To You, My Lad* (1904), set in a fictionalised Felixstowe named Burnstow.

Dunwich Church, 1801

DUNWICH

IP17 3DT

The coastal village of Dunwich was the Anglo-Saxon capital of the Kingdom of East Anglia. Once a seat of power for pagan kings and Christian bishops, much of the village has already fallen prey to coastal erosion. The ruins of Greyfriars Abbey are of particular interest. The gravestones teetering on the cliff-edges are thought to have inspired the 1968 television adaptation of author M.R. James' ghost story *Oh, Whistle, And I'll Come To You, My Lad*, in which a hapless scholar unearths a whistle from an eroded grave. All eight of the town's original churches have been claimed by the sea, the last one collapsing in 1914. Visitors are encouraged to listen to the sound of the waves for ghostly echoes of the lost bells.

Demon Dogs of East Anglia

FOR centuries, demonic dogs have been seen roaming the landscapes of East Anglia. The Black Shuck—his name taken from the Saxon "succa", meaning devil—usually has malevolent flaming eyes, though it is sometimes described as headless or one-eyed. Invariably, these apparitions are thought to bring calamity or death.

The first recorded sighting happened around 1127, when a group of monks at Peterborough Abbey—now the cathedral of Peterborough, in Cambridgeshire—witnessed a monstrous procession of huntsmen accompanied by black hounds. The incident is thought to be an example of the Wild Hunt, a vision seen across Europe, said to herald a great calamity.

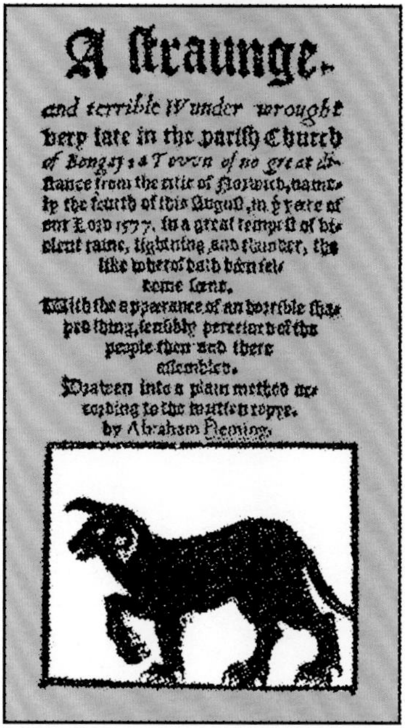

A straunge.
and terrible Wunder wrought
very late in the parish Church
of Bongay: a Towne of no great di-
stance from the citie of Norwich, name-
ly the fourth of this August, in ye yeere of
our Lord 1577. in a great tempest of vi-
olent raine, lightning, and thunder, the
like whereof hath been sel-
dome seene.
With the appearance of an horrible sha-
ped thing, sensibly perceived of the
people then and there
assembled.
Drawen into a plain method ac-
cording to the written copye.
by Abraham Fleming.

View of the east end, Holy Trinity Church

HOLY TRINITY CHURCH, BLYTHBURGH

Church Ln, IP19 9LP

Known as the Cathedral of The Marshes, this church has stood for a thousand years. On the 4th of August 1577, a storm hit the church, and a monstrous dog was witnessed charging down the aisle, leaving scorch marks on the door. These marks are visible today, cited as evidence of the Devil's fingernails.

Monk confronting the Devil

CHURCH OF ST BOTOLPH, IKEN

Woodbridge, IP12 2ES

The Ikanhoe fens were said to be teeming with demons and ghosts before Saint Botolph (610–c.680) drove them out and established a monastery there. Some of the demons were reported to speak like men while possessing feminine, mermaid-like bodies. The monastery no longer stands, but the tiny Church of St Botolph preserves an aura of mystery and a Saxon Cross that may have been a memorial to the holy man. After his death, Botolph's bones toured the country, driving out demons wherever they were taken.

St Botolph's church

Spirits of the Fens

THEIR isolation made these fertile, marshy areas excellent sites for religious communities in the medieval period, but the fens of East Anglia can be dangerous places, notorious for disappearances and outbreaks of malaria. They're also prone to self-igniting gases known as will-o-the-wisps, which have sparked many legends and superstitions.

Whistling in the fens is frowned-upon, as it attracts the lantern men, glowing spirits who lure victims to drown in the reed beds. If you see the eerie light of a lantern man, the solution is to lie face-down, mouth open to the mud, until the phenomenon subsides.

The Toadmen of the Fens were said to have sold their souls to the Devil with a ritual that involved catching a male toad and hanging it until its bones had been picked clean. Once dried, the bones were thrown into a running stream on a full moon at midnight. All bones except one would be swept downstream. The remaining bone would guarantee psychic control over horses, a useful skill to have in these marshy areas.

Witchfinder General

BASED on the bloody exploits of 17th-century witch-hunter Matthew Hopkins, folk horror classic *Witchfinder General* (1968) was one of the most controversial horror films of its day. It was largely shot in Suffolk, in locations with true witchcraft ties.

ORFORD CASTLE
Castle Hill, IP12 2ND / £
The cellar of this imposing 12th-century keep was used as a set for the bloody climax of the film. Orford Castle has a long history of strange goings-on. Around 1167, a fisherman caught a naked "wild man" covered in hair and sent him to the castle for six months of questioning. Refusing all food but raw fish, the wild man eventually escaped to the sea, keeping his secrets to himself.

LAVENHAM
CO10 9PZ
A wealthy Medieval settlement built on the success of wool trade, Lavenham is possibly the best preserved Medieval village in Britain. Its 16th-century guildhall presents a daisy wheel mark on the chimney lintel and a mummified cat, both of them thought to protect against evil. The building was the backdrop to the witch burning scenes of the film, shot in the market square. Actor Ian Ogilvy has recalled how some of the residents of the square claimed to have heard unexplained clanking and screaming the night after the filming, attributing the disturbances to angry ghosts.

KENTWELL HALL
Long Melford,
CO10 9BA / £
This moated Tudor house was used as the magistrate's home, and in many publicity shots featuring a menacing Vincent Price. Kentwell is open to the public, and hosts regular historical re-enactments and an annual Halloween show with techniques from stage magic, such as trapdoors, mirrors, and the Pepper's Ghost illusion.

Familiar, "The Discovery of Witches" (1647)

Norfolk

GRIMES GRAVES

Thetford, IP26 5DE / £

These Neolithic flint mines turn the Norfolk breckland into a moonscape of craters. Like many landmarks in England's Danelaw territory, the site's name is thought to refer to one of the Norse god Odin's guises: Grimnir, "the masked one". Roughly 4500 years ago, a settled community dug 400 of these pits with simple antler picks and brought up flint for tools, weapons, and ceremonial objects. Excavations in the late nineteenth and early twentieth centuries uncovered subterranean altars bearing decorated cups, unused antler picks, and phallic carvings. Skeletons were discovered carefully arranged in backfilled barrows, including those of a young man and a dog, suggesting ritual activity, perhaps with the aim of replenishing the mines. Further excavations in the 1930s yielded a crude chalk "Venus" statuette. The exciting find is rumoured to be a forgery planted by a disgruntled archaeologist, but the British Museum continues to store the statue, hoping for similar discoveries to verify its provenance or a long-awaited confession to emerge.

Neolithic flint implements found in Norfolk

TUNSTALL

St Peter and St Paul's Church, Tunstall Rd, NR13 / TG417080

Less than a mile from the ruins of St Peter and St Paul's Church in Tunstall lies a boggy pool. Abandoned from the 1660s onwards, the church was vulnerable to looters, leading to a tale of the Devil making off with the bells. In his hurry to escape the angry parson, the Devil clawed a never-ending tunnel through the marshy earth, creating Hell Hole, which still bubbles to this day as the bells make their eternal descent. Listen carefully for the sound of ghostly ringing.

The ruined tower

V. West Midlands

Herefordshire, 122
Worcestershire, 124
Warwickshire, 128
Staffordshire, 132
Shropshire, 138

V. WEST MIDLANDS

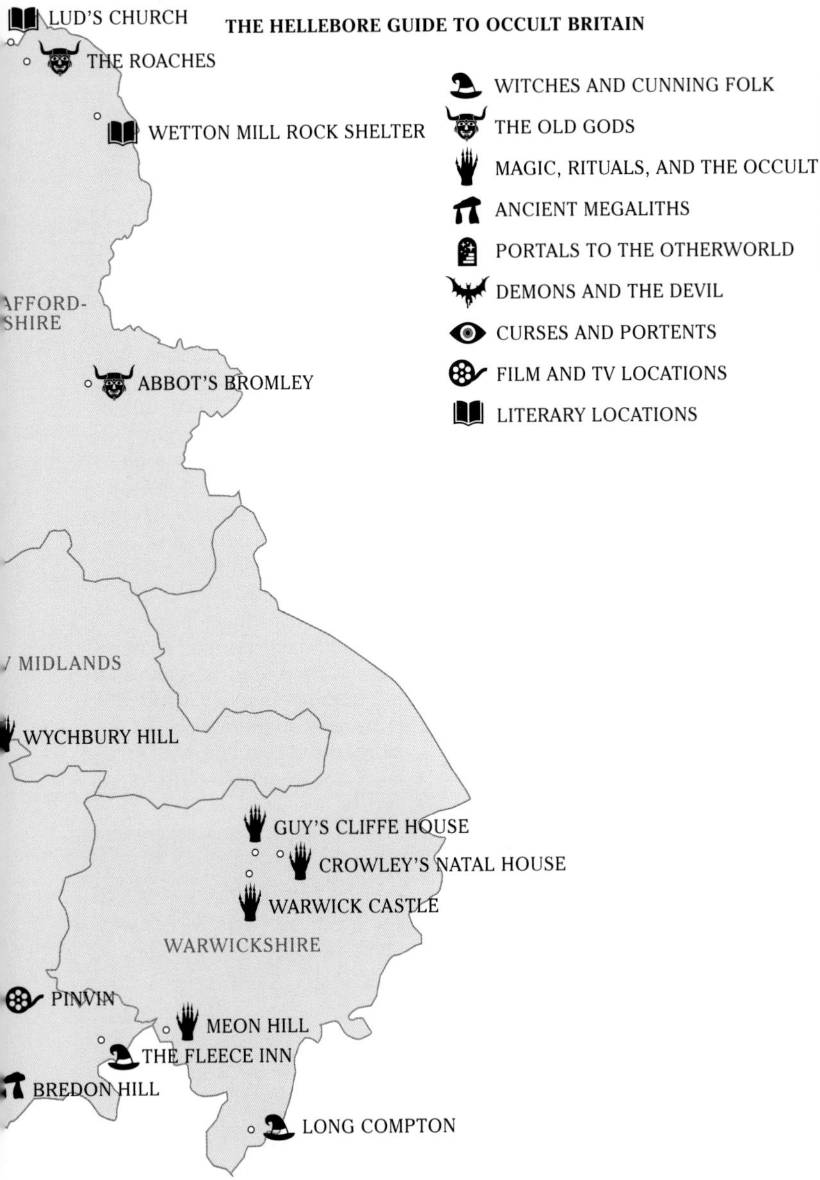
THE HELLEBORE GUIDE TO OCCULT BRITAIN
WITCHES AND CUNNING FOLK
THE OLD GODS
MAGIC, RITUALS, AND THE OCCULT
ANCIENT MEGALITHS
PORTALS TO THE OTHERWORLD
DEMONS AND THE DEVIL
CURSES AND PORTENTS
FILM AND TV LOCATIONS
LITERARY LOCATIONS
LUD'S CHURCH
THE ROACHES
WETTON MILL ROCK SHELTER
AFFORD-
SHIRE
ABBOT'S BROMLEY
MIDLANDS
WYCHBURY HILL
GUY'S CLIFFE HOUSE
CROWLEY'S NATAL HOUSE
WARWICK CASTLE
WARWICKSHIRE
PINVIN
MEON HILL
THE FLEECE INN
BREDON HILL
LONG COMPTON

Herefordshire

Tower of St Michael

Dextra Dei, the hand of God

ST MICHAEL'S CHURCH, GARWAY

Hereford, HR2 8RJ

St Michael's Church is one of the churches the Templars built in England, inspired by that of the Holy Sepulchre in Jerusalem. Its 12th-century circular nave was replaced with its current rectangular version by the Knights of St John in the 15th century, but the round foundations can still be seen today on the north side of the church. The exterior walls are engraved with a variety of mason's marks, including a Maltese Cross, a winged dragon, and a *Dextra Dei* (the hand of God) emerging from a cloud. Inside, the Templar chancel arch incorporated eastern elements and motifs, such as Moorish-style stone and "water leaves", both presumably inspired by the Templars Crusader origins, as well as a Green Man, horned and grinning, with foliage emerg- ing from his mouth.

Green Man relief

The Evil Squire of Hergest Court

SIR THOMAS VAUGHAN (1400–1469) passed to posterity as Black Vaughan, supposedly due to his evil nature, though some argue that the sobriquet referred to his hair colour. He fought for the Yorkists in the War of the Roses and was beheaded at Banbury. After his burial, his spirit tormented the inhabitants of Kington taking various shapes, one of them an angry bull that broke into the church while a mass was being held. In 1912, folklorist Ella Mary Leather recorded that 12 parsons with 12 candles and a woman with a newborn baby "whose innocence and purity were perhaps held powerful in exorcism" gathered to exorcise Black Vaughan, while the squire's wraith yelled "I was fierce when I was a man, but fiercer now, for I am a devil". His spirit was driven into a snuff box which remains buried under a large stone at the bottom of Hergest pool. It was said that Black Vaughan left two footmarks under an oak tree near Hergest Court where the grass never grew back, and that after the oak tree was cut down, the man who felled it went mad and died in an asylum.

Hergest Court

Hergest Road, HR5 3EL

The 13th-century fortified manor house that was Black Vaughan's home is privately owned, but it is visible from Hergest Road and from the Hergest Croft Gardens, which are open to the public. The estate is said to be haunted by a black dog that manifested every time a member of the Vaughan family was about to die.

Hergest Court

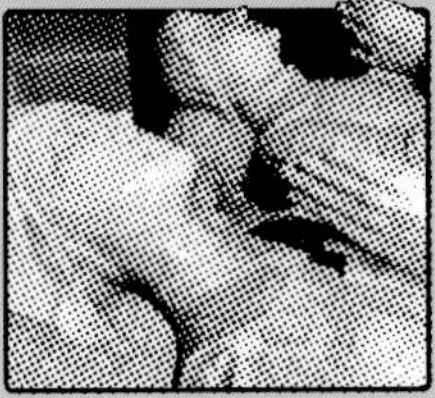

Ellen Gethin "the Terrible"

St Mary's Church, Kington

Church Rd, HR5 3AG

A beautiful 15th-century alabaster tomb in St Mary's Church contains the headless body of Black Vaughan. He lies next to his wife, Ellen Gethin "the Terrible", who once dressed as a man to fire an arrow through the heart of her cousin in retaliation for her brother's murder.

Worcestershire

The Fleece Inn

THE FLEECE INN, BRETFORTON

The Cross, Evesham, WR11 7JE

This 15th-century half-timbered building became a pub in 1848, remaining in the same family until 1977, when it was bequeathed to the National Trust. The three white circles in front of the fireplace in the dining room were painted over previous chalk or white-wash versions, so regularly drawn they left indentation marks. Their purpose was to prevent witches from entering the building via the chimney.

BREDON HILL

THE 18TH-CENTURY Parson's Folly dominates the landscape from the summit of Bredon Hill. Here, excavations at the site of an Iron Age hillfort—now visible as earthworks—revealed the skeletons of at least 36 individuals (including seven children) from around 100 BCE, the cut marks in the bones suggesting they were the victims of a violent attack. In spite of the tragedy, the hill and its ancient standing stones have become the focus of many rituals through the centuries.

Penda's Fen

Pinvin: Pershore, WR10 2EU
Chaceley: Gloucester, GL19 4EH

The visionary coming-of-age TV drama *Penda's Fen* (1974) shows how a young boy comes to reject the conservative values that suffocate him, aided by visions of a masked incubus; a Blakean angel; his idol, composer Edward Elgar; and the last pagan ruler of England, King Penda, who blesses him with these unforgettable words: "Be secret. Child, be strange, dark, true, impure, and dissonant. Cherish our flame." Mystical, moving, and still extraordinarily prescient, the drama was shot in Pinvin—whose name is thought to mean Penda's Fen—and Chaceley, where the Village Hall and the Old Vicarage became the Parish Hall and the Rectory.

The last pagan ruler of England, King Penda

A masked incubus

Bambury Stone

GL20 7PH · SO957402

A landslide split the so-called Bambury Stone into three, giving it the appearance of a kneeling elephant as well as its alternative name, the Elephant Stone. On Good Friday, the locals would climb the hill to kiss the stone for good luck. When the clock strikes twelve—or when the bells of Pershore Abbey ring, depending on the account—the stone is said to walk to the river Avon for a drink, which leaves exposed the treasure beneath it.

Bells of the abbey

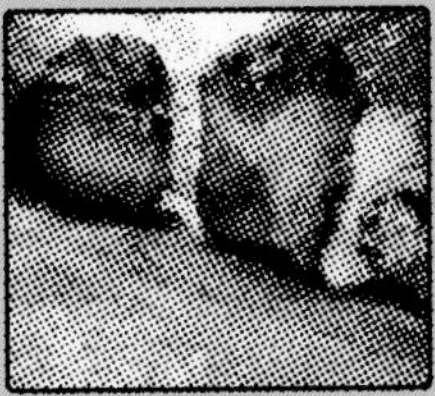
The King and Queen Stones

The King and Queen Stones

GL20 7JH · SO946386

This set of three standing stones is thought to be the remains of a collapsed long barrow. Healing rituals were performed around the site: crawling through the passage between the stones was said to cure diseased or deformed limbs and reverse a witch's enchantment, while passing children through it would protect them from rickets. Pregnant women would sit on the stones to ensure safe pregnancy and birth.

Mortsafe guarding grave

CHURCHYARD OF ST ANDREW'S, DOWLES

Dowles Rd, Bewdley, DY12 2RG

St Andrew's Church was demolished in 1956, but a copse of trees enshrouds the remains of its churchyard, accessed via an ancient corpse road. As well as a child's grave guarded by a mortsafe to fend off resurrectionists, the churchyard contains the remains of one Susan Wowen from Bewdley, whose story was recorded by John Richard Burton in the 19th century. She was known for the horns that grew up to three inches long at the back of her head, which were shed every three years. A Mr Soley of Sandbourne had one of them tipped with silver, while another one was sent to Oxford for study. Susan passed to posterity as a witch, her horns seen as a materialisation of her wickedness.

St Andrew's Church

WYCHBURY HILL

Margaret Murray

MARKED BY the earthworks left by an Iron Age hillfort, the westernmost of the Clent Hills has lingered in the popular imagination due to the "Who put Bella in the Wych Elm?" mystery. The 1943 discovery of the remains of an unknown woman inside a wych elm in the nearby Hagley Woods, part of the estate of Hagley Hall, inspired many lurid theories, both because of the mystery surrounding it and because of the insistent graffiti that appeared in the area following the grisly discovery. Anthropologist Margaret Murray posited the crime as a ritual murder carried out in order to produce a hand of glory—a magical tool made from a real human hand and said to offer invisibility and the ability to rob without being caught. Murray's theory, almost immediately dismissed, was based on the victim's hand having been severed and on the fact that her remains were concealed within a tree, supposedly to avoid supernatural revenge. An alternative theory suggests the victim was an escapee from a Nazi spy ring in Birmingham. Sadly, her identity is still unknown and the crime remains unsolved.

THE WYCHBURY OBELISK

Hagley, Stourbridge,
DY9 9JY

Close to the summit of the hill, erected in 1747 as a family monument by the then owner of the nearby Hagley Hall, the 1st Baron Lyttelton, this obelisk is more recently known for the graffiti that has sporadically appeared on it since the 1970s, "Who put Bella in the Wych Elm?". This followed a spate of similar graffitied questions which began to appear in the Birmingham area in 1944.

HAGLEY ESTATE

Four Stones: Clent, Stourbridge,
DY9 9PE · SO933803

Temple of Theseus:
A456, Stourbridge DY9 9LE ·
SO921813

Within Hagley Estate are several follies built in the 18th century under the orders of Lord Lyttelton. The Four Stones were erected "in imitation of a Druidical monument", and are also known as Ossian's Tomb after the blind 3rd-century bard dubbed the Homer of the North. The Temple of Theseus is a miniature replica of a Greek Doric temple, England's first example of Neo-Classical architecture, but it is now fenced off.

Warwickshire

LONG COMPTON

CV36 5LA

THERE is an old saying that states "there are enough witches in Long Compton to draw a load of hay up Long Compton Hill", a claim supported by the village's history and folklore. It might all have started with an episode of Christian necromancy in 604 CE, when a local lord was excommunicated by St Augustine for refusing to pay his tithes. Later, when Augustine requested that no excommunicated man should be present at mass, a dead man crawled out of his tomb at the entrance to the church, explaining he probably shouldn't be there because he'd been excommunicated in life. Augustine calmly raised the dead priest who had shut him out and the three had a civilised chat before the sinner repented and both dead men returned to their graves.

Long Compton was said to be rife with shapeshifting witches, some of whom gathered at the King's Stone in the nearby Rollright Stones (on the border with Oxfordshire). At a field near the church, then known as The Close, a young man sold his soul to the Devil, receiving twelve imps as familiars after drawing a circle in the middle of the field and reciting the Lord's Prayer backwards.

St. Augustine of Canterbury

Many of these tales were collected in the 19th century by the Reverend Harvey Bloom, a local clergyman and folklorist.

The Witches of Long Compton

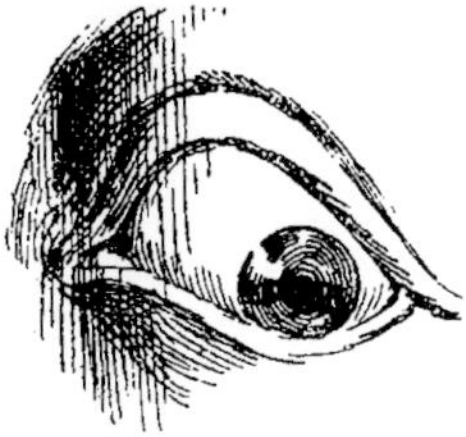

In 1875, 79-year-old Ann Tennant, from Long Compton, was stabbed to death with a pitchfork by James Haywood, a local farm labourer who believed that Ann had the power of the evil eye, and that she had bewitched him so that he suffered from cramps and pains. On walking home one evening he crossed paths with Ann, and stabbed her in an attempt to draw her blood and release him from her spells—whether or not it was his aim, she died soon after from her wounds. Haywood, who alleged there were 16 other witches in Long Compton, was found not guilty of murder by reason of insanity and was sent to Broadmoor Asylum. Even in the 1920s, belief that witches abounded in the village was still prevalent, as noted by a statement written in 1928 by Richard Clarke, the son of an eyewitness to Haywood's crime, who believed the killer's suspicions to be fully justified.

CHURCH OF ST PETER AND ST PAUL

Main St, Long Compton, Shipston-on-Stour, CV36 5JJ

The church is famous for its unusual lych gate, dating from about 1600, when it was the end of a now demolished row of cottages. In its porch lies the 14th-century recumbent effigy of a woman, said to have once covered the tomb of a witch. The small animal resting at her feet, possibly a fox or a cat, supposedly represents her familiar.

MEON HILL

Granbrook Ln, Chipping Campden, GL55 6TQ

THE DEVIL is said to have accidentally created Meon Hill by throwing a clump of earth to thwart the construction of Evesham Abbey in 717CE. He missed his target due to the intervention of St Egwin, the abbey's founder. The Devil's clump of earth became the hill, later the site of an Iron Age hillfort. The soil regularly yielded Iron Age and Romano-British coins and currency bars, which undoubtedly contributed to the stories of buried treasure.

The Pitchfork Murder

MEON HILL is associated with stories of the Black Dog, whose appearance heralds the death of those who see him. In the 1920s, the folklorist Rev. Bloom wrote about how in 1885 a young man from Lower Quinton named Charles Walton met the Black Dog "nine times on successive evenings… on the ninth encounter a headless lady rustled past him in a silk dress, and on the next day he heard of his sister's death". In 1945, the same Charles Walton, by then 74 years old, was found killed on Valentine's Day in what came to be known as the Pitchfork Murder. The press linked the case to occult practices and the experts weighed in: Margaret Murray argued his death was a blood sacrifice to ensure strong crops, given the proximity of the date to Candlemas Day, while Gerald Gardner pointed at the victim's old age to refute her claims—the "sacrificial king" had to be a person at the peak of youth and strength. Yet there might be an occult link after all: Walton's encounters with the Black Dog, his solitary demeanour, and his uncanny way with animals could have made him the target of a hate crime driven by fears of witchcraft. Unlike Ann Tennant's, his murder remains unsolved.

Black Dog, Yellow Fairy Book, 1894

GUY'S CLIFFE HOUSE

Warwick, CV34 5YD

A fire in 1992—while Granada TV was filming the episode of "The Last Vampyre" for its *Sherlock Holmes* series—seriously damaged this 18th-century house built by a slave owner and named after the legendary Guy of Warwick. Sir Guy, a knight who defeated the most fearsome beasts and went on a pilgrimage to the Holy Land, is said to have spent his last days in a cave at the foot of the cliffs. A statue commemorates him in the Chapel, which has been used for Masonic ceremonies since the 1950s. The house is also said to replay the deadly fall of a woman from one of its balconies in a classic Stone Tape-style, and many have attempted to find the tunnels that supposedly lie beneath the grounds, unsuccessfully.

Guy's Cliffe House

The Last Vampyre, 1992

The Cradle of the Great Beast

Crowley's natal house: 30 Clarendon Square, Leamington Spa, CV32 5QX
Warwick Castle: Warwick, CV34 4QU / £

BORN in Royal Leamington Spa, Aleister Crowley (1875–1947) studied at Trinity College, Cambridge, before becoming the most notorious occultist of his time, learning Hindu and Buddhist practices in India, mountaineering in Mexico and the Himalaya, honeymooning in Cairo, establishing the Abbey of Thelema in Sicily, attempting to raise Pan in Algeria, faking his death at the Boca do Inferno in Lisbon, and scandalising polite society all over the world until his death at Netherwood, Hastings, aged 72.

Unsurprisingly, many locations with occult ties in the Midlands—or elsewhere, for that matter—were allegedly frequented by Crowley. He held séances at the extremely haunted Kenilworth room in Warwick Castle, and tales of his visits to Guy's Cliffe House and of the rituals he supposedly performed at Keele's amphitheatre (an old quarry that once was part of a Templar estate, now Keele University in Staffordshire) are still whispered in occult circles, even though there is no evidence to support them.

Staffordshire

ST NICHOLAS' CHURCH, ABBOT'S BROMLEY

Rugeley, WS15 3BP

Each year on Wakes Monday—the day following the first Sunday after the 4th of September—the streets of Abbot's Bromley host a horn dance thought to be the oldest folk dance in Britain. Starting at 8am, a group of six deer-men, a Fool, a Hobby Horse, a Bowman, and Maid Marian, dance across the area to the tune of a melodeon. The ceremonial antlers used in the dance are on display in St Nicholas Church during the rest of the year, and some of them have been carbon dated at over 1,000 years old.

Abbot's Bromley, c. 1900

ST JOHN THE BAPTIST'S CHURCH, BURSLEM

Stoke-on-Trent, ST6 3JY

Jackdaw (Coloeus monedula)

A 17th-century grave at the churchyard is the focus of a Halloween rite of passage: children run around it three times, singing "Molly Leigh, Molly Leigh, chase me round the apple tree, Molly Leigh, Molly Leigh, you can't catch me" to summon the spirit of the woman who lies beneath, the so-called Witch of Burslem. Molly Leigh was born in 1685 in a cottage in the village's outskirts. She was quiet and strange-looking, the only child of a dairy farming couple, always followed by a black bird. For decades the locals shunned her, and in 1746 the local parson accused her of not attending church like a good Christian. After attempting to shoot her pet bird, the reverend spent several weeks bedridden in terrible pain, which led him to accuse Molly Leigh of witchcraft. Molly died before she could stand trial and was buried in consecrated ground, but the reverend claimed he'd seen her in her cottage, risen from the dead. He gathered a group of local parsons to open her grave and drove a stake through her heart to prevent her from returning again. Her pet bird—which the reverend believed to be her familiar—was buried alive with her, and her grave was turned around north to south, othering Molly Leigh even after death.

The Staffordshire-born witch Sybil Leek (1917 – 1982), who lived in the New Forest village of Burley, claimed to be Molly Leigh's descendant. Like her ancestor, Leek kept a pet jackdaw who always followed her around.

Church graveyard, Burslem

St John's Church

James Bateman

Biddulph sphinx

BIDDULPH GRANGE

Grange Road, Biddulph, ST8 7TZ / £

In this Grade I-listed garden, rare and exotic plants grow among ornamental buildings that conjure faraway lands and esoteric beliefs. Victorian plant hunter James Bateman and his wife Maria were assisted by artist Edward Cooke in creating a landscape that reflected their beliefs in a universe that was intelligently designed, where geological processes formed different environments and plants. But there seems to be something of the Victorian occult revival too, particularly in the China garden, which boasts a gilded bovine statue with a sun disc reminiscent of Apis, and in the Egyptian court, with its pair of sphinxes guarding a dark pyramidal temple inhabited by an Ape of Thoth. Its pioneering stumpery, where upside-down oak tree roots and ferns flank a sunken path, echoes ideas of rusticity in English gardens that seem influenced by antiquarian druidism and ornamental hermits.

Biddulph Grange

THE ROACHES

Bawdstone: ST13 8TY · SK007619
The Winking Man: ST13 8UH · SK020623
Doxey Pool: ST13 8UA · SK004628

This rocky escarpment and its surroundings are populated by weirdly shaped rocks around which folk rituals and beliefs have developed. The Bawdstone was the destination of a Beltane procession formed by the inhabitants of Leek and other nearby villages. Those who were sick or who believed themselves cursed would crawl under it in order to knock the Devil off their backs. Before the 1920s, the rock was also ritually whitewashed on Beltane day. The Winking Man is a natural rock formation that resembles a man's profile and that is said to wink to some passers-by—allegedly, as a sign of fertility. The winking effect is a consequence of parallax, due to the alignment of a rock behind it.

Just above the Roaches is Doxey Pool, a small pool said to be home to a malevolent water spirit, the blue nymph Jenny Greenteeth, who lures unsuspecting victims into her watery grave.

The Winking Man

Doxey Pool

In search of the Green Chapel

"This oratory is evil. With herbs overgrown,
it is a fitting place for the man in green
to deal here his devotions after the Devil's manner…
This is a chapel of misfortune—evil betide it!
It is the most cursed kirk that ever I came in."
—*Sir Gawain and the Green Knight.*

IN THE 14TH-CENTURY chivalric romance *Sir Gawain and the Green Knight*, Sir Gawain faces his greatest challenge in Camelot and decapitates the mysterious Green Knight, but, picking up his own bleeding head, his adversary demands they meet again for a second duel a year and a day later in the Green Chapel. The mysterious location is revealed after an incessant search, when the hero arrives at a foreboding place that is "nought but an old cavern, or a cleft in an old crag", where the Devil's presence is overwhelming. So vivid are the descriptions of the Green Chapel that many scholars argued it was based on a real location. Since the dialect of the poem matched that of the Staffordshire/Cheshire border at the time in which it was written, the general consensus is that the Green Chapel might have been inspired by one of these two locations—or that perhaps it is a conflation of both.

1 LUD'S CHURCH

Buxton, SK17 0SU · SJ986656

It is said that direct sunlight only enters this deep chasm on Midsummer's Day. Hidden in the depths of Back Forest, ornamented with moss, ferns and overhung trees which paint it a dark emerald green, the evocative site is said to have been used in the 15th century as a secret place of worship for Lollards, reformed Christians considered heretical. It is thought that Sir Walter de Lud-Auk, a Lollard who was captured here by passing soldiers, may be the origin of the name.

2 WETTON MILL ROCK SHELTER

Wetton, DE6 2AG

Perched above Wetton Mill Farm in the Manifold Valley, this cavern is a less popular candidate for the Green Chapel, but perhaps a more fitting one. From its entrance, a natural cavern known as Hob Hurst's House (said to be the haunt of the Peak District goblin after whom other local monuments are named) is visible across the valley. Wetton Mill rock shelter was used as a location in Ken Russell's adaptation of Bram Stoker's *The Lair of the White Worm.*

Shropshire

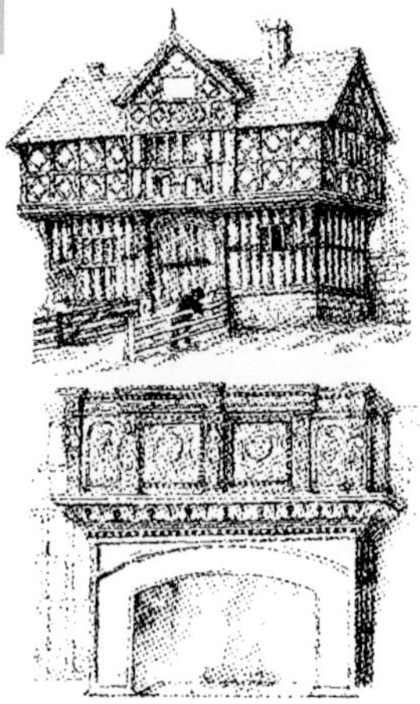

Gatehouse and fireplace

STOKESAY CASTLE

Ludlow Rd, Craven Arms,
SY7 9AH / £

The 17th-century woodwork in the gatehouse of this fortified manor house is carved with intriguing depictions of the Devil, the Biblical serpent, dragons, and nude figures. The castle is a rare example of a near complete set of Medieval buildings that have survived with very little alterations since the 13th century. Legend has it that a treasure is buried underneath, now guarded by a monstrous raven after the two giants who owned it lost the key to it and became so upset they died of grief.

Stone at Mitchell's Fold

MITCHELL'S FOLD

Stapeley Hill, White Grit, SY15 6DE · SO304983

Half of the thirty original stones of this Bronze Age stone circle still remain. The tallest of these was originally part of a pair which formed an entrance into the circle. There may have also been a central stone, which folk tales identified with a petrified witch. The story goes that during a time of famine, a fairy provided the community with a magic cow which gave an endless supply of milk as long as people only took a single bucket to be filled. When a witch milked the cow into a sieve, the cow galloped away. As a punishment, the witch was petrified and the circle of stones was built around to prevent her from ever leaving Stapeley Hill.

The Legend of Wild Edric

EADRIC THE WILD, also known as Wild Edric and Eadric Cild, was an 11th-century Anglo-Saxon thegn who led an opposition to William the Conqueror. After his rebel army was defeated in 1069, Edric submitted to William, eventually accompanying him on his attack on Scotland. He became a legendary figure, haunting the Shropshire area, where he is associated with several landmarks.

STIPERSTONES

SY5 0PG · SO367986

Legend has it that after Edric's surrender to the Normans, his followers imprisoned him, along with his wife, Lady Godda, and his fighters, in the lead mines under the rocky hill of Stiperstones. They were cursed with the inability to die until all wrongs were righted, so when England is under threat, the group can be seen riding across the sky, in a ghostly cavalcade reminiscent of the Wild Hunt. Sightings of Wild Edric and his host have been reported during the Crimean War and before the two World Wars.

The Stiperstones ridge is also associated with demonic forces. On the longest night of the year, witches and demons gather around the ridge to choose their king. Another story tells how the Prince of Darkness was carrying stones from Ireland in order to fill in Hell Gutter, a valley on the other side of Stiperstones. As the Devil sat on the northernmost tor, now known as the Devil's Chair, the strings of his leather apron snapped, and the stones fell around the chair. Legend says that if the rocks are driven into the ground, disaster will befall England, so the Devil sits there still, using his weight to bring this about. It is said that if you climb the Devil's Chair on a hot day, you can smell brimstone in the air.

BOMERE POOL

SY5 7AP · SJ499080

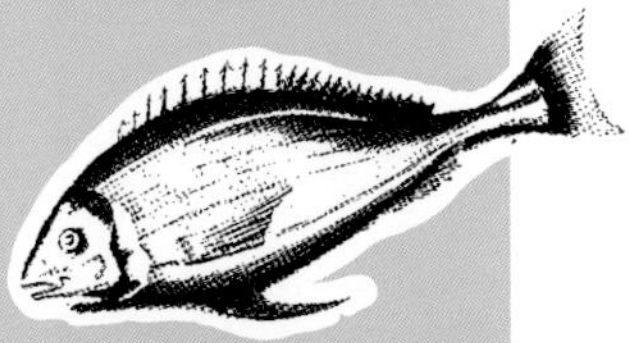

This lake is home to a legendary monster-fish who will carry the belted sword of Wild Edric until it is claimed by the true heir to Condover Hall, the house where Edric was born.

Bomere Pool is also said to contain the remains of an entire ancient city drowned in a single night because its inhabitants (variously described as Romans or Anglo-Saxons) refused to convert to Christianity. The bells of the church built by the priest who failed to convert the village have been heard ringing at midnight on Christmas Eve.

Grave of the last sin-eater

ST MARGARET'S CHURCHYARD, RATLINGHOPE

Shrewsbury Road, Ratlinghope, SY5 8DJ

The graveyard of St Margaret's Church houses the grave of Richard Munslow, the last sin-eater in England. Munslow was a local farmer who died in 1906. Like other sin-eaters from the area of the Marches, he was tasked with consuming the food and drink handed to him over a coffin, taking on the sins of the deceased so they would arrive purified before God. Given the weight of these sins upon the soul of the sin-eater, they were usually very poor people prepared to pay this high spiritual price in return for food and drink. Despite the service they provided to the local community, they were often shunned and lived in isolation. However, Munslow was a well-established farmer who provided this service out of love for his community, a service he allegedly began after the death of his four children. In recognition and gratitude, his grave was repaired in 2010 after a local fundraiser.

Taking on the sins of the deceased

CAYNTON CAVES

Caynton Road, Beckbury, TF11 9DF · SJ775028

The various entrances to these man-made caves on the grounds of Caynton Hall look like a series of rabbit holes, but inside the complex are carved archways and pillars, niches for candles, intriguing symbols, and a font. All of this fuelled the rumour that the caves were built for the Knights Templars to host their secret rituals. However, Historic England believes the date of their construction to be the late 18th or early 19th century, long after the order was dissolved. The caves were sealed off in 2012 due to vandalism and alleged black magic rituals on the site, but they've since been re-opened.

Caynton Caves

MORETON CORBET CASTLE

B5063, Shrewsbury, SY4 4DW

The dramatic ruins of Moreton Corbet Castle, whose earliest remains date to the 13th century, are a fitting setting for a narrative of curses, religious dissent, and a furious Puritan spectre. Established in about 1100 by a Saxon family, the castle went into the hands of the Corbets in the 13th century, who remodelled it extensively three centuries later. A pair of mythological creatures—a chimera and a wyvern—are carved into the Elizabethan frontage. In the 17th century, during the reign of King James I, Sir Vincent Corbet, then lord of the manor, took in a Puritan neighbour named Paul Holmyard, offering him protection at a time of prosecution. But after Holmyard became increasingly fanatical, Sir Vincent asked him to leave. Holmyard took to the woods, returning to curse the castle and its inhabitants: "Rejoice not in thy riches, not in the monuments of they pride, for neither thou nor thy children, nor thy children's children shall inhabit these halls." Sir Vincent was so terrified that neither he nor his son ever set foot on the castle again, and the spectre of Paul Holmyard is said to roam the ruins still.

Chimera on west corner

Wyvern on east corner

Moreton Corbet Castle

VI. East Midlands

Northamptonshire, 146
Leicestershire and Rutland, 148
Lincolnshire, 151
Nottinghamshire, 155
Derbyshire, 159

VI. EAST MIDLANDS

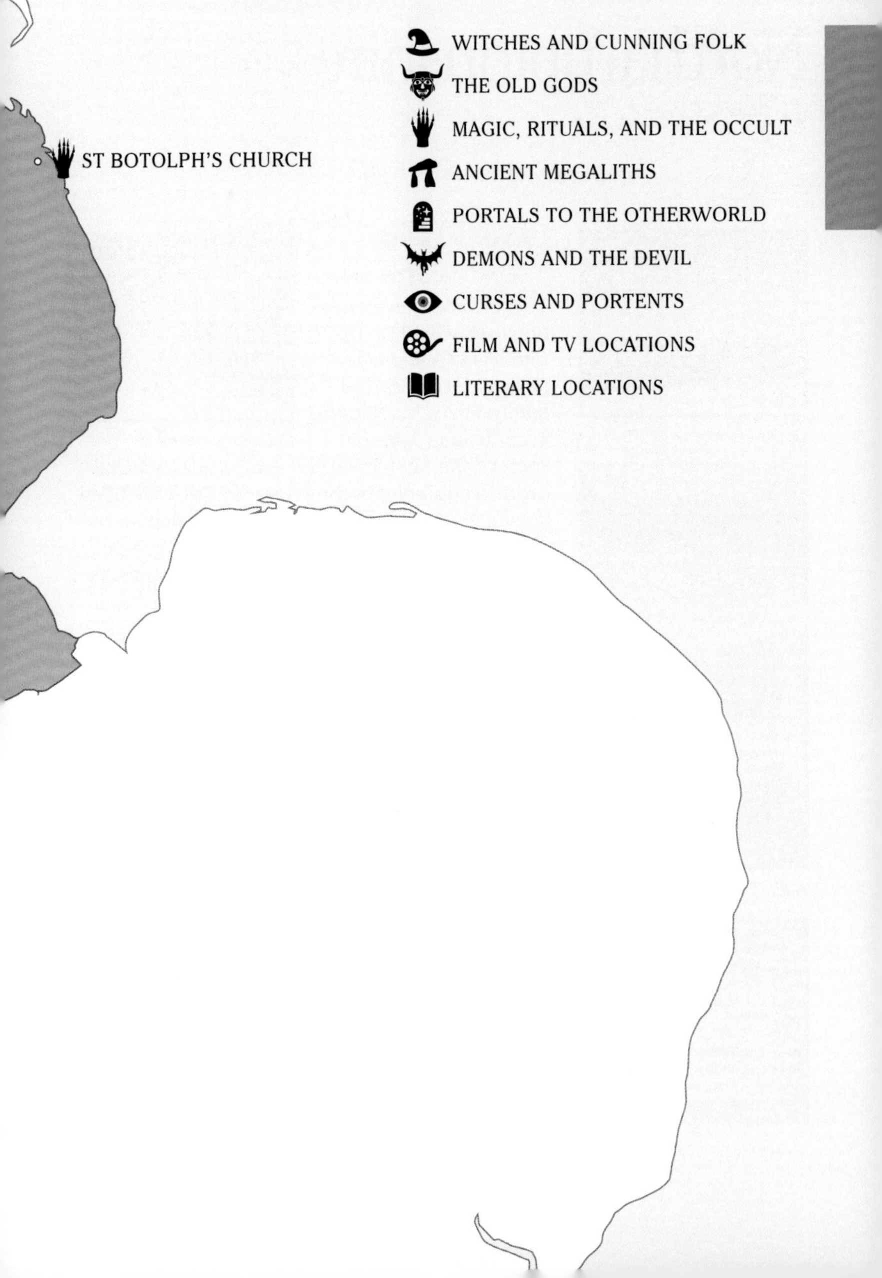
WITCHES AND CUNNING FOLK
THE OLD GODS
MAGIC, RITUALS, AND THE OCCULT
ANCIENT MEGALITHS
PORTALS TO THE OTHERWORLD
DEMONS AND THE DEVIL
CURSES AND PORTENTS
FILM AND TV LOCATIONS
LITERARY LOCATIONS
ST BOTOLPH'S CHURCH

Northamptonshire

Canons Ashby

Hidden Masonic imagery

CANONS ASHBY

Daventry, NN11 3SD / £

Courtyard entrance

This Elizabethan manor house was built on the remains of a Medieval priory for the Dryden family. In 2013, a National Trust worker found a secret chamber whose entrance was concealed inside a cupboard in the Winter Parlour. It's been speculated that the tiny room, untouched for 400 years, was used to hide ceremonial objects from public view—the Drydens were thought to be members of a society that evolved into what we now know as Freemasonry, and the Winter Parlour might have been their Temple. The crests in the lower level on its walls are believed to belong to the families connected with the lodge, and include some hidden Masonic symbols, and the buffet is a representation of the Temple of Solomon in Jerusalem. Further Masonic imagery can be seen in The Tower, where two carved compasses ornate the fireplace, and in the murals in the Spenser room, which include an all-seeing eye and a wreath of clouds.

GUILSBOROUGH

NN6 8QL

A village sign was dedicated in 2000 to commemorate the trial and subsequent hanging of Agnes Brown and Joan Vaughan who, according to a pamphlet of 1612, were accused of malefice against Elizabeth Belcher, a local noblewoman, and her brother-in-law, Master Avery. Another story, less historically documented, tells of Mother Roades, an elderly witch who died before her trial. Her friends, whom she had promised just before her death she would see again before the month was out, were arrested riding from Guilsborough on the back of a sow—a scene commemorated on the sign and on a tapestry in the village hall. They were subsequently hanged, so Mother Roades was reunited with them after all.

Tapestry in the village hall

ALL SAINTS' CHURCH, BRAUNSTON

71 High St, Daventry, NN11 7HR

A curious carved stone figure stands in the churchyard of All Saints' Church in Braunston. Referred to as "The Goddess", it was discovered in the 1920s, as the underside of the stone which was being used as the church doorstep. Neither a gargoyle nor a Sheela-na-Gig, it has been interpreted as a fertility figure due to the prominent breasts and lips, but its original date and purpose are uncertain.

"The Goddess"

All Saints' Church, Braunston

Leicestershire and Rutland

Tomb of Sir Roger Smith

EDMONDTHORPE

Melton Mowbray, LE14 2JX

The church of St Michael and All Angels holds the 17th-century alabaster tomb of Sir Roger Smith and his two wives. The effigy at the lower tier is that of Lady Ann Smith, his second wife, rumoured to be a shapeshifting witch. It is said that the red marks on her alabaster hand are a depiction of the injuries her butler inflicted on her paw while she was a cat, which remained on her when she became human again.

The Legend of Black Annis

Leicester Castle: 7 Castle View, Leicester LE1 5WH

LOCAL LORE tells of the flesh-eating witch Black Annis, who lived in a cave in the Dane Hills. With her blue skin and her claw-like fingers, she wore the tanned skins of her victims—largely children and lambs—around her waist, and had the ability to turn into a monstrous cat known as Cat Anna. An underground tunnel was said to communicate her cave with the cellars beneath Leicester Castle, and in the 19th century children were told she hid near the Turret Gateway, ready to snatch them away. Folklorist Katherine Briggs recorded that, until the end of the 18th century, a dead cat drenched in aniseed and symbolising Cat Anna would be dragged before a pack of hounds on Easter Monday. The strange parade, held to celebrate the end of winter, would start at Black Annis' Bower and end at the Mayor of Leicester's house.

The figure of the legendary witch might have been conflated with the Medieval anchoress Agnes Scott, who lived in a cave in the Dane Hills. Historian Ronald Hutton believes she may have been turned into a bogeyman figure at the time of the Protestant reformation, thus becoming Black Annis.

THE HUMBER STONE

10 Waterside Rd, LE5 1TL

Only the tip of this isolated, 3-metre-tall stone is visible. Standing near the traffic island of Thurmaston Lane and Sandhill Avenue, in the 18th and 19th centuries it was known by numerous names, such as the Hoston Stone, Hostin, Holly Stone, Holy Stone or the Hellstone. 19th-century amateur historian John Dudley believed it to have been an altar for druidical sacrifice, noting that the name Hellstone was related to Hela, the Norse goddess of death.

The Humber stone is said to be cursed: should anyone interfere with it, bad luck will follow. After parts of it were broken off in the 18th century to allow for easier ploughing of the land, the landowner's fortunes dwindled, and he died in 1810 in a parish workhouse. In 1878 the Victorian geologist William Pochin removed a piece of the stone for analysis; shortly afterwards, he accidentally shot off half his hand. In 1925, a farmer built a haystack on the stone; the haystack promptly burst into flames. After it was extinguished by the fire brigade, it reignited and burned for three days.

Stone excavation, 1878

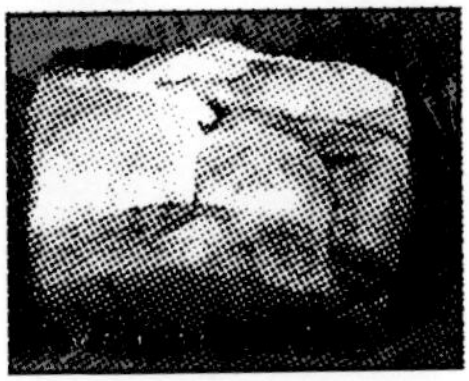

The Humber Stone

THE WING MAZE

7 Glaston Rd, Wing, Oakham, LE15 8RU

On the edge of the village of Wing is a cut turf maze—technically a labyrinth—that measures 14m across and that may date from the Medieval period. A listed ancient monument, only seven others survive in England. Folklore associates it with fertility rites and apotropaic purposes, and with a ritual that involved penitents crawling its path on their hand and knees in atonement for their sins. The 1846 Leicester and Rutland directory was more prosaic, describing it "an ancient maze, in which the rustics of the parish run on feast days".

The Wing Maze

The Old Maze, Rutland

The Witches of Belvoir

Belvoir Castle: Grantham, NG32 1PE / £

IN 1613, Joan Flower and her two daughters, Margaret and Philippa, from Bottesford, were working as servants at Belvoir Castle. Their family had been employed by the earls of Rutland for several generations, but, despite being in favour with the earl and his wife, the countess, they were not popular in the local community. Joan in particular was deemed a "monstrous malicious woman" and rumoured to be a witch.

When fellow servants lodged a complaint against Margaret accusing her of stealing, Margaret was dismissed. Her mother did not take it well, particularly when the earl did not argue in her favour.

The earl and countess became ill, and in the summer of 1613, the earl's eldest son also became ill and subsequently died, soon followed by his younger brother, which left the family with no heirs. Between this and the resentment and accusations of the other servants and villages, the earl was gradually swayed to the idea that the Flowers women were witches, and that Joan had placed a curse on his family.

Just before Christmas 1618 the three women were arrested and charged with witchcraft, and tales of their coven meeting on Blackberry Hill started to circulate. Joan died on the way to Lincoln gaol, allegedly choking on bread after demanding trial by corsned, an old method that involved eating a piece of unleavened bread while receiving the Sacrament—if the person choked and died, they were guilty. She was buried at Ancaster. Margaret and Philippa continued to Lincoln. Both confessed to witchcraft and admitted to have used the elder son's glove to bring about his death through magic, and to have cursed the earl and countess so they would have no more children. The sisters were found guilty and hanged in Lincoln gaol.

ST MARY THE VIRGIN'S CHURCH, BOTTESFORD

Rectory Ln, Bottesford, NG13 0DA

PARTS of St Mary the Virgin's church in the village of Bottesford date back to the 12th century. Changes were made over the course of the following centuries, including a memorial to Francis Manners, the sixth Earl of Rutland, who died in 1632. His memorial is also known as the "Witchcraft Tomb", as it is the only known tomb in England to record a death by witchcraft. An inscription reads "In 1608 he married Lady Cecilia Hungerford... by whom he had two sons, both of whom died in infancy by wicked practice and sorcerye". The sons, Henry and Francis, are depicted on the tomb carrying skulls to indicate they died before their parents.

Lincolnshire

WOOLSTHORPE MANOR

Water Ln, Grantham, NG33 5PD / £

The birthplace and family home of revolutionary scientist Sir Isaac Newton (1642 – c. 1726). Here visitors will find the apple tree that inspired Newton's theory of gravity, as well as several interesting hexafoil or "daisy wheel" witch protection marks common to old English houses and strange hieroglyphics purportedly made by the genius. Newton was a student of alchemy and astrology, with a strong belief in his own powers of prophecy. In Newton's opinion, the world will not last beyond the year 2060.

Woolsthorpe Manor

Sir Isaac Newton

BELTON HOUSE

High Rd, Belton, Grantham, NG32 2LW / £

The carved limestone sundial at the heart of the Dutch Garden of this 17th-century stately home became a portal to the past in Helen Cresswell's *Moondial*, adapted as a children's TV series in 1988. With a pedestal showing Cronus, the god of Time, and Eros, the god of Love, the sundial was sculpted by Christopher Wren's collaborator Caius Gabriel Cibber. The house is a fine example of Carolean architecture, and it's now managed by the National Trust, with a statue walk, a maze, a mirror pond, and a temple embellishing the grounds.

Belton House sundial

The Lincoln Imp

The Lincoln Imp

Woodwose

LINCOLN CATHEDRAL

Minster Yard, Lincoln, LN2 1PX / £

Among the 28 carved angels of the Angel Choir on the cathedral's façade, a squat figure sporting bull's ears and devil horns stares at the visitors with a mocking grin in his lips. This demonic creature is known as the Lincoln Imp, and its peculiar location has inspired several legends. One of the most popular tells how Satan sent two imps to earth to cause mischief. They went to Chesterfield and twisted the spire of the church there before heading to Lincoln cathedral, where their shenanigans were interrupted by an angel. One of the imps escaped the angel's wrath, but the second was turned to stone. He still remains in its place, just above the buttress on the Bishop's Door.

CHURCH OF ST ANDREW'S, STAINFIELD

Market Rasen, LN8 5JA

This 18th-century church is speckled with references to a woodwose known as the Wild Man of Stainfield. A wooden figurine depicting the beast, naked except for foliage around his waist, and holding a club, once surmounted a helmet that belonged to the Tyrwhitts, a prominent local family.

The first written record of the legend appears in 1915, when Rev. James Alpas Penny, dating the story to the 18th century, tells how one Francis Tyrwhitt-Drake released the locals from the dangerous creature who lived in the woods around the hamlet. The nobleman stabbed the wild man with his sword, and the creature bled so profusely that the field was stained red and thereafter called Stainfield. In return, Tyrwhitt-Drake was granted the wild man's estate.

Other stories claim the wild man was a knight who returned from the Crusades and, on finding his lands had been stolen, took to the woods.

A variant states the wild man was killed by a group of local farmers known as the Hardy Gang, in order to protect their livestock. The stories might have developed to explain the presence of the emblazoned helmet, as well as a pair of gauntlets and a sword that once hung next to it in the church. All of them were said to belong to the knight who killed the wild man. Unfortunately, the items—with the exception of the crest—were stolen from the church in 1995.

Saint Andrew's Church

ST BOTOLPH'S CHURCH, SKIDBROOKE

Church Ln, Skidbrooke, Louth, LN11 7DQ

Deep in the Lincolnshire marshlands stands an abandoned 13th-century church rumoured to be a regular venue for black magic rituals. The Grade I-listed building was dubbed "the demon church" by the press, and paranormal investigators regularly report strange occurrences, from orbs to shadowy figures and thunderous noises on clear nights.

Interior of St. Botolph's

PELHAM MAUSOLEUM

Great Limber, Grimsby, DN37 8JN

With a design inspired by the Temples of Vesta at Rome and Tivoli, the 18th-century Pelham Mausoleum in the gardens of Brocklesby Hall provided a striking setting for the 1973 TV adaptation of M. R. James' *Lost Hearts*. Here, the young Stephen, staring at the chanting cherubs on the lantern glazing, is spooked by a ghostly laugh and follows an elusive ragged figure that disappears behind the columns. The nearby South Ormsby Estate stood in for Mr Abney's house, Aswarby Hall.

Pelham Mausoleum

Doorway of the gatehouse

Oriel window, east side of the gatehouse

Thornton Abbey's gatehouse

THORNTON ABBEY

Ulceby, DN39 6AG / £

After the Dissolution of the Monasteries, this 12th-century Augustinian abbey, rebuilt in the 13th and 14th century, became a secular college for priests and later a private house. Very little remains of the original building, but its fortified gatehouse is one of the best preserved in Britain.

Antiquarian William Stukeley (1687–1765) wrote of a grisly discovery at the abbey shortly before 1722: the remains of an abbot, seated at a table with a book and a candlestick before him, were found during construction works, when one of the walls was pulled down, suggesting he'd been bricked up alive. The abbot's identity is uncertain, but the 16th-century abbey chronicle suggests two possible candidates. The first one is Thomas de Gretham, deposed in 1393 "for some unknown reason". His reputation was so dire that a later owner of the manuscript tore out the pages relating to this abbacy to prevent "scandal to the church". Rumours abound that Gretham dabbled in black magic and that he succumbed to the sins of the flesh. The second candidate is Walter Multon, who, in 1443, "died, but in what maner or by what death I know not. He hath no obit, as the other abbots have, and the place of his burial has not been found". Or at least it had not before the 18th century. The ghostly monk who haunts the abbey ruins is said to be the restless spirit of the immured abbot.

Green man in vaulting of Thornton Abbey Gatehouse

Nottinghamshire

HEMLOCK STONE, BRAMCOTE

Coventry Ln, Stapleford, NG9 3GH

Folklore attributes the origin of this 8.5-metre high monolith to a temper tantrum thrown by the Devil. The prayers and bell-ringing of the monks at the nearby Lenton Priory were so vexatious to him that he threw the stone from Castleton, Derbyshire, over 40 miles away, but his aim was poor, and the rock landed on Stapleford Hill, where it has remained ever since. Its name has led to many stories about it being a gathering place for witches—hemlock is one of the plants thought to have been used in the witches' flying ointment.

Recent geological surveys support the theory that the rock is a natural formation, but discussions about its nature are likely to continue. In the 19th century, writer, homeopath and mesmerist Dr Timothy Spencer Hall, writing as "the Sherwood Forester", alleged it was used in druidic rituals, a practice he thought was echoed by "the lighting of a fire upon it annually on Beltane Eve, as old people in my young days could remember and describe". This practice was also recorded by James Frazer in his magnum opus *The Golden Bough*.

Postcard, Hemlock Stone

Rev. George Oliver

CHURCH CEMETERY, NOTTINGHAM

49-51 Forest Rd E, NG1 4HT

This 13-acre graveyard was founded in 1851, on a hillside formerly used as a quarry then as a site of execution. It is known familiarly as Rock Cemetery, due to the many sandstone caves that run through the sloping side of the barren hill.

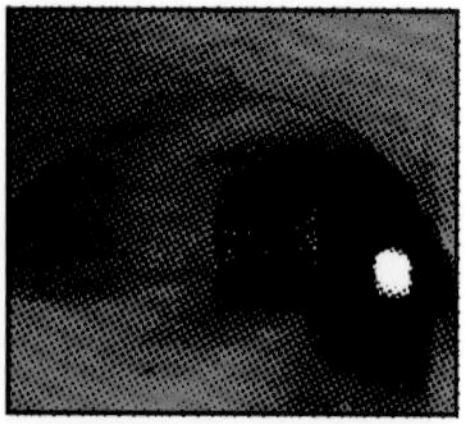

Tunnel in Rock Cemetery

Robin Hood

Newstead Abbey, west front

The presence of the caves, tunnels and other manmade features in the sandstone led local vicar, antiquarian and Freemason Rev. George Oliver to believe that an ancient druid temple had previously existed on the site, which is why he tried to halt the site's development in the 19th century.

A series of terraces, pathways, ramps and tunnels interconnect the separate sections of the cemetery. One area, Saint's Anne's Valley, is a natural hollow, extended and strengthened by the city's unemployed poor, where buttressed gothic arches are set into the exposed bedrock, and a row of paupers' graves lines the bottom of the ramp. At the other end of the social scale, notable interments include the architect Watson Fothergill. The caves to the north east of the cemetery are known as Robin Hood's Caves, as folklore claims that this was the site where the legendary outlaw would stable his horses.

NEWSTEAD ABBEY

Newstead Village, NG15 8NA / £

After the Dissolution, Newstead Abbey was purchased by the Byron family, who turned it into their home. For several generations the Byrons were beset by bad luck, which some have ascribed to the curse that follows those who use a religious building as their private residence. The ghost of a friar known as the Goblin Friar, immortalised in the epic poem *Don Juan* by George Gordon, Lord Byron (1788–1824), was said to appear every time a family member was about to suffer a disgrace. The rooks or crows who live in the property are said to be the spirits of the monks haunting the grounds. Other ghosts unconnected to the curse are the Rose Lady, the White Lady, and the ghost of Boatswain, the poet's beloved dog.

At an area of the Great Garden known as Devil's Wood stand a pair of statues of satyrs, one of them female, both attributed to Jan Van Nost, who also sculpted the statue of Pan in Painswick.

Female satyr, Great Garden

DRUID STONE, BLIDWORTH

Mansfield, NG21 0QR · SK579558

There is no evidence to support druidical activity at this natural glacial formation, but early O.S. maps marked its location with the legend "Druidical Remains". The narrow manmade passage cut through its centre may have been used to pass sick children through to cure whooping cough or rickets. In the 19th century, the local vicar Rev. Richard Whittworth claimed that on the day of the summer solstice the rising sun passed through the stone's artificial hole. Although modern study has disproven this particular hypothesis, it is possible that the sun would appear over the rock at the Beltane sunrise, on 1st May. The stone lies on private land but it is visible from the public footpath leading to Ravenshead and to Lord Byron's ancestral home, Newstead Abbey.

Druid Stone, Blidworth

Blidworth Rock

Green Man relief

SOUTHWELL MINSTER

Church St, NG25 0HD

This 12th-century minster standing on the site of an earlier Saxon church is carved with many interesting symbols. A Sheela-na-Gig, possibly from the first half of the 12th century, hails visitors among other Romanesque motifs in the right hand tower, and Green Men carvings flourish at the Chapter House.

Ironstone implement

CRESWELL CRAGS

Crags Rd, Worksop, S80 3LH / £

Nestled between the counties of Derbyshire and Nottinghamshire is the limestone gorge of Creswell Crags, whose opposing cliffs are honeycombed with caves. As well as fossils, bones, and artefacts that provide evidence for Neanderthal use 60,000 years ago, over 80 engravings and reliefs created around 13,000-15,000 years ago have been discovered in the caves. These images—depicting animals such as bison, horses, and birds, as well as female anthropomorphic figures—are the oldest to be found in Europe this far north. Several hundreds of "witch marks" were also carved in the 17th and 18th centuries to offer protection against evil. They're particularly concentrated in the darkest recesses of the caves, thought to be the dwelling place of demons and evil spirits.

Caves at Creswell Crags

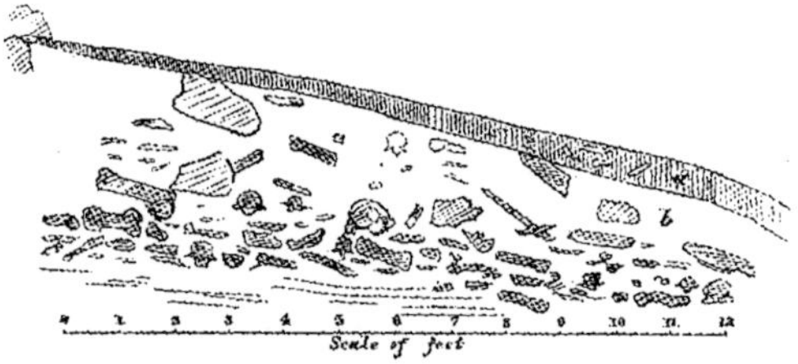

The bones of Creswell Crags

Derbyshire

ARBOR LOW STONE CIRCLE

Long Rake, Monyash, Bakewell, Derbyshire, DE45 1JS / £

This Neolithic henge monument is one of the most important prehistoric sites in the East Midlands. Within a bank and ditch, a circle of some 50 limestone slabs, now fallen, surround a central cove of at least 6 stones. The skeleton of a man in an extended position was unearthed near the cove in 1901, the same year in which WM Turner recorded the belief that the stone circle should be avoided at night, as it is the dwelling of boggarts. Today the site is owned by English Heritage, and can be accessed through a working farmyard.

300m southwest of the henge lies Gib Hill, a Neolithic oval barrow with an Early Bronze Age round barrow built over. An 1848 excavation inside revealed a burial cist containing the remains of a Bronze Age cremation burial, along with pottery, flint, and stone tools. The hill takes its name from its use as a hanging place in the 18th century, and fairy lights have been seen dancing around it at night.

Arbor Low Stone Circle

Burial mound, Gib Hill

NINE STONE CLOSE STONE CIRCLE

Harthill, Matlock, DE45 1LJ · SK225626

In spite of its name, only four of the original stones of this Bronze Age circle remain upright, one of which bears cup marks on both of its sides. A fifth stone has been used a gatepost in the field since the late 18th century. Curiously, the nine from its name may not be a number, but a corruption of "noon", perhaps related to the belief that the stones dance at midday or at midnight—hence its alternative name, "The Grey

Standing stones, Nine Stone Close

Ladies". The site was also thought to be a dancing ground for faeries. A local legend tells of a farm labourer who discovered a clay pipe at the stones; on smoking it, he was able to see through the earth and down into the realm of faerie.

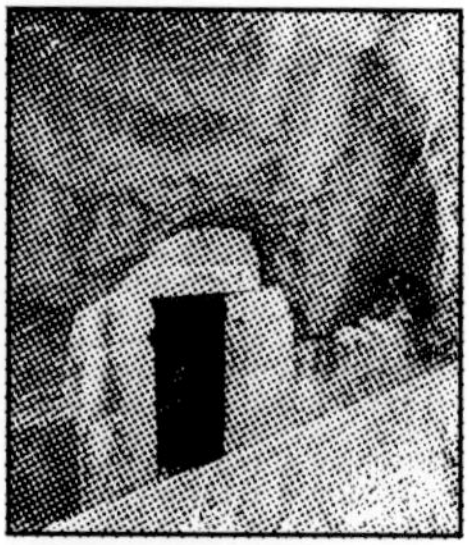
Rowtor Rocks

Stereographic photo, Rowtor Rocks, c. 1859–1863

ROWTOR ROCKS

Birchover, Matlock, DE4 2BQ · SK235621

This gritstone outcrop was described in the 18th century as having druidical associations, but the only proven one is that the nearby pub, the Druid Inn in Birchover, was the meeting place for the Ancient Order of Druids (established in 1781).

The rocks at the western end of the outcrop display Late Neolithic or Early Bronze Age engravings, such as cup and ring marks, but most of its rock features, including caves, "altars", stairways and pillars, were the work of Thomas Eyre (d. 1717), a local parson who lived in Rowtor Hall and on whose ground the outcrop stood. Eyre allegedly "entertained his company on this elevated spot", and some locals believed he practised druidic ceremonies and even black magic—contemporary antiquarians had popularised the idea that druids performed human sacrifices. The private chapel Eyre built under the rocks is now the parish church of St Michael's.

The Nine Ladies

The standing stones

STANTON MOOR

Nine Ladies Stone Circle: Lees Rd, Stanton in Peak, Matlock, DE4 2LS · SK248635

Doll Tor Stone Circle: Birchover Rd, Matlock, DE4 · SK238628

This upland heather moor has been occupied since the Bronze Age. Two stone circles, the possible remains of three others, and over 70 burial cairns dot the landscape, with most of the larger monuments forming an uneven but possibly deliberate line running SSW/NNE across the moor.

• Folklore regards the **Nine Ladies Stone Circle** as a group of nine women petrified for dancing on the Sabbath. A tenth stone was discovered in 1976, fallen flat to the east of the circle.

The King Stone, an outlier to the west of the Nine Ladies, is said to be the fiddler who accompanied them. Damaged by a vehicle in 1990, the stone is inscribed with graffiti dating from the 19th century, as recorded by Charles Dickens in *The Pickwick Papers*.

• The six stones of the **Doll Tor Stone Circle** were erected in the Bronze Age. A cairn to the east side of the circle incorporates one of the circle's stones within it. Excavations at the cairn revealed a Bronze Age grave pit with a female cremation, as well as four other cremations around it, with urns, cups, and faience beads.

The King Stone

The Doll Tor Stone Circle

MAM TOR

Hollins Cross: Hope Valley, S33 8WA · SK135845

St Edmund's Church: Castle St, Castleton, Hope Valley, S33 8WE

Landslips on the eastern face of this hill have generated smaller hills beneath, a recurring process that explains its name: Mam Tor literally means "Mother Hill"; locally, it is also known as "The Shivering Mountain". In the Iron Age, its summit was the site of a settlement of over a hundred timber houses. Two Bronze Age bowl barrows—one of them allegedly excavated in the 19th century, revealing human bones and a bronze item—and two hillforts—one of them the earliest in Britain and also one of the largest—also stood there.

A roughly paved road known as the Great Ridge runs over the Tor. Prior to the 19th century, the people of Edale had to carry their dead over the ridge so they could be buried in St. Edmund's Church in Castleton. They would stop at Hollins Cross, a crossroads at the lowest point on the Great Ridge, to offer their prayers, before continuing through the Coffin Road until they reached Castleton. The mourners then had to enter the church by the Devil's Door, which was the entrance also reserved for paupers.

The trig point on Mam Tor

Rough path up to Mam Tor

VII. The North West

Cheshire, 166
Greater Manchester, 170
Merseyside, 173
Lancashire, 178
Cumbria, 182
Isle of Man, 188

VII. THE NORTH WEST
ISLE OF MAN
PEEL CASTLE
CHURCH OF ST TRINIANS
MALEW CHURCH
WITCHES' MILL
THE ANCIENT MARKET CROSS
WITCHES AND CUNNING FOLK
THE OLD GODS
MAGIC, RITUALS, AND THE OCCULT
ANCIENT MEGALITHS
PORTALS TO THE OTHERWORLD
DEMONS AND THE DEVIL
CURSES AND PORTENTS
FILM AND TV LOCATIONS
LITERARY LOCATIONS

CUMBRIA
LONG MEG AND HER DAUGHTERS
ELVA HILL STONE CIRCLE
CASTLERIGG STONE CIRCLE
EAGLE CRAG
CALGARTH HALL
SWINSIDE STONE CIRCLE
LEVENS HALL
DEVIL'S BRIDGE
BIRKRIGG
STONE CIRCLE
BEETHAM FAIRY STEPS
LANCASHIRE
PENDLE
THE WRITTEN STONE
ST. LEONARD'S CHURCHYARD
GREATER
MANCHESTER
WARDLEY HALL
CHETHAM'S LIBRARY
JOHN RYLAND'S LIBRARY
CRANK CAVERNS
MERSEYSIDE
BIDSTON HILL
THE CALDERSTONES
THE ANCIENT CHAPEL
OF TOXTETH
ALDERLEY EDGE
MINERVA'S SHRINE
CHESHIRE

Cheshire

ALDERLEY EDGE

For several generations the name of Alderley Edge has conjured up tales of mystery and magic, largely due to the work of Alan Garner, who drew inspiration from local legends for his children's novels *The Weirdstone of Brisingamen* and *The Moon of Gomrath*. Sitting at the base of the red sandstone escarpment known as The Edge, the village and the surrounding landscape boast several landmarks redolent of these myths.

STORMY POINT

SJ860778

The ground beneath The Edge is riddled with tunnels where copper was mined from the Bronze Age until the 1920s, making it the oldest known metal-mining site in England. Stormy Point is an outcrop with an entrance to an old copper mine, now sealed with iron bars, from which eerie music is said to emerge.

The spot is also known as The Devil's Grave, and local legend says that if a person walks around it widdershins (anticlockwise), they may summon the Devil from his slumber below.

THE HOLY WELL

SJ859778

Reputedly in use since Anglo Saxon Times, this well was thought to have healing properties and the power to grant wishes to those who made propitiatory offerings. The iron gates in the legend of the Wizard were said to be located somewhere between Stormy Point and the Holy Well.

THE WIZARD'S WELL
SJ854780
Under a moss-covered, bearded face etched into the rock, are engraved the words "Drink of this and take thy fill, for the water falls by the Wizard's will". Like the Druid's circle, these were reputedly made by Alan Garner's great-great-grandfather, but there is something otherworldly in this spot all the same.

THE ARMADA BEACON
SJ858777
A Bronze Age burial mound once stood at The Edge's highest point. In 1588 this was the site of a beacon whose function was to signal the coming of the Spanish Armada.

THE DRUID'S CIRCLE
SJ860777
Although its location—deep in the woods between Stormy Point and the Armada Beacon—might suggest otherwise, this stone circle is a modern folly, purportedly erected by Alan Garner's stonemason great-great-grandfather.

The Wizard of Alderley Edge

THE TALE of The Wizard of Alderley Edge was published in the *Manchester Mail* in 1805, in a letter recording a story often recounted by Parson Shrigley, the former Clerk and Curate of Alderley, before his death in 1776.

The story told of a farmer on his way to sell a milk-white mare at Macclesfield market. As he was travelling through Alderley Edge, he encountered a tall and mysterious figure who carried a black staff. This man—known only as The Wizard—wished to buy the horse, but the farmer declined, thinking he might get a better price at the market.

Though all were impressed with the fine white horse, none at Macclesfield market would buy it. As the farmer made his way back across The Edge by moonlight, he was met once again by The Wizard, who had been waiting for him. He wielded his magical staff to reveal a set of iron gates embedded in a great rock. Following him through the gates and down into the earth, the farmer beheld a sleeping army of 140 knights in silver shining armour. These "Caverned Warriors", The Wizard explained, were kept in magical slumber until the day when they must awaken to defend Britain. Beside every knight but one slept a milk-white steed, and it was for this last horseless warrior that their guardian wished to procure the farmer's mare. The farmer was paid in ancient coins and hastily ushered out of the cavern. Though he heard the iron gates close behind him, when he looked back there was nothing but stone. For centuries now, people have searched for the iron gates, but no one has ever found them.

The Enchanter Merlin, Gustave Dore, 1888

The King and Queen of the Witches

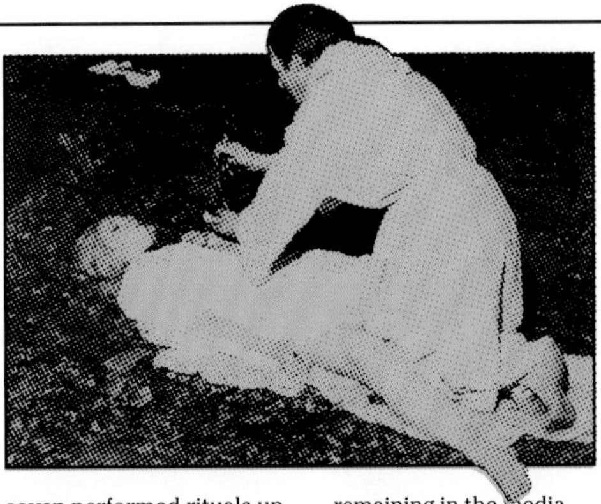

IN HER 1976 autobiography *Maxine: The Witch Queen*, Maxine Sanders (b. 1946) recalls how at the age of fifteen she was initiated into a secret magical lodge in rituals performed on The Edge. In 1964, she met her future husband Alex Sanders, whom she would marry in a handfasting ceremony on The Edge the following year. The couple co-created what came to be called Alexandrian Wicca, and were known as The King and Queen of the Witches. They lived together in Alderley Edge village for a time, and their own coven performed rituals up on The Edge, photographs of which appeared in The Cheshire Comet in the mid-60s, causing something of a local scandal. They also appeared in films, such as *Legend of the Witches* (1970), *Witchcraft '70* (1970), *Secret Rites* (1971), and numerous documentaries, remaining in the media spotlight throughout the 60s and 70s. Images of the ceremonial magic they performed together, with participants often naked or semi-naked, became part of the core occult imagery associated with the British Witchcraft of that era.

MINERVA'S SHRINE

Handbridge, Chester, CH4 7JE

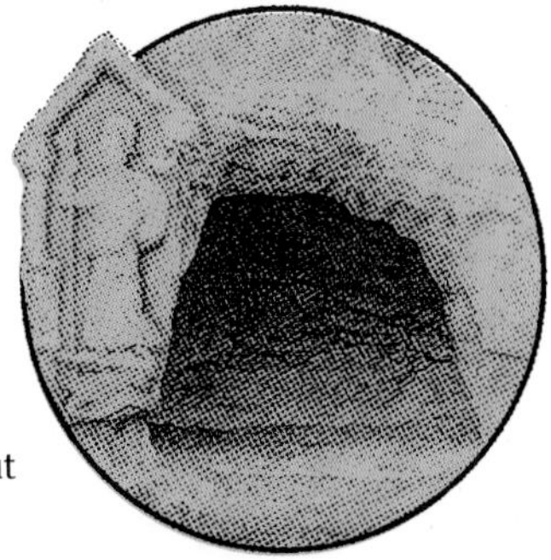

In Edgar's Field, a small public park on the south bank of the River Dee, stands an incredible remnant of the Roman occupation of Chester. During the early 2nd century it was used as a sandstone quarry, and its workers carved a shrine to Minerva—goddess of war, knowledge, learning, craftsmanship, and the arts—out of the rock. It is believed that offerings to the goddess would have been left in the small cave next to her shrine, which is known as Edgar's Cave. Today, Minerva's Shrine—extremely weathered and protected by a 19th-century stone surround—is the only monument of its kind in Western Europe which remains in its original location.

Greater Manchester

Wardley Hall, 1890

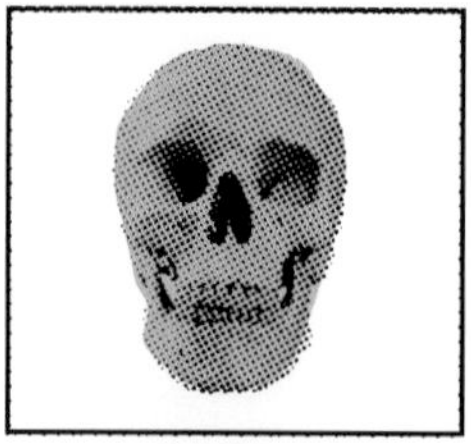

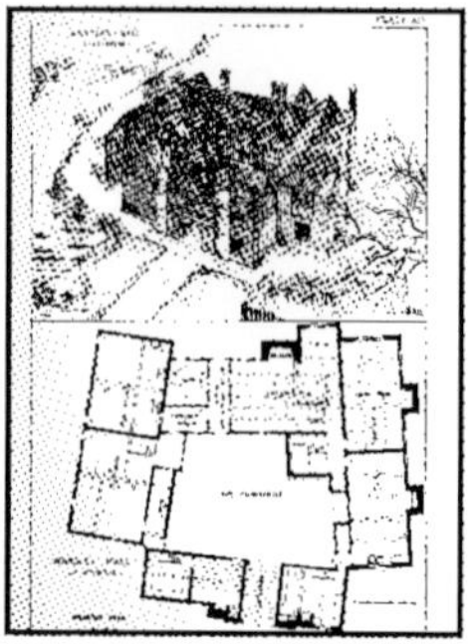

Plans of Wardley Hall, 1884

WARDLEY HALL

Wardley, Worsley, M28 2ND

Saint Ambrose Barlow

Housed in a glass-fronted, locked niche at the top of a staircase within Wardley Hall is a strange relic believed to be one of Britain's screaming skulls. It is allegedly the head of Saint Ambrose Edward Barlow, a Benedictine monk and Catholic martyr who was hanged, drawn, and quartered at Lancaster Moor in 1641. His remains were boiled in oil, save for his head, which was exposed on a pike at Manchester and, somehow, ultimately made its way to this medieval manor house, where it was kept as a secret relic. In 1745, Matthew Moreton, who leased the hall at the time, discovered the skull in a box within a wall, but a maid-servant threw it into the moat, mistaking it for the head of an animal. The same night there was a furious storm, which Moreton ascribed to the indignity to which the relic had been subjected. He recovered the skull and restored it to its place. From then onwards, any attempts to remove the skull from the manor house are said to have resulted in similar disturbances, and efforts to destroy the relic have proved it indestructible. Wardley Hall is currently the official residence of the Roman Catholic Bishop of Salford, and can be visited via previous arrangement.

CHETHAM'S LIBRARY

Long Millgate, M3 1SB

The oldest free public reference library in the English-speaking world was founded in 1653 in a 15th-century building initially erected to accommodate a college of priests. Among its impressive collection of books and manuscripts, Chetham houses a 16th-century copy of the *Tractatus de Nigromantia* believed to have belonged to shorthand pioneer John Byrom, and five books that once belonged to Dr John Dee, several of which contain marginalia written by the man himself. Chetham's has been used as a location in the 2013 BBC adaptation of M. R. James' *The Tractate Middoth*, and in the 1986 episode *The Priory School* of Granada's *The Return of Sherlock Holmes*.

Bookshelf, Chetham's Library

Dr Dee's Demons

BEFORE Chetham's Library came into existence, the space now known as the Audit Room was set aside for the use of the warden of Christ's College. Between 1595 and 1605, this honour corresponded to the infamous Elizabethan polymath Dr John Dee (1527–c.1608). The ancient refectory table in the Audit Room bears a strange semi-circular mark in one corner, supposedly left by the fiery hoof of a demon conjured by Dee during his tenure. At the timber ceiling, a carved "Mouth of Hell" mask with a sinner ensnared in its jaws warns visitors of infernal perils.

Green Man wall relief, John Ryland's Library

JOHN RYLAND'S LIBRARY

150 Deansgate, M3 3EH

This Victorian Gothic marvel is one of the most beautiful buildings in Manchester, with interiors worthy of a tale of ghosts and scholars. Since it opened to the public in 1900, the library has accumulated several works of occult interest, such as a fragment of a 15th-century copy of the *Concordantiae Caritatis*, the so-called Latin MS 105, and an album of doppelgängers and spectres containing examples of Victorian photographic trickery.

Interior of John Ryland's Library

Merseyside

BIDSTON HILL

Boundary Rd, Birkenhead, Prentonx, CH43 7PF

Sun Goddess and Moon Goddess: SJ288900

Horse carving: SJ286900

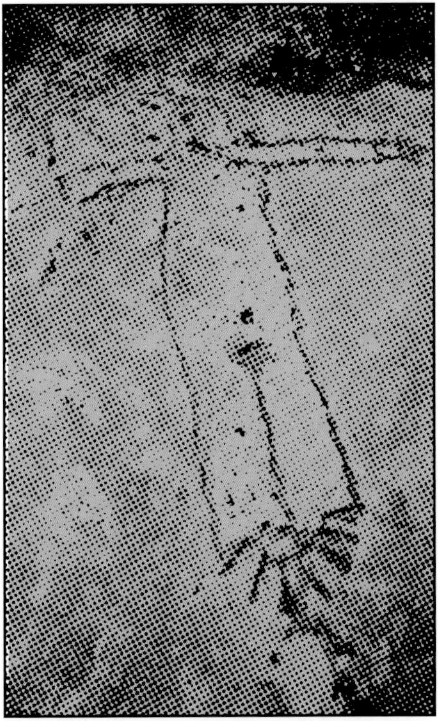

With a peak of 70m, Bidston Hill is one of the highest points on the Wirral Peninsula. The true age and meaning of its mysterious rock carvings has never been ascertained, but it's been suggested they were made by Norse-Irish settlers who arrived in the area circa 800 CE.

The Sun Goddess is 1.4-metre-tall humanoid figure with arms outstretched forming right angles. The sun at her feet aligns with the Midsummer sunrise. Her counterpart, the Moon Goddess, is a figure of similar design and size with a moon at her feet, though her head is said to resemble that of a cat. The stone on which the Moon Goddess is carved has been deliberately left to become overgrown in recent years, in order to protect the delicate rock art from damage. A carving of a horse's head with a sun design upon its neck is also to be found near the 19th-century observatory—now an Artistic Research Centre—erected in the park that surrounds the hill.

Cotton Mather

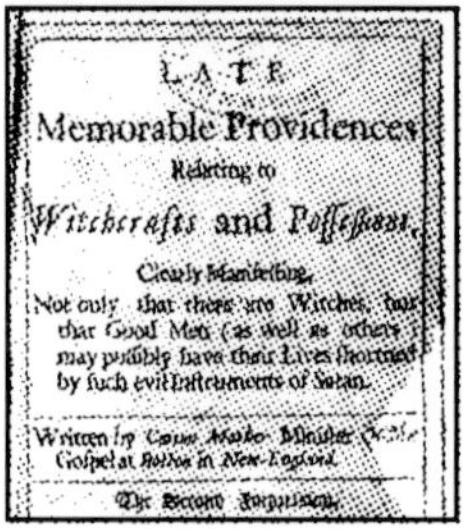

LATE
Memorable Providences
Relating to
Witchcrafts and Possessions,
Clearly Manifesting,
Not only that there are Witches, but that Good Men (as well as others) may possibly have their Lives shortned by such evil Instruments of Satan.

Written by Cotton Mather Minister of the Gospel at Boston in New-England.

The Second Impression.

Cotton Mather's Memorable Providences.

THE ANCIENT CHAPEL OF TOXTETH

371 Park Rd, Toxteth, Liverpool, L8 4UE

This little sandstone chapel is the oldest dissenting place of worship still in use in the UK. It was built in 1618, next to a modest schoolhouse erected by a small Puritan community. The first schoolmaster there was also the chapel's first minister: a man named Richard Mather who, along his wife, Katherine, emigrated to Boston, Massachusetts in 1635. Their transplanted Liverpool Puritan community flourished in North America; their son, Increase, and their grandson, Cotton, becoming ministers in their time. Both of their names are best known today in connection with the infamous Salem Witch Trials of 1692. Cotton's 1689 work *Memorable Providences, Relating to Witchcrafts and Possessions* was blamed by many for contributing to New England's Witch Panic, while Increase published his *Cases of Conscience Concerning Witchcraft* the year following the Salem executions.

The Ancient Chapel of Toxteth

The Prince and His Witch

IN JUNE 1644, during the English Civil War, a force of ten thousand Royalist soldiers under the command of Prince Rupert of the Rhine descended on the city of Liverpool. Local lore has it that Rupert's Cavaliers made camp in the churchyard of the Ancient Chapel of Toxteth, en route to lay siege to Liverpool Castle.

Prince Rupert was rumoured to be a witch, and a 1642 pamphlet alleged that his pet Boy, a large poodle, also possessed supernatural powers. Some believed that Boy was a shape-shifting witch or the Devil himself, and that he was immortal, but he eventually met his end at the Battle of Marston Moor, hit by a purpose-made silver musket ball, only a month after he and his master took Liverpool.

THE CALDERSTONES

The Calderstones: Mansion House, Calderstones Park, Liverpool, L18 3JB

The Archer Stone: 40 Archerfield Rd, Liverpool, L18 7HT

These six megaliths are the remains of a Neolithic passage grave that once stood just outside today's Calderstones Park. Carved into the stones are circles and spirals dating from around 3000 BCE, a Bronze Age depiction of a dagger, and eight well-defined individual foot or handprints from the same era. One of these has an extra digit, a trait regarded in some ancient societies as a mark of auspiciousness, good fortune, and healing abilities.

A seventh stone, believed to be a displaced portion of the tomb, is enclosed in green-painted iron railings a mile or so southeast of Calderstones Park. It is known as the Archer Stone or Robin Hood's Stone, due to the belief that a series of grooves weathered into its surface were once used for sharpening arrowheads—though 19th-century antiquarians argued that the channels were used in pagan bloodletting rituals. Photographic evidence from 1928, when the monolith was moved to its present location, shows that Neolithic carvings lay buried beneath the concrete.

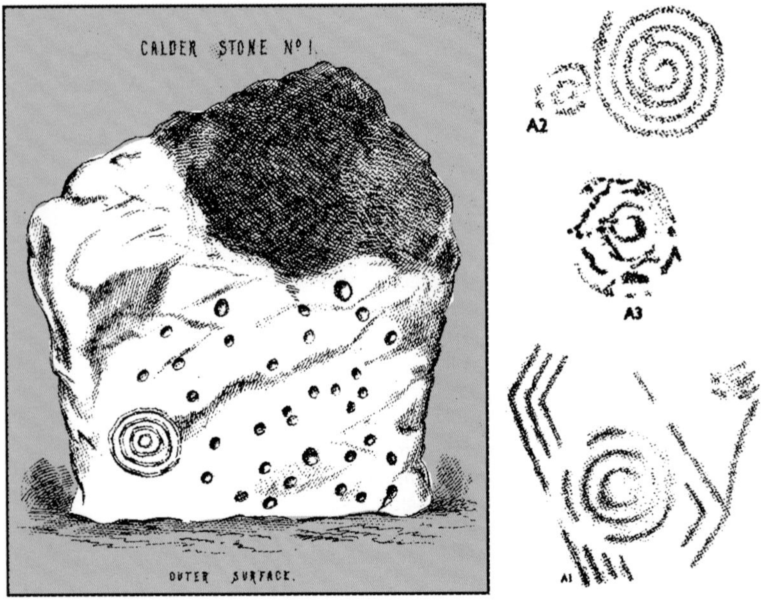

Calderstone no. 1 and close-up of carvings

CRANK CAVERNS

Crank, Saint Helens, WA11 · SJ510995

This abandoned tunnel system has long been an area of interest for amateur explorers as well as a source of local legends. It was formerly known as the Rainford Delph Quarry, a sandstone quarry excavated at multiple levels between the mid-1700s and the early 20th century. The mines broke through into pre-existing caverns and tunnels, said to have been used to hold secret Catholic masses during the Reformation.

There are tales of an above-ground Christian church accidentally undermined and sunk, virtually intact, into the hollow below. A 1933 report chronicled the descent of two reporters into the tunnel-system in search of the source of these legends. There, after hours of searching, they found a "dark, majestic and lofty" cavern with a "cathedral-like interior", including a gallery which bore a striking resemblance to an altar, complete with steps. Some explorers, however, claim to have seen ancient and thoroughly unchristian altars and statues carved into the rock.

The caverns can currently be accessed from a public footpath, though due to their instability there have been several attempts to close them to the public. Enter at your peril.

Lancashire

PENDLE

The Pendle Witches

IN 1612, twenty people living in the area surrounding Pendle Hill were accused of witchcraft and taken to prison to await what came to be known as the Lancashire Witch Trials. Eight of them, the so-called "Samlesbury Witches", were acquitted of all charges. The others were not so fortunate. Elizabeth Southerns, known as "Mother Demdike", died in Lancaster prison at the age of eighty, while awaiting her trial. Margaret Pearson was sentenced to be pilloried on four market days, followed by a year in prison. The other ten were taken to the moors at the edge of the city of Lancaster and hanged. They were buried at unmarked graves and their place of execution is now lost. Centuries later, the so-called Pendle Witches have become folk heroes, remembered for the injustice and suffering they were subjected to.

PENDLE HILL

Nelson, BB9 6LG

Rising above an ancient hunting ground, Pendle Hill is infamous as the site where the so-called Pendle Witches allegedly held their sabbaths. Its 557-metre summit, known as The Big End, is also the site of a Bronze Age burial mound.

PENDLE HERITAGE CENTRE

Park Hill, Colne Road, Barrowford, BB9 6JQ / £

The starting point of the Lancashire Witches Walk, this museum and visitor centre houses a permanent exhibition on the Pendle Witches.

NEWCHURCH
St Mary's Church: 5 Cross Ln, Burnley, BB12 9JR
Painted on the tower of St Mary's Church to ward off evil, the Eye of God watches over the churchyard. A gravestone inscribed with the name "Nutter" is often mistaken for Alice Nutter's grave, but, having been hanged as a witch, she wouldn't have been buried in consecrated ground. At the Pendle trials, Anne Whittle, known as Old Chattox, was accused of digging out skulls from this churchyard in order to extract teeth for her incantations.

FAUGH'S QUARRY
Well Head Road, Newchurch-in-Pendle, Burnley, BB12 9LW · SD820392
Elizabeth Southerns claimed to have met the Devil here, "in the shape of a boy wearing a coat half black, half brown." The quarry is now disused, but carved apotropaic eyes and the mysterious bearded figure known as the Wizard of the Stone Pit keep watch.

ROUGHLEE
Nelson, BB9 6NS
To mark the 400th anniversary of the trials, a statue of Alice Nutter, one of the Pendle Witches, was erected near Crowtrees Farm, the house where she lived.

THE LANCASHIRE Witches Walk is a 51-mile trail running between Barrowford village and Lancaster Castle, where the Pendle Witch Trials took place. In 2012, ten cast iron way-markers inscribed with a verse of a specially commissioned poem were installed along the way.

ST LEONARD'S CHURCHYARD

16 Church Brow, Walton-le-Dale, Preston, PR5 4BH

St Leonard's Churchyard was the scenario of the most famous episode of necromancy in England. In the 16th century, Edward Kelley and an associate arrived at the churchyard on a mission to divine the future of a lord, who had come accompanied by his servant. Kelley exhumed the body of a man who had been buried that morning, and summoned an "evil spirit" to possess the corpse and reveal, speaking through his organs, the future of the aristocrat. The story was recorded in the 17th century by English antiquary John Weever, as told to him by the lord's servant, who had witnessed the gruesome episode. Though Kelley's assistant was named as Peter Waring in Weever's original account, later retellings often include Dr John Dee in his place—and some go further, insisting that whatever spoke through the dead man in the churchyard that night foretold the hour and manner of Kelley and Dee's own deaths.

RENAISSANCE occultist and spirit medium Edward Kelley (1555–1597) is best known today for his association with Dr John Dee. Kelley claimed to be able to communicate with spirits and angels via the act of scrying. Enochian—the language of angels, which was dictated to Kelley—was the key to Enochian magic, whose secrets included the philosopher's stone, god-like wisdom, and eternal life.

THE WRITTEN STONE

Written Stone Lane, Preston, PR3 2ZL

Lying at the side of an old Roman road known as Written Stone Lane is a sandstone slab inscribed with these words: "RALFFE: RADCLIFFE: LAID: THIS STONE TO LYE: FOR: EVER: A.D. 1655". It is said that beneath the stone lies a boggart who terrorised the Radcliffe family of Cottam House—now Written Stone Farm—in the 17th century. If the stone is ever moved, the evil spirit will be unleashed.

Postcard of The Written Stone

Cumbria

BEETHAM FAIRY STEPS

Slack Head, Milnthorpe, LA7 7BD

These weathered and ancient stone steps, set in a steep limestone cleft, lead east of the village of Beetham into the woodlands beyond. The steps are small and narrow, and the gap between the walls to either side less than 30 cm in width at their narrowest point, which led to the belief that they were built for and by fairies. Local lore says that those who climb the steps without touching the walls will be granted a wish, and may even catch a glimpse of the Little People.

The Fairy Steps are situated on one of Lakeland Fell's old corpse roads, along which the coffins of those who died in more remote parts of the neighbourhood would have been carried for burial. These sacred routes through the landscape—sometimes also known as Spirit Ways—are often linked to Fairy Paths, and were once believed to have been used by the living and the dead, the natural and the supernatural, alike.

Fairy Steps, 1907

DEVIL'S BRIDGE

Bridge Brow, Kirkby Lonsdale, Carnforth LA6 2DF

Spanning the River Lune to the south and east of the town of Kirkby Lonsdale is a triple-arched 12th-century bridge known as Devil's Bridge. Local legend says the Devil agreed to build it for an old woman whose cow had strayed over to the opposite bank of the river. The price he named was the soul of the first living thing that crossed it. The old woman outwitted the Prince of Darkness, who expected her soul in exchange, by throwing a bun across the bridge to bait a small dog across ahead of her. The coping stone of the bridge bears a mark known as The Devil's Hand-print, evidence of the bridge's diabolic origin.

The Devil's Bridge, 1898

Ancient Stones of Cumbria

BIRKRIGG STONE CIRCLE

Ulverston, LA12 9RD

This Early Bronze Age monument consists of two concentric rings of limestone stones, and is also known as the Druid's Circle and the Druid's Temple. Excavations have revealed that the ground within the rings was once cobbled. Five cremations have been uncovered at the site, as well as a pestle, a palette, and a piece of red ochre, assumed to have been used for ritual purposes.

SWINSIDE STONE CIRCLE

Millom, LA18 5LD

Two well-spaced stones on the south-eastern side form the entrance to this circle of approximately fifty-five slate stones, also known as Swineshead and Sunkenkirk. Local folklore claims that Christians attempted to build a church on the site, but the Devil destroyed it by night, driving the ends of the stones into the earth in their current formation. The exact number of stones is supposed to be impossible to count correctly.

CASTLERIGG STONE CIRCLE

Castle Lane, Keswick, CA12 4RN

Castlerigg was erected in 3000 BCE, which makes it one of the earliest stone circles in the country. Well-known for its dramatic setting, overlooking the Thirlmere Valley, Castlerigg doesn't contain any formal burials. Within the circle, which has a slightly flatter circular shape than later examples, there is rectangle of standing stones. There isn't much folklore associated to it, apart from the usual uncountability of the stones, but its entrance aligns with the midwinter sunset.

ELVA HILL STONE CIRCLE

Cockermouth, CA13 9SQ

The name Elva Hill might derive from the Old Viking for "place of the elves". On the southern slope of the hill stand the 15 remaining stones of a Neolithic stone circle, the tallest of which is just under one metre—a size fitting for the Little People, who are said to dwell on this fairy hill.

LONG MEG AND HER DAUGHTERS

Hunsonby, Penrith, CA10 1NW

The largest stone circle in Cumbria—and the second largest in England—is believed to have been arranged circa 1500 BCE, though local legend claims it was formed when Scottish wizard Michael Scot (1175 – c.1232) turned a dancing Witches' Sabbath to stone. The tallest of the stones is popularly known as Long Meg, supposedly the matriarch of the coven. While her "daughters" are made of granite, Meg is made of red sandstone, carved with intricate spirals and circles, and is said to bleed if anyone damages it.

Any attempts to move the stones have resulted, according to oral folklore, in severe storms, but if anyone can successfully count the same number of stones twice in a row, they may hear some whispered words from Long Meg when they press their ear to her stone.

Long Meg standing tall

Levens Hall and topiaries

Levens Hall, 1907

Screaming Skulls of Calgarth Hall, 1925

LEVENS HALL

Kendal, LA8 OPD / £

Levens Hall is famous for its topiary gardens, laid out by French gardener Guillaume Beaumont between 1689 and 1711, but legend has it that, around the time the gardens were created, a starving Roma woman asked the family for shelter from the bitter cold. They refused, and she died after uttering a curse: "No son will inherit the hall until the River Kent doesn't flow anymore and a white fawn is born in the park." The first male heir was said to be born many years later, in 1896, when the River Kent froze and a little white fawn was born to the herd. A shadowy figure believed to be the ghost of the Roma woman has been seen on the road outside the Hall. The deer park is also home to a herd of majestic Bagot goats.

CALGARTH HALL

Old Hall Road, Windermere, LA23 1HZ

This Georgian villa overlooking the Windermere saw Romantic poets Wordsworth and Coleridge converse in its halls. In the turbulent times of WW1 it became a hospital, and it has recently been converted into retirement flats, but Calgarth Hall was originally built by a bishop in the late 18th century, on the spot of a 16th-century cottage said to have belonged to a couple of farmers, Kraster and Doreen Cook. The story goes that magistrate Myles Philipson coveted their land, and upon the couple's refusal to sell it, he framed them for theft. Abusing his power, Philipson himself sentenced them to death and decreed that their land should pass over to his hands. Thus, Doreen Cook cursed the magistrate's family: as long as they occupied their land, she and her husband would haunt them, and they would never prosper. When the Philipsons moved in, they found two skulls in a window upstairs. Thomas West writes in *A Guide to the Lakes* (1779–1821) that the skulls were "buried, burnt, powdered, and dispersed in the wind, and upon the lake", but they always returned to their ledge, uttering terrible shrieks and tormenting the new residents. After Myles Philipson's death, the skulls only appeared at Christmas, on the anniversary of the death of the Cooks. The disturbances ceased—and the skulls vanished—when the Bishop of Llandaff performed an exorcism.

Calgarth Hall, entrance

EAGLE CRAG

Borrowdale, Keswick · NY275122

The impressive fell of Eagle Crag is the setting of the legend of 16th-century heiress Lady Sybil, who lived near the cliff, in the long-since ruined Bernshaw Tower. Lady Sybil loved nature above all else. In one of her regular visits to Eagle Crag, she bargained away her soul in exchange for the ability to change her form. Meanwhile, her suitor Lord William sought the advice of local witch Mother Helston about how to win the reluctant lady's heart. The witch sent a familiar of hers in the form of a great hound to help Lord William, and asked him to hunt near Eagle Crag for a white doe. Caught, and brought back to the lord's home, the doe transformed into Lady Sybil.

The Witch of Eagle's Crag, John Heywood, 1895

The pair were married, but the lady could not give up her shape-shifting ways. One night, while wearing the form of a white cat, Lady Sybil was badly injured, having one of her paws severed. In the weeks that followed she weakened more and more. The clergy, under orders of Lord William, tried their best to break her unholy bargain, and to free the lady's soul before she passed away. Local legend says that on the eve of All-Hallow's a hound and a milk-white doe can still be seen standing upon Eagle Crag.

Lady Sybil at Eagle Crag

ISLE OF MAN

WITCHES' MILL, CASTLETOWN
Arbory Road, IM9 1HA · SC259676
The Witches' Mill was the original site of Cecil Williamson's Museum of Witchcraft, which had Gerald Gardner, the father of modern Wicca, as its resident witch in the early 1950s. To Gardner, the Isle of Man was a centre of natural witchcraft, and he claimed that the burned-out ruins of the mill tower had been used by the Arbory witches as a dancing ground since the late 19th century.

THE ANCIENT MARKET CROSS, CASTLETOWN
The Parade, IM9 1LG
A plaque at the site of the ancient market cross commemorates Margaret Ine Qane (or Quaine) and her son, condemned for witchcraft and burnt at the stake in 1617, but little is known about their case.

MALEW CHURCH
Malew Road, IM9 1TE · SC268694
An intriguing 1850s grave attracts curious visitors to the churchyard of Malew. Cornered by four iron stakes joined by metal chains, the final resting place of Matthew and Margaret Hassal is known as The Vampire's Grave. The story goes that Matthew's corpse emitted a bloodcurdling groan during his wake, so the congregation installed the chains to impede his return as a revenant.

PEEL CASTLE
West Quay, Peel, IM5 1TB / £
The demonic black dog known as Moddey Dhoo is said to haunt the grounds of the 11th-century Viking castle dominating St Patrick's Isle. The fortress was built over Celtic monastic buildings. Excavations at the Christian cemetery unearthed the remains of the so-called Pagan Lady, a 10th-century wise woman with high status grave goods, including a miniature pestle and mortar and a necklace with beads sourced from all over the world, now kept at the Manx Museum in Douglas.

CHURCH OF ST TRINIANS
Peel Rd, IM4 2DN · SC317801
Beneath the dark forests of the Greeba mountain stand the remains of the 14th-century church of St Trinians, whose roof was ripped off three times by the legendary Buggane, furious that a Christian temple was erected in his territory. This Buggane was a shape-shifting creature, at times looking like an ogre and at others like a demonic black calf with glowing red eyes and cloven feet.

"The Phynodderree, and other legends of the Isle of Man", 1882

1903

VIII. The North East

Yorkshire, 194
County Durham, 204
Tyne And Wear, 206
Northumberland, 208

VIII. THE NORTH EAST

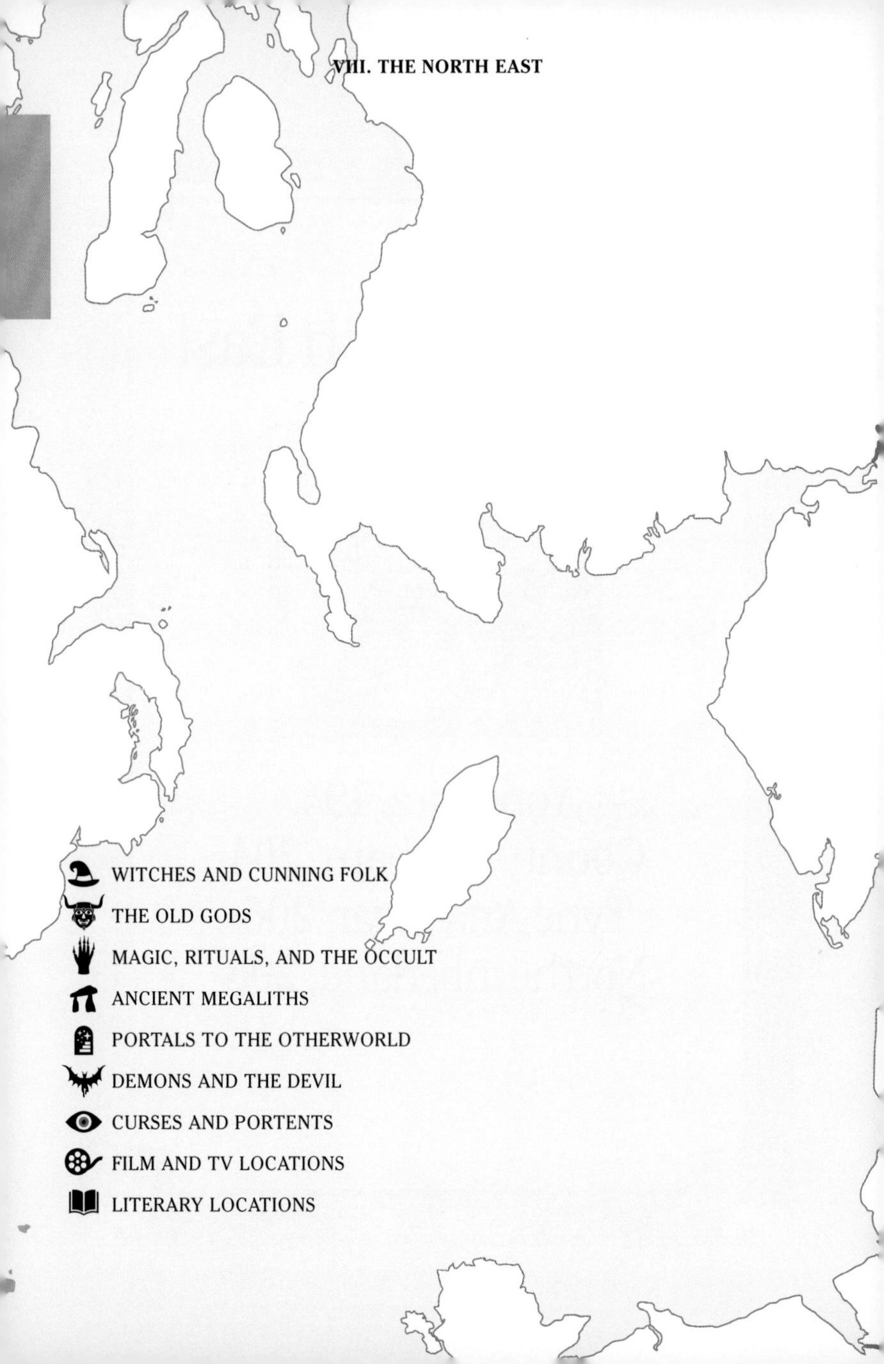

DUDDO FIVE STONES
LINDISFARNE
BAMBURGH CASTLE
DUNSTANBURGH CASTLE
NORTHUMBERLAND
CARRAWBURGH MITHRAS TEMPLE
TYNE & WEAR
WORM HILL
PENSHAW HILL
ST EDMUND'S CHURCH
DURHAM CATHEDRAL
DURHAM
GISBOROUGH PRIORY
HOB HOLES
ALL SAINTS CHURCH
WHITBY
RYEDALE FOLK MUSEUM
ST MARY'S CHURCH
DRUID'S TEMPLE
BRIMHAM ROCKS
RUDSTON MONOLITH
BURTON AGNES HALL
MOTHER SHIPTON'S CAVE
ROMBALDS MOOR
YORKSHIRE

Yorkshire

Swastika Stone, Ilkley Moor

ROMBALDS MOOR

Ilkley LS29 9QQ · SE095469

Said to be named after Rombald, a legendary local giant, this cluster of moors is famous for its abundance of ancient rock carvings. Perhaps the most intriguing feature is the so-called Swastika Stone on the northern edge of Ilkley Moor, whose Bronze Age carving is unique in Britain. Its similarity to Iron Age Camunian rose designs of Italy has led to speculation that it may have been carved by Romans in imitation of those in their homeland. The motif is thought to be a solar symbol.

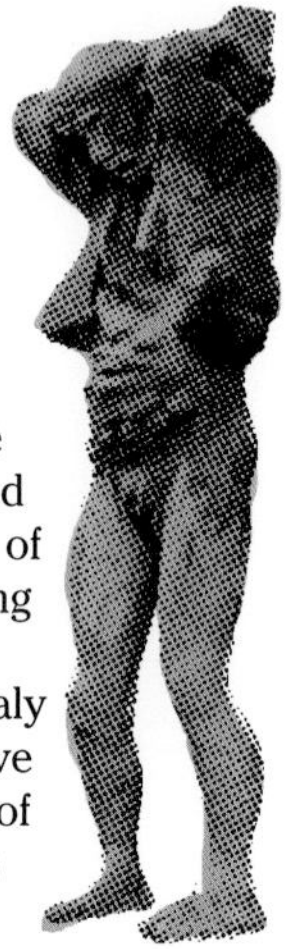

Trigpoint, Rombalds Moor

MOTHER SHIPTON'S CAVE

Prophecy Lodge, High Bridge, Knaresborough, HG5 8DD/ £

THIS CAVE at the picturesque market town of Knaresborough is associated with the legendary prophetess Mother Shipton, who was either born or brought up here, according to different versions of the legend. Mother Shipton's Cave has been a tourist attraction since the 1630s, when interest in the prophetess seems to have first spread beyond the boundaries of Knaresborough. In the parkland near the cave is a petrifying well, which turns to stone any item kept submerged in its waters for an extended period of time.

The Prophetess Of York

MOTHER SHIPTON (c.1488–1561) was born Ursula Sontheil to a 15-year-old mother and an unknown father—her father, some versions of her legend say, was none other than the Devil himself. By the time she married Tobias Shipton at the age of twenty-four, Ursula was already known as a herbalist, wise woman, and fortune teller. Tobias died only a few years after they were wed, and the couple had no children. Instead, it was because of her bent and aged appearance that Ursula came to be known as Old Mother Shipton.

PUBLISHED IN 1641, eighty years after her death, *The Propheceyes of Mother Shipton* recorded some of the predictions Ursula had apparently made during her lifetime, including the defeat of the Spanish Armada in 1588, the Great Fire of London in 1666, and the end of the world in 1881. She became a legendary figure, her prophecies often invoked during times of crises and used as political propaganda and cautionary tales.

Wishing Stone and Pulpit, 1914

BRIMHAM ROCKS

Brimham Moor Road, Summerbridge, HG3 4DW

Although Brinham Rocks is a natural landscape, during the 18th and 19th century it was believed that many of its features had been carved, or partially carved, by druids—though some other legends attribute their formation to the Devil. The names given to the rocks reflect these ideas: Druid's Skull, Druid's Pulpit or Druid's Telescope. Perhaps the most amazing of these is Druid's Idol or Idol Rock, a huge boulder which appears to be balanced on a tiny, 12-inch diameter pedestal. The Wishing Stone, which has a hole in it, was thought to have been used as an oracle.

Local folklore tells that somewhere among the rocks there is a cave inhabited by a witch known as the Great Sybil, who had the power of predicting the future.

The natural rock stack on a high point west of the Brinham Rocks site was known as the Noonstone, next to which Midsummer fires were lit.

Druid's Temple

DRUID'S TEMPLE

Knowle Ln, Ripon HG4 4JZ · SE174787

Set in woodland in the heart of the Yorkshire Dales, this folly was built in 1820 under orders of scholar and philosopher William Danby near his home of Swinton Park. The Stonehenge-inspired complex included a tomb and a sacrificial altar, in line with antiquarian views of the time, which saw stone circles as druidic temples where ritual sacrifices were performed.

Danby paid otherwise unemployed labourers the considerable sum of a shilling a day for their work on the temple, and, after its completion, attempted to hire a hermit to reside in it. He stipulated that the hermit should live alone in the temple, without shaving or speaking a word. The longest anyone lasted in the post was four and a half years.

Though the folly is a mere two centuries old, local folklore says that the Druid's Temple has long been a meeting place of a Satanic coven. Those who try to spend the night at the temple will, according to local lore, be driven out before daybreak.

Burton Agnes Hall

BURTON AGNES HALL

Rudston Rd, Burton Agnes, Driffield, YO25 4NB / £

Entombed within the walls of this Elizabethan manor house is the skull of the daughter of Sir Henry Griffith, the man who built it. Katherine "Anne" Griffith died at the Hall in 1620, following a violent attack and robbery when she was en route to visit some friends. Before she expired, she made her two sisters promise that her head should be taken and preserved in her beautiful home "as long as it shall last". Even though her sisters agreed—likely to pacify her—Anne was laid to rest in the local churchyard, and soon Burton Agnes Hall was haunted by a thoroughly unfriendly ghost. The hauntings ceased when the parish priest agreed to the opening of Anne's coffin, and to her head being returned to her home. Subsequent inheritors of Burton Agnes Hall tried to rid themselves of the grisly relic, but since its removal always resulted in a return of Anne's unhappy spirit, it was decided that the skull should be concealed within the walls of the Great Hall. Hanging from the Inner Hall, the portraits of Anne and her sisters watch the visitors.

Burton Agnes hall and stairway, 1904

RUDSTON MONOLITH

Rudston, Driffield, YO25 4UY

In the northern side of the churchyard of the 12th-century All Saints Church stands England's tallest monolith, over 7 metres in height. Local folklore says that the huge stone was flung by the Devil at the church, but, repelled by God's protection, it missed and embedded in the churchyard.

Monolith at Rudston, 1894

Carved symbol in fireplace to ward off witches

Restored cottage from 1704

Carvings in the crypt of St. Mary's Church

The Rudston Monolith is thought to have been placed in its current position in the Late Neolithic or Early Bronze Age. Excavations by 18th-century antiquarian William Stukeley uncovered several skulls, which he believed were signs of prehistoric sacrifices made at the stone.

RYEDALE FOLK MUSEUM

Hutton-le-Hole, YO62 6UA / £

DAEMONOLO-
GIE, IN FORME
of a Dialogue,
Divided into three Bookes.

This open-air museum includes several historic buildings, and displays three wooden posts carved with apotropaic symbols. They would have been positioned near the fireplace of homes in North East Yorkshire and Lancashire, protecting a building's hearth from witches and their familiars. King James's *Daemonologie* (1597) specified the importance of these protective measures: witches and demons "will come and pierce through, whatever house or church, though all ordinary passages be closed", gaining entrance via any opening "the air may enter in at".

Also worth seeing are the 18th-century spell tokens—love charms to attract suitors—inscribed with initials, dates, and symbols.

ST MARY'S CHURCH, LASTINGHAM

Lastingham, York, YO62 6TN

The impressive, vaulted crypt beneath St. Mary's Church in Lastringham was constructed between 1078 and 1086 CE. An oaken door lintel in the crypt is believed to have belonged to the original 7th-century monastery church which once stood there. This lintel is carved with symbols that have been interpreted as pre-Christian or pagan, which may represent the absorption—rather than out and out destruction—of pagan, nature-worship beliefs, symbols, and customs by the English church at the time.

WHITBY

"Right over the town is the ruin of Whitby Abbey, which was sacked by the Danes… It is a most noble ruin, of immense size, and full of beautiful and romantic bits; there is a legend that a white lady is seen in one of the windows."
—Bram Stoker, *Dracula* (1897)

THE SPECTRAL ruins of Whitby Abbey dominate the seaside town of Whitby, the Gothic capital of the UK, a reputation that began to brew in 1890, when Bram Stoker (1847–1912) stayed in Mrs Veazey's guesthouse at 6 Royal Crescent. But there is more to Whitby than its association with *Dracula*: the town hosted the 7th-century synod that determined the fate of Christianity in England, where it was decided that the English Church should follow Roman, rather than Celtic practices. Its shoreline occasionally returns the snakes that St Hilda was said to have turned to stone—though we now know them as ammonite fossils, not as petrified demons.

WHITBY ABBEY

Abbey Ln, YO22 4JT / £

The remains of this Anglo-Saxon monastery, later a Benedictine abbey, stand on a headland that has been settled since the Bronze Age. The original monastery—for both men and women—had St Hilda (614–680) as its first abbess. Both the town and the monastery were abandoned in the 9th century, probably as a result of Viking raids, but a new Benedictine community flourished here between 1078 and 1539. After the Dissolution, the buildings were bought by the Cholmleys, who abandoned them in the 18th century.

The Abbey is said to be haunted by the nun Constance de Beverley, bricked up alive in its walls after the other nuns discovered she was romancing a knight. Local lore says those who gaze into the Abbey's Well at midnight might find in the waters the reflection of St Hilda, but those who aren't pure of heart will see the face of the Devil, who will drag them to Hell.

DRACULA'S STEPS

St Mary's Church: Abbey Plain, Whitby, YO22 4JR

One hundred and ninety nine steps lead up from the River Esk to the graveyard of the Church of Saint Mary. It was from this cemetery that the Demeter, the ship carrying Count Dracula, was first sighted in Bram Stoker's 1897 novel. It was up these steps that the Count ran, transformed into of a huge black dog. "What it was," said Mina Harker when she saw her sleepwalking friend Lucy Westenra with a strange figure bent over her, "whether man or beast, I could not tell".

The steps, the churchyard, and the nearby abbey, have featured in numerous screen adaptations of *Dracula* including the 1977 BBC TV film *Count Dracula*, and Steven Moffat and Mark Gatiss' 2020 TV mini series *Dracula*.

BRAM STOKER'S BENCH

Khyber Pass, YO21 3DQ

Not far from the Whitby Whalebones stands a bench with a memorial plaque commemorating the Irish author, who envisioned the arrival of Dracula in England when he sat at this vantage point.

The Hand of Glory

Whitby Museum: Pannett Park, YO21 1RE / £

WHITBY MUSEUM houses England's last surviving Hand of Glory, discovered in the early 20th century by stonemason and local historian Joseph Ford in the wall of a thatched cottage in Castleton village. The Hand of Glory—the hand of a criminal cut from the dead body while it still hung from the gallows, then pickled and turned into a kind of candle—is said to have magical powers: no one sleeping in a house where one of them is lit will wake, allowing those in possession of it to steal from that dwelling with impunity. The burning hand can only be extinguished, and the spell broken, with blood or milk.

The Barghest of Whitby

STOKER'S choice of having Count Dracula arrive in Whitby in the form of a huge black dog was no doubt influenced by the barghests of local folklore—ghostly or spectral black dogs seen as omens of death, or guardians of certain paths or places. The word "barghest" means either "town-ghost" or "bear-ghost", on account of the size and ferocity of the spectre. Black dog folklore in England is often connected with sites of Norse invasion, and Whitby Abbey, at the time known as Streonshalch monastery, was laid waste by Danes in successive raids between 867 and 870 CE.

HOB HOLES, RUNSWICK BAY

Saltburn-by-the-Sea, TS13 5HU

The caves in the cliffs near Runswick Bay were said to be inhabited by a strange creature known as the boggle. Fishermen's wives used to bring their children here to be cured of whooping cough, invoking the creature with the words "Hob-hole Hob, my bairn's gettin' t' kink-cough, tak't off, tak't off!"

Hob Holes cave entrance

GISBOROUGH PRIORY

Church St, Guisborough, TS14 6HG

Local legend says that treasure is hidden somewhere beneath this impressive ruin of an 11th-century Augustinian priory. In 1866, William Henderson recorded that the chest of gold was guarded by a raven, which might hint at "the Scandinavian origin of the legend". By the mid 20th century the guardian raven seems to have been replaced in the local lore with the figure of a monk wearing a black robe, who would appear at midnight on the year's first new moon to check that the treasure was still in place. In 1966 and 1967 large crowds gathered at Gisborough Priory at the appointed hour and apparently witnessed the appearance of the figure.

The ruins of Gisborough Priory

County Durham

Ruins of the All Saints Church

SOCKBURN

All Saints Church, Sockburn, Darlington, DL6 2JB
Durham Cathedral, Durham, DH1 3EH

Sockburn was once an eminent Northumbrian parish that saw the coronations of Highbald, Bishop of Lindisfarne, and Eanbald, Archbishop of York in the late 8th century. The ruins of All Saints Church host the 13th-century carving of a cross-legged knight in armour. This carving marks the final resting place of Sir John Conyers, said to have killed the fearsome dragon-like beast known as the Sockburn Worm in the 15th century. The weapon with which Sir John Conyers slew the Sockburn Worm—a falchion sword believed to have been the inspiration for the Vorpal Sword in Lewis Carroll's *Jabberwocky*—is currently on display at Durham Cathedral, and for centuries it's been used in the ceremony to induct a new bishop.

The Jabberwock

Northumberland, County Durham, and Yorkshire are rife with folk tales about wyrms (in Old English, wyrm means dragon or serpent). Some have seen in these beasts an allegory for Viking invasions, though an esoteric interpretation is also possible. These legends—in particular, that of the Sockburn Worm—provided inspiration for the poem *Jabberwocky*, by Lewis Carroll (1832–1898), of *Alice in Wonderland*'s fame. Carroll grew up in the rectory at Croft, about five miles from Sockburn.

ST EDMUND'S CHURCH

Church Lane, Edmundbyers, DH8 9NQ

Hung on the west interior wall of this 12th-century church is an unassuming gravestone commemorating a woman called Elizabeth Lee, who died in 1792 aged 87. Local legend says she was a witch, descended from some of the women who were tried for witchcraft in Newcastle-upon-Tyne in the 1670s. When Elizabeth Lee died, she was buried in St Edmund's churchyard in the same grave as her late husband. But the idea of a woman "known" to be a witch being buried on holy ground did not sit well with some parishioners, so her grave-marker was eventually moved to the interior of the church for fear of vandalism or even exhumation.

A roundel stained glass window, installed in the west wall of the church circa 1800, depicts the Eye of God at the centre of a sun, surrounded by a six pointed star. Though probably Masonic, it is said that this window was installed to watch over the witch's grave.

Eye of God stained glass

Gravestones outside St. Edmund's Church

St Edmund's Church

Tyne and Wear

The legend of the Lambton Worm ◉

THE LAMBTON FAMILY occupied Lambton estate, three miles west of Penshaw Hill. The story goes that, as a boy, John Lambton (1505–1582) caught a strange salamander, which he threw down a well and forgot about. Through the years the creature grew and grew, poisoning the water and emerging as a gigantic serpent-like dragon which terrorised the area, seemingly immortal due to its powers of regeneration. When John returned from the Crusades, he sought the advice of a wise woman to defeat the monster. She told him to cover his armour with spear-heads so that, when the worm tried to crush him, it would split itself into too many pieces to be able to recover. But she also warned John that, once the worm was dead, he must kill the first living thing he saw, or in nine generations no lord of Lambton Castle would die peacefully in his bed.

The battle took place in the River Wear, and the Lambton Worm was defeated. Overjoyed at John's victory, his father forgot about the wise woman's words and rushed to congratulate him. The knight could not kill his father, and so the Lambtons were cursed.

The legend of the Lambton Worm was transmitted in the traditional song of the same name, and was the basis for Bram Stoker's 1911 novel *The Lair of the White Worm*. Screenwriter Anthony Shaffer, who penned *The Wicker Man* (1973), wrote a Lambton Worm-inspired film treatment for a sequel that would have Sergeant Howie fight the monster. Drawing heavily from witchcraft and sorcery and laden with folkloric references, for better or worse the film was never made.

WORM HILL
Worm Hill Terrace,
Washington,
NE38 8AQ

The story goes that the Lambton worm wrapped itself seven times around Worm Hill, and that the marks it left there can be seen to this day.

PENSHAW HILL
Chester Rd, Penshaw,
Houghton le Spring,
Sunderland, DH4 7NJ

Some versions of the story record that the Lambton Worm wound itself around Penshaw Hill, now crowned by a 19th-century replica of the Temple of Haephestus in Athens—a memorial to John Lambton, 1st Earl of Durham (1792–1840), and, according to the legend, one of the first Lambtons to be born free of the curse.

Illustration by John Dickson Batten, More English Fairy Tales, 1894

Northumberland

Altar dedicated to Mithras, Carrawburgh

CARRAWBURGH MITHRAS TEMPLE

Humshaugh, Hexham, NE46 4DB

This temple to Mithras—mysterious god of light, of kings, of war, and justice—was built by soldiers stationed at Carrawburgh Roman Fort circa 200 CE. Carrawburgh was one of sixteen Roman forts along Hadrian's Wall, and housed a garrison of approximately five hundred soldiers from south-west France and southern Belgium.

Replicas of three 2nd-century altars found there now stand within the temple ruin. One of these depicts Mithras himself wearing a crown of light. Three holes drilled into the stone would once have allowed lamp or candlelight to shine through the altar, giving the god a shining halo. The temple's original dark, cavern-like appearance, designed to mimic the cave in which Mithras slew the sacred bull, is now roofless and open to the elements. A full-scale reconstruction of the temple as it would once have been can be found in the Museum of Antiquities at Newcastle.

Dunstanburgh Castle

DUNSTANBURGH CASTLE

Dunstanburgh Rd, Alnwick, NE66 3TT / £

The dramatic ruins of this 14th-century fortification stand on a remote headland that was also the site of an Iron Age fort. Legends tell of Sir Guy the Seeker, who, having been caught in a storm, sought shelter in the fortress. There he met a wizard who led him into a large room, where a noble lady in a crystal tomb was guarded by a sleeping army. The wizard asked Sir Guy to choose either a sword or a hunting horn—only the right choice would wake the lady. Sir Guy chose the horn, but when he blew it, he woke the sleeping knights, who rushed at him. He found himself alone outside the ruined castle, and spent the rest of his days attempting to find a way back inside, unsuccessfully—to this day, his ghost is said to haunt the ruins, looking for the lady in her crystal tomb.

More fearsome than the ghost of Sir Guy, however, is the ghost of the nobleman who built the castle: Thomas Plantagenet, 2nd Earl of Lancaster, executed for treason in 1322. The manifestation appears to carry his own head, awfully mangled due to the executioner's botched job.

The field north-west of the castle is reputedly barren, according to another legend: a child was imprisoned in the castle but managed to escape by procuring the key to her dungeon. When she fled, she threw it into that field, which caused it to become barren.

Sir Guy the Seeker

Execution of Thomas Plantagenet, Earl of Lancaster

BAMBURGH

Bamburgh Castle: NE69 7DF / £
Spindlestone: NU153339
Laidley Worm's Trough: NU155339

Bamburgh Castle was built in the 11th century on the foundations of a 5th-century Celtic Brittonic fort destroyed by Vikings. In the 15th century, Sir Thomas Mallory identified it as the home of Sir Lancelot of Arthurian legend. According to the ballad *The Laidly Worm of Spindleston-Heugh* (first recorded in the 18th century, allegedly transcribed from a 13th-century manuscript), Bamburgh Castle was the home of a king who took a witch as his second wife. Jealous of the beauty of the king's daughter, the witch cursed her to become a Laidly Worm—a serpent-like dragon. The monster wound itself around a nearby rock called the Spindlestone, and was fed from a natural bowl in the stone, still marked on

Bamburgh Castle, 1815

The Laidly Worm of Spindleston, 1892

Robin of Sherwood, Bamburgh Castle

Lindisfarne Castle on Holy Island

the OS map as "Laidley Worm's Trough", though nothing is visible here now. The curse was broken when the young girl's brother returned from overseas and kissed the worm three times. The wicked stepmother was transformed into a toad and was cast into the sea, and the returned son became king in his father's stead.

In the 1960s, excavations at the castle and in the adjacent Anglo-Saxon burial ground uncovered the Bamburgh Sword—a 7th-century high status weapon speculated to have belonged to a king or one of his close associates—and a small gold plaque of similar date, depicting a strange, multi-legged creature with snaking, entwined limbs. Known as the Beast of Bamburgh, the plaque is currently on display in the castle's own archaeology museum.

Bamburgh Castle has featured as a location in many films and TV series including Ken Russell's *The Devils* (1971), Roman Polanski's *Macbeth* (1971), and the *Robin of Sherwood* HTV/ITV series (1984–86).

LINDISFARNE

Holy Island, TD15 2RU

Whirlwinds, lightning, and fiery dragons were seen above the Holy Island of Lindisfarne before the Viking raids in 875, when the monks at the monastery fled with the remains of St Cuthbert—said to have miraculous properties—, wandering for seven years before they eventually settled in Chester-le-Street. Cuthbert's ghost stayed on the island, famously telling Alfred the Great he'd one day sit on the throne of England. A cell returned to Lindisfarne in 1093, and in the 12th century a new church was built, the ruins of which are still standing. As in other sites raided by Vikings, the island is haunted by a demonic dog, but what makes this one peculiar is that it's snowy white. Still, seeing it jump from the castle ruins is said to be a portent of death or calamity.

DUDDO FIVE STONES

Duddo, Berwick-upon-Tweed, TD15 2PT

Four miles south of the Scottish Border is a small but impressive Early Bronze Age stone circle known as Duddo Five Stones. Though only five remain, excavations in the late 1800s uncovered the sockets where two other stones once stood. One alternate name for the stones is The Women, supposedly owing to their tapered waists and to the notion that the sound the wind makes when it whistles between them is like that of feminine singing. The stones are also known as The Turnip Pickers, said to be the petrified remains of men caught harvesting the vegetables on the sabbath.

Two of the megalithic stones at Duddo

Sunset over the Duddo Five Stones

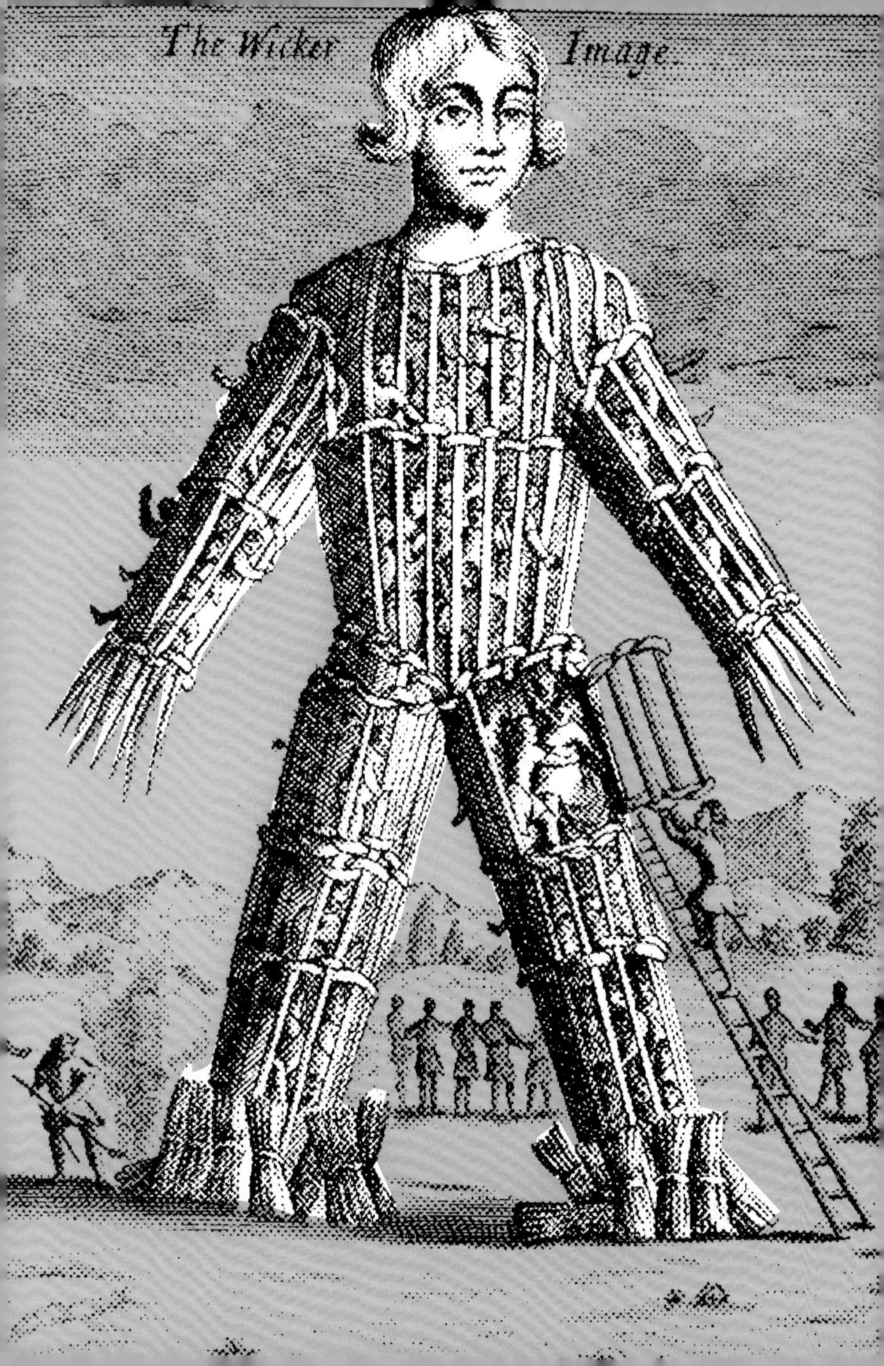
The Wicker Image

IX. Wales

Gwent, 216
Glamorgan, 220
Dyfed, 224
Powys, 226
Gwynedd, 228
Clywd, 236

IX. WALES

- WITCHES AND CUNNING FOLK
- THE OLD GODS
- MAGIC, RITUALS, AND THE OCCULT
- ANCIENT MEGALITHS
- PORTALS TO THE OTHERWORLD
- DEMONS AND THE DEVIL
- CURSES AND PORTENTS
- FILM AND TV LOCATIONS
- LITERARY LOCATIONS

Y MEINI HIRION
ISLE OF ANGLESEY
BRYN CELLI DDU
BARCLODIAD Y GAWRES
TREMEIRCHION
ST DIGAIN'S CHURCH
CLWYD
DINAS EMRYS
HUW LWYD'S PULPIT
DINAS BRAN
GWYNEDD
BALA LAKE
NANNAU PARK
BARDSEY ISLAND
STONE OF GRONW
DINAS MAWDDWY
OLD COURTHOUSE, DOLGELLAU
CADAIR IDRIS
POWYS
DYFED
ST MARTIN'S CHURCH
CWRT-Y-CADNO
PENTRE IFAN
ST NICHOLAS' CHURCH
CHURCH OF ST ISSUI
THE SKIRRID
GWENT
TRELLECK
TWMBARLWM
ARTHUR'S STONE MAEN CETI
THE SWANSEA DEVIL
CAERWENT
GLAMORGAN
GOAT'S HOLE
TREDEGAR HOUSE
CASTELL COCH
OGMORE CASTLE
TIKINSWOOD

Gwent

Machen Country

Widely regarded as one of the fathers of weird fiction, Welsh author Arthur Machen (1863–1947) was born in Caerleon-On-Usk. He grew up in The Old Rectory in Llandewi, fascinated by his grandfather's dabbling in archaeology and by the idea that that the soil regularly yielded remains of its pagan past. He moved to London and then to Buckinghamshire, but the landscapes of Wales continued to haunt his writings.

TWMBARLWM

Risca, Newport, NP11 6FY · ST244927

"Twym Barlwm, that mystic tumulus, the memorial of peoples that dwelt in that region before the Celts left the Land of Summer."
—ARTHUR MACHEN

Twmbarlwm was the inspiration for Machen's "Hill of Dreams", the hill crowned by the old Roman fort where Lucian Taylor, the hero of his semi-autobiographical novel, is taken by the decadent visions of a pagan past.

With its distinctive shape—the locals know it as "the pimple" or "the nipple"—, this "mystic tumulus" is the focus of many legends. The mythical king Brân the Blessed is said to be buried under the cairn by the hillfort, next to his treasure, protected by a swarm of bees, and waiting to rise out the earth when Wales needs him.

Folklore also regards Twmbarlwm as a sacred site for the druids, who used it as their place of judgement. Those who were found guilty would be dragged down into the valley below, Duffryn y Gladdfa, the Valley of the Dead. Ghostly green Celtic warriors are said to wander the area at night, their sightings an omen of death.

The wind on the southern slopes of the hill produces an effect known as "mountain organ". This might be related to the legend of the young girl who, at the end of the 19th century, was lured by a strange music that came from the hill, and who disappeared never to be seen again.

CAERWENT

NP26 5AU

"Caerwent, also a Roman city, was buried in the earth, and gave up now and again strange relics—fragments of the temple of Nodens, god of the depths. I saw the lonely house between the dark forest and the silver river, and years after I wrote "The Great God Pan," an endeavour to pass on the vague, indefinable sense of awe and mystery and terror that I had received."
—ARTHUR MACHEN

Caerwent was an important settlement of the Silures, an ancient tribe that became Romanised following the Roman conquest of Britain. Its ruins are among the best-preserved in Europe, with excavated houses, 5-metre-tall walls, and vestiges of a Romano-British temple. Machen mistakenly believed this temple was consecrated to the god Nodens—the Temple of Nodens, however, was the one excavated by Mortimer and Tessa Verney Wheeler in Lydney Park, Gloucestershire.

Bronze plate of Nodens

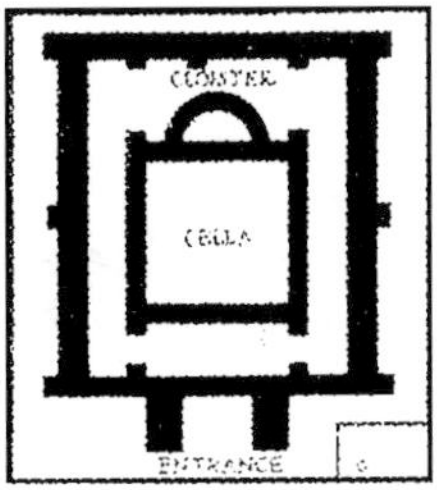

Plans of the temple

Excavations at Caerwent, 1903

Viscount Tredegar with his pet parrot

Tredegar House, side entrance

Carving at Tredegar House

TREDEGAR HOUSE

Pencarn Way, Newport, NP10 8YW / £

Evan Morgan, 2nd Vicount Tredegar

The earliest surviving part of Tredegar House dates back to the 15th century, but the current red brick building is one of the most significant Restoration houses in the country. In 1934 it passed to the hands of Evan Morgan, 2nd Viscount Tredegar (1893–1949). The viscount was both a papal chamberlain at the Vatican and a keen occultist, known as the "Black Monk" or the "Adept of Adepts" to his infamous friend Aleister Crowley—hence the rumours that the crucifix in his room was inverted or straightened depending on his mood.

Morgan kept a menagerie of exotic animals and hosted notoriously wild parties for his circle of friends, which included poet Robert Graves, writers Aldous Huxley and H. G. Wells, and The Great Beast himself. The latter declared the viscount's bedroom the best equipped "magick room" he'd ever seen.

During the Second World War, Morgan became a high-ranking officer in MI8, but he was court martialled after revealing departmental secrets to two women. When his commanding officer died of a mysterious illness shortly afterwards, his death was rumoured to be the result of a cursing ritual the viscount had staged with the help of his friend Crowley.

TRELLECK

Monmouth, NP25 4PE

King Harold's Stones

Tump Turret

Once an important market town, the village of Trelleck gets its name (meaning "three stones") from a Bronze Age alignment of standing stones thought to mark the place of death of three tribal chieftains. They're known as King Harold's Stones, reflecting the belief that they were erected by the monarch. Other tales claim they were the result of a hurling contest between the Devil and Jack o' Kent, who won the match. The Preaching Cross in the local churchyard is said to have been built on an ancient druidic altar, and the flat-topped mound behind Court Farm, likely a Medieval motte, is known as Tump Turret, and believed to be the burial place of the three chieftains or a burial site for plague victims.

The Feats of Jack o' Kent

St Nicholas' Church: The Rectory, B4347, Grosmont, Abergavenny, NP7 8LW

IN LOCAL LORE, this legendary character is known for outsmarting the Devil in bizarre and often humorous feats, and for having sold his soul to Satan in exchange for supernatural powers. The folk figure likely drew from several historical characters, among them, the 14th-century Franciscan friar Dr John Gwent; the astronomer Dr John Kent of Caerleon, who wrote a treatise on witchcraft in the 13th century; and John Kent, a Robin Hood-type figure marauding across the Welsh Marches. Jack o' Kent is said to be buried under the walls of St Nicholas' Church in Grosmont, so the Devil couldn't claim his soul. An old cross on the north side of the churchyard marks the spot of his grave.

Grosmont, Mon. The old cross in the Churchyard

Glamorgan

Paviland Cave

GOAT'S HOLE

Paviland Cave, Rhossili, Swansea, SA3 1PE · SS436858

High above sea level, overlooking the Bristol Channel, is a limestone cave considered one of the most important archaeological sites in Britain. An 1823 excavation carried out by William Buckland, Professor of Geology at Oxford University, revealed the 34,000-year-old remains of the so-called Red Lady of Paviland—the oldest ceremonial burial in Western Europe. Seeing the bones had been dyed with red ochre and decorated with periwinkle shells, ivory rods, bone beads, and a mammoth skull, Buckland proffered he'd found the burial place of a prostitute or a witch. Subsequent analysis revealed that the so-called Red Lady was a 25-year-old male. Much

Section of the cave, Goat's Hole

has been written about the remains, including a possible shamanistic connection. The bones are currently stored at the University of Oxford Museum, but Swansea Museum holds a replica. To access the cave, approach at low tide and wear sturdy boots.

Arthur's Stone

ARTHUR'S STONE · MAEN CETI

Swansea, SA3 1AE · SS491905

The ancient sandstone ridge of Cefn Bryn—known as the Backbone of Gower—is peppered with several cairns, the most famous of which is Arthur's Stone, a Neolithic two-chamber tomb not far from its summit. Its folk name comes from the belief that it was a stone unceremoniously thrown by King Arthur after it got in his shoe. On a full moon, the armour-clad figure of the legendary king is said to rise from beneath it, but there are other legends attached to it: that the stone regularly walks down to the Burry estuary to have a drink, and that it can help young maidens attract a faithful suitor if they perform a ritual under a full moon: bring an offering of cake, and crawl three times around the stone on hand and knees—the first person to appear on the spot will make a devoted partner.

Engraving of of Arthur's stone with goats, 1840

THE SWANSEA DEVIL

Swansea Museum: Victoria Rd, Maritime Quarter, Swansea, SA1 1SN

This three-foot-tall wood carving of the Devil decorated the office building across the road from St Mary's Church for many years. It was the work of a 19th-century architect whose designs for the church had been rejected, and who allegedly uttered this prophecy: "When your church is destroyed and burnt to the ground, my devil will remain laughing". St Mary's Church was bombed during WWII, but the carving of Old Nick—now kept at Swansea Museum—is still grinning.

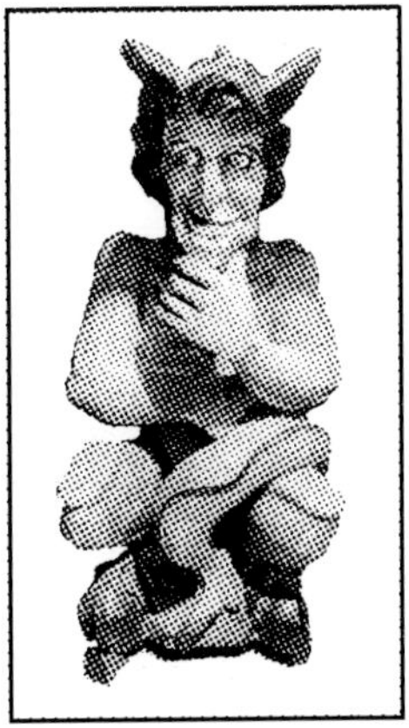

The Swansea Devil

Stepping stones across the River Ogmore

OGMORE CASTLE

Bridgend, CF32 0QP

A set of ancient stepping stones crosses the River Ogmore, haunted by the souls of those who died without revealing the location of their hidden treasures. It is said that they will only rest when their riches are thrown downstream into the water.

The treasure hidden under the 12th-century Ogmore Castle has its own supernatural guardian wandering the ruins, Y Ladi Wen (the White Lady). When a man once dared approach her, she led him to a cauldron filled with gold, buried under the old castle tower, and offered him half of it. The lure of gold was too powerful, and the man returned shortly afterwards to dig out the rest. He was found badly mauled and delirious, and died days later, after confessing his greed.

Engraving of the ruins of Ogmore Castle, 1776

TIKINSWOOD

Duffryn Ln, Cardiff, CF5 6ST · ST092733

Tikinswood is one of the best-preserved chambered cairns in Britain and was used to bury the remains of at least fifty people in the Neolithic era. A short walk away, to the west of the hamlet of St Lythans, is St Lythan's burial chamber, whose capstone is said to twirl three times on Midsummer Eve while the rest of the stones go down to the river. Those who visit it on Hallowe'en can whisper a wish to the stones and it might come true.

Both sites are associated with the same legend: that whoever spends the night here on the eve of Beltane, Midsummer, Samhain, or Midwinter will either die, go mad, or become a poet.

Tikinswood Cairn

St Lythan's burial chamber

THE RED CASTLE · CASTELL COCH

Cardiff, CF15 7JS

The High Victorian, Medieval-inspired interiors of this 19th-century fancy are a reflection of the interests of John Patrick Crichton Stuart (1847 – 1900), the third Marquess of Bute. Stuart was a Catholic convert fascinated by ancient religions, astrology, and the occult, who held regular séances and telepathic experiments at his estates in Cardiff and Scotland, and served as Vice Chairman of the Physical Research Council. He used his family fortune to leave an impressive architectural legacy, commissioning architect William Burges to turn Cardiff Castle—his main residence—and the ruins of the 13th-century Castell Coch—which would become his rural retreat—into sumptuous, Medieval-inspired wonders.

John, 3rd Marquess of Bute

The original Castell Coch was a Norman motte-and-bailey castle, and later a stone keep owned by Ifor Bach, a 12th-century Welsh leader who kidnapped the earl of Gloucester and his family, holding them hostage until he recovered the land he'd lost. Bach and his treasures are purportedly buried in a secret chamber under the castle, guarded by two stone eagles who spring to life to scare off grave robbers—the eagles are said to be two of Bach's men, whom the nobleman petrified by using black magic.

Entrance to Castell Coch

Castell Coch courtyard

Dyfed

Pentre Ifan seen at twilight

PENTRE IFAN

Nevern, Crymych, SA41 3TZ · SN099370

This imposing Neolithic dolmen is made of the same bluestones that conform Stonehenge, sourced from the Preseli Hills just above. Fairies in red caps have been glimpsed dancing around the stones, and some legends regard it as a druidical site for rituals of initiation. The dolmen is also known as "The Womb of Ceridwen", a Welsh sorceress and a goddess.

The Golden Idol of Trewern

Trewern Hall: SA41 3XE · SN088381

THE MANOR house on the edge of the Pentre Ifan wood belonged to the wealthy Warren family, and local lore says it had to be exorcised several times. When the last of the Warrens died, Trewern remained empty for many years. It was then rented to a Baptist minister, David George, who became rich shortly after he moved in. After George's death, his servants revealed the secrets of his newly found fortune: in one of the walls of the house he had discovered a "pagan idol" made of gold, allegedly unearthed by one of the Warrens near Pentre Ifan, and he was selling fragments of it to finance his lifestyle. Oddly, the Trewern hauntings ceased only when the last gold shaving was sold off.

Roman anthropomorphic handle

CWRT-Y-CADNO

Pantcoy: Pumsaint, Llanwrda, SA19 8YG

Caio Parish Church: Church Street, Cynwyl Gaeo, Caio, Carmarthenshire, SA19 8RD

National Library of Wales: Penglais Rd, Aberystwyth, SY23 3BU

Pantcoy saw the birth of physician and cunning man John Harries in 1785, well-known in his lifetime for his accomplishments in medicine, astrology, and magic. Harries reputedly owned a thrice-padlocked grimoire he only opened once a year in a secluded part of the nearby wood. His annual ritual triggered a severe storm, but also gave him unlimited power—a renewal of his pact with the Devil, it was claimed.

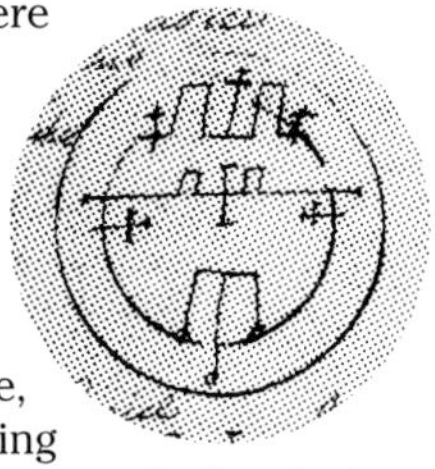

Harries could foresee people's deaths, including his own. When the date came, he stayed in bed all day, hoping to avoid his fate, but the house caught fire during the night and he perished. As the pallbearers approached the churchyard in Caio, where Harries was to be buried, his coffin suddenly became lighter. The Devil already owned his soul, but he took possession of his body just before it reached consecrated ground—or so the story goes. A gravestone with his name and that of his son, Henry, also a famous physician and cunning man, suggests otherwise.

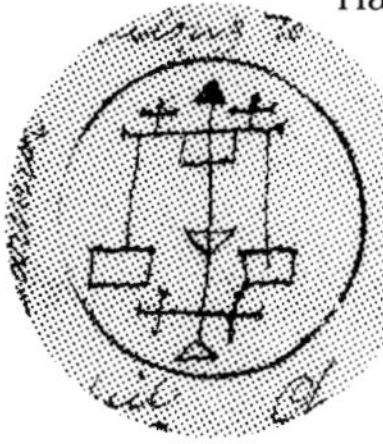

The Pant-coy now standing isn't the original thatched house where Harries was born and where he met his death, but a reformed farm building. As for the Harries' books, they're now at the Library of Wales, most of them rebound. It's been suggested that the padlocked conjuring book now forms the first 22 pages of MS 11117B.

Entrance to Caio Church

Compendium Maleficarum

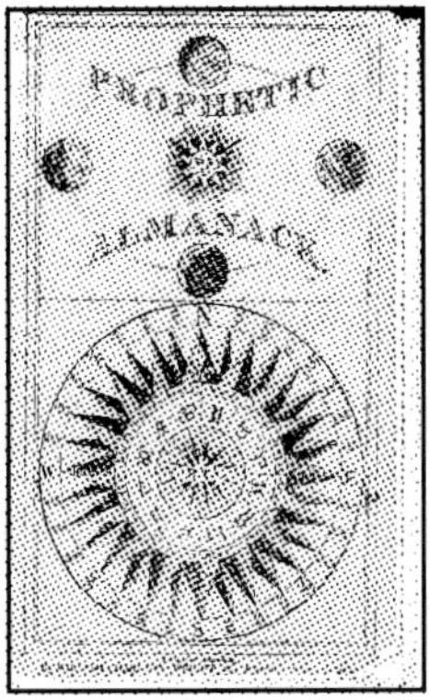

Symbols and manuscript, library of John Harries

Powys

THE BLACK MOUNTAINS

EXTENDING from southeast Wales into Herefordshire, the Black Mountains are one of the four mountain ranges that comprise the Brecon Beacons. The feeling of remoteness they elicit has often been exploited in classics of rural horror—see, for example, L T C Rolt's short tales "Cwm Garon" and "The House of Vengeance", and the rural scenes of *An American Werewolf in London*, which were filmed at Crickadarn and Hay Bluff, at the northern edge of the range. Plan your visit carefully and beware the moon.

THE SKIRRID · YSGYRYD FAWR

Abergavenny, NP7 8EN · SO331183

Biblical imagery pervades legends about the Skirrid mountain, known locally as the Holy Mountain. Its distinctive shape was said to be the result of a landslide that occurred at the time of the Crucifixion. Other tales allege it was caused by Satan stomping on top of it, furious after the Archangel Michael's refusal to follow his evil ways.

The peak of the Skirrid harbours the ruins of an Iron Age fort and the Chapel of St Michael, where services were held until the mid-19th century. The distinctive natural plinth on the north-western slopes is known as The Devil's Table, where the Prince of Darkness played cards with the legendary Jack o' Kent. In some stories, the latter is held responsible for the Skirrid's landslide.

ST MARTIN'S CHURCH, CWMYOY

Abergavenny, NP7 7NT

The famous tower of this Gothic-style church is said to be crooked as a result of the landslide of the legends, but geologists have ascertained that its foundations were built on glaciation debris. The 11th-century cross in the nave, which bears a rare carving of Christ, would have stood in the churchyard to be venerated by Medieval pilgrims.

Carving of Christ

CHURCH OF ST ISSUI

Abergavenny, NP7 7LP

The west wall of this 14th-century church contains a painted depiction of the Day of the Judgement—a Doom, where a skeleton with a scythe, an hour-glass and a spade greets the visitors. Legend has it that any attempts to whitewash the paintings have been futile, as the grinning skeleton always reappears to warn the viewers of their fate.

The church was built on the site of the cell of a 6th-century hermit named Issui or Ishow who was robbed and murdered by a traveller. His cell and the healing well nearby became a site of pilgrimage before the church was built.

Gwynedd

Cadair Idris, 1781

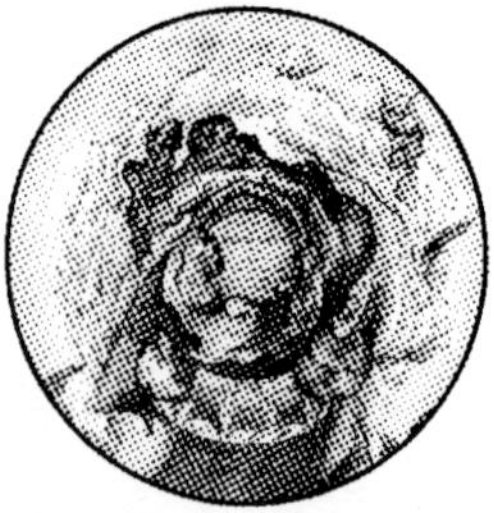

A panoramic view of Cadair Idris and adjacent mountains, 1865

Old Courthouse, Dolgellau

CADAIR IDRIS

Dolgellau, LL36 9AJ · SH711130

Known as the seat of Idris, a giant in ancient Welsh literature, the peak of this mountain is yet another place in Wales said to turn pernoctating visitors into either poets, madmen, or corpses. The Devil's cloven hooves left a mark at the so-called Rock of the Evil One as he joined the locals in a game of cards on the south side, and the whole area is said to be a regular haunt of the hounds of Gwyn ap Nudd and the hounds of Annwn—the Welsh version of the Wild Hunt, who foretell the death of those who meet them.

OLD COURTHOUSE, DOLGELLAU

Queen's Square, LL40 1AW

Dark scenes were captured in the plasterworks of this old courthouse, now a restaurant and tea rooms: a witch's trial by ducking, a hooded necromancer in a magic circle summoning a corpse from its tomb, and a winged demon with a grinning face in his groin. In the past, they might have served as a warning of the perils of black magic.

NANNAU PARK

Precipice Walk, Dolgellau, LL40 2NG

In this 18th-century landscaped parkland once stood a hollow oak tree known as The Haunt of Demons. In 1402, Nannau belonged to Hywel Sele, a supporter of the English crown and the cousin of Owain Glyndwr, who instigated a fierce

The Owl Service

Dynas Mawddwy: SY20 9JF

Edward Rowlands' Stone of Gronw: SY20 9AH · SH908192

ALAN GARNER'S 1967 novel *The Owl Service* concerns three teenagers who find themselves re-enacting the Welsh myth of Blodeuwedd (the Flower-Faced, a woman magically made of flowers and oak), from the medieval compilation of Welsh myths known as the *Mabinogion*. Impressionistic and complex, the ambitious eight-part TV adaptation from 1969 caused something of a stir with its themes of sexual jealousy, class struggle, and supernatural possession. The intertwining of myth and landscape affecting the lives of the main characters granted both the book and the series a space in the folk horror canon.

For the TV series, the action was moved from Llanymawddwy—the epicentre of the events in the novel—to the nearby village of Dinas Mawddwy, with the scenes in Llanymawddwy's Bryn Hall shot in Poulton Hall, near Liverpool. The stone of Gronw, carved by local stonemason Edward Rowlands and signed by the artist to avoid it being mistaken for an ancient monument, still stands by the River Dovey.

revolt against the English. A hunting expedition at Nannau took a sinister turn when Sele shot an arrow to his cousin—whether in purpose or accidentally depends on the account. Wearing a chainmail vest, Owain Glyndwr wasn't hurt, but he killed Sele in retaliation and concealed his body in the trunk of an oak tree. Eventually, Glyndwr confessed to the family and Sele's skeleton was found, but for centuries afterwards, a spine-chilling wailing sound was said to come from inside the tree.

The Haunt of Demons was hit by a storm in 1813, and its wood was used to make tables, cabinets, and drinking vessels, some of which are held at the National Museum of Wales in Cardiff. Several houses in the area claim to contain an engraving of the tree in a frame made with its wood.

Discovery of Hywel Sele in the Nannau Oak

An engraving of the oak

Bardsey Island

View of Bala Lake, engraving, 1799

The Vaughan family, who lived at the estate between the 18th and the 20th century, created a series of leisure walks around the estate to entertain their guests. The Nannau Deer Park Walk leads to the place where The Haunt of Demons stood, now marked with a pillar by the garden wall. The 2.5-mile circular Foel Offrwm Walk runs around the base of the luridly named Hill of Sacrifice, the site of an Iron Age hill fort.

BARDSEY ISLAND

Pwllheli, LL53 8DE

The legendary wizard Merlin lies in a glass coffin surrounded by the thirteen treasures of Britain and his nine bardic companions on this island that has also been identified with Avalon. In the Medieval era Bardsey was a place of pilgrimage, the burial site of 20,000 holy men and royals, hence its epithet "the Rome of Britain". Today it is a wildlife reserve with an aura of sacredness, crammed with prehistoric remains and the ruins of a 13th-century monastery.

BALA LAKE • LLYN TEGID

Llyn Tegid, Bala, LL23 7YH

Science says the largest natural lake in Wales is home to a rare fish species, and folklore that it shelters a sunken town. Bala Lake takes its Welsh name from Tegid Foel, the husband of Ceridwen the Enchantress in the Mabinogi. Tegid, who ruled the old town of Bala, was known for his cruelty and excess, but he and his family met his comeuppance when he was holding a celebratory banquet for the birth of his first grandson and the whole town was engulfed by water. Only a harpist survived, guided to safety by a magical bird who insistently chirped "Vengeance will come!" Local lore says that, on certain nights, the lights of the palace and the old town of Bala glow under the surface.

HUW LWYD'S PULPIT

Bont Newydd, Gwynedd, LL41 4PU · SH705412

Huw Lwyd's Pulpit

A footpath leads from the village of Llan Ffestiniog to the waterfall of Rhaeadr Cynfal. A little further, below a belvedere, stands the natural stone pillar known as Huw Lwyd's Pulpit. Here, the sorcerer would stand to preach to those who gathered in the gorge, casting spells to exorcise his patients. Black shadows would be seen coming out of their bodies, dragged by the fast-flowing waters and crashing at the bottom of the waterfall. To this day, the waterfall is still known as Rhaeadr Ddu—the Black Falls.

The Welsh Wizard

Cynfal-fawr: Rhos-wen, Maentwrog, Bont Newydd, LL41 4RA · SH702406

HUW LWYD (c.1568–c.1630) was a mercenary soldier for King James I, as well as a writer, alchemist, healer, bard and harpist. His magical skills were said to be the result of his being the seventh son of a seventh son. Devoted to the craft, he styled himself as a preacher, befriending Dr John Dee, who became his pen pal, and acquiring a reputation as a sorcerer. On his deathbed, Lwyd purportedly told one of his daughters to throw all his books of Black Arts into a lake, where they were collected by a pair of ghostly hands. No record of his death exists, which inevitably led to the belief that he never really died. His house, Cynfal-fawr, still stands, not far from Llan Ffestiniog.

DINAS EMRYS

From Craflwyn Car Park, Beddgelert, LL55 4NG · SH600491

Dinas Emrys, engraving

The Welsh Red Dragon

Ruins of what is considered to be an 11th Century tower

This wooded hillock raising over the Glaslyn river valley is said to have served as the retreat of the Celtic king Vortigern when he escaped the Anglo-Saxon invaders in the 5th century. His men's efforts to build a fortress there were thwarted by a supernatural force, so Vortigern was advised to sacrifice a young boy not conceived by a mortal man—Myrddin Emrys, the Merlin of Arthurian legend. Before Vortigern could kill him, Merlin said the castle could not stand because two dragons were battling each other in a pool beneath the hill, and predicted the triumph of the Welsh Red Dragon over the White Dragon of the Saxons.

Myrddin Emrys

Vortigern and his men released the dragons, and when Merlin's prophecy was fulfilled, the king was finally able to build his fortress. The red dragon returned to his lair under the hill and became a national symbol of Wales.

A cave in Dinas Emrys supposedly hides Merlin's treasure. When its right heir is near, it will open of its own accord, but unworthy seekers will feel the ground rumble and the sun cloud over their heads. Although Merlin's treasure has never been found, excavations in the 1940s corroborated the ancient legends: archaeologists found a subterranean lake and the remains of a 5th-century fortress rebuilt several times.

ANGLESEY

"On the shore stood the forces of the enemy, a dense array of arms and men, with women dashing through the ranks like the Furies… A circle of druids, pouring forth dire imprecations with their hands uplifted towards the heavens, struck terror into the soldiers."
—Account of the Roman attack on Ynys Môn (Anglesey), from Tacitus' *Annals*.

THE ISLAND of Anglesey is haunted by a past that might only be real in Roman accounts. In the popular imagination, the island remains associated with druids after the writings of the Roman historian Tacitus, who portrayed the druids of Anglesey as savages who practised magic, soothsaying, and human sacrifice.

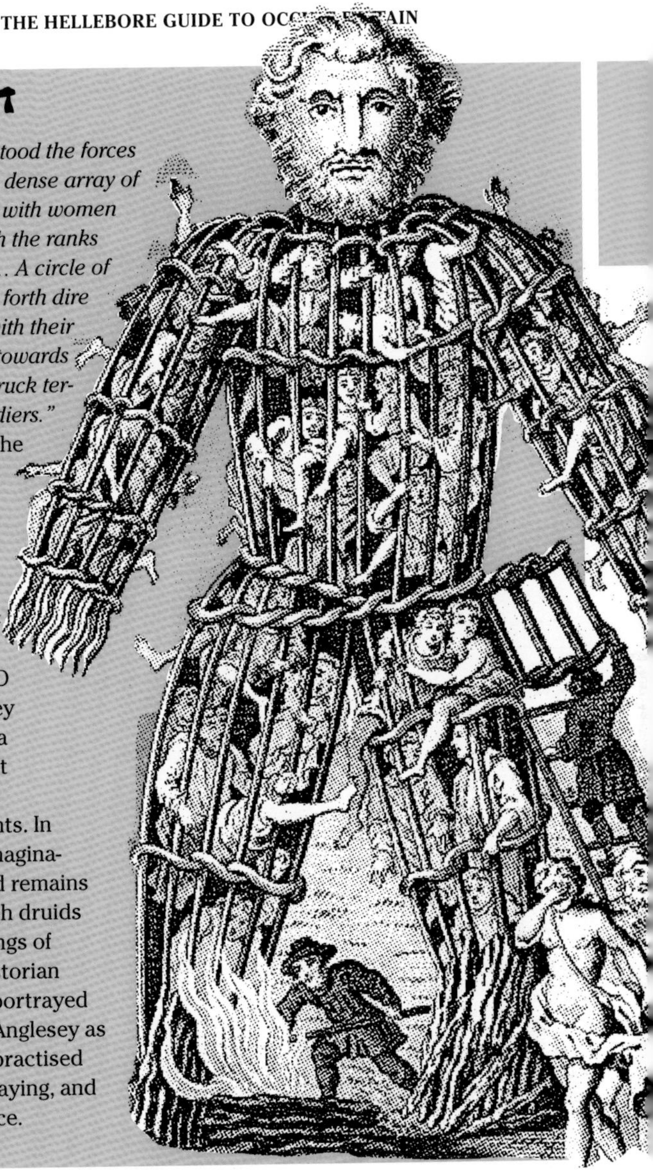

THE MOUND IN THE DARK GROVE · BRYN CELLI DDU
Llanddaniel Fab, Llanfair, LL61 6EQ
This Neolithic burial mound was designed to align with the rising sun on the summer solstice, when the light shines down its passageway to illuminate the chamber within. Human bones and arrowheads have been found inside, and carvings appear inside and on a standing stone outside the burial.

THE GIANTESS' APRON · BARCLODIAD Y GAWRES
Ty Croes, LL63 5TE
The name of this c.3000 BCE Neolithic passage comes from its legendary origin: the stones were supposed to have dropped from the apron of a giantess, who was going to build a house with them.

The stones inside the tomb are carved with spiral patterns, zigzag lines and lozenges.

A 1950s excavation uncovered the remains of two men who had been cremated, and traces of a fire inside the tomb, which was covered by a mixture of water, eel, frog, toad, mouse, grass-snake, shrew, and hare, and was topped with shells.

Y Meini Hirion

THE DRUIDS' CIRCLE · Y MEINI HIRION

Amlwch LL68 0RH · SH363921

There are many legends attached to this Neolithic stone circle, said to have been a gathering place for witches and druids. The so-called Stone of Sacrifice, with a cavity on the top, is said to replay cries and moans on stormy nights, echoes of a supposed sacrificial use—newborn babies, however, were placed on its ledge to be blessed with good fortune. The ill-tempered Deity Stone brutalises those who use offending language within the circle. One cautionary tale tells of a famously blasphemous man whose battered corpse was found at the base of the stone.

Meini Hirion standing stones

Clwyd

Gogmagog the giant

Dinas Bran castle

DINAS BRAN

Llangollen, Denbighshire, LL20 8D

This conical hill commanding the Dee Valley is said to hide the gates of Annwn, the otherworldly dwelling of Gwyn ap Nudd, king of the Fair Folk. The dramatic ruins visible today date from the 13th century, when they were built over an Iron Age fort.

In the 12th-century *Romance of Fulk Fitzwarine*, Dinas Bran is a ruined fortress teeming with evil spirits, the domain of the mace-wielding giant Gogmagog. Norman knight Payn Peveril and his 15 men defy all warnings and stay overnight. Before Peveril kills Gogmagog, he learns the castle was built by King Brân in order to defeat the brutish giant.

Dinas Bran is both translated as the Castle of Crows and as Brân's stronghold—Brân, the name of the legendary king whose head is said to be buried under the Tower of London, also means "crow" or "raven". In the *Romance of Fulk Fitzwarine*, Gogmagog reveals there's treasure buried under the castle, but some other tales refer specifically to a silver harp and even to the Holy Grail itself.

ST DIGAIN'S CHURCH

1 Uwch Afon, Llangernyw, Abergele, LL22 8PR

Every All Hallows' Eve at dead of night, the morbidly curious in Llangernyw may stand under the east window of this 13th-century church waiting for the arrival of the Angelystor—the

Recording Angel. This supernatural being is said to appear in the church to recite the names of the parishioners who will die within the next year.

Two standing stones, one with an incised cross possibly dating from the 7th-9th century, can be found south of the church. The boulders that flank one of the tombs at the graveyard are said to be an ancient pagan altar, while the enormous yew tree in the graveyard is reputedly the oldest living thing in Wales.

St Digain's Church

TREMEIRCHION

St Marcella's Parish Church: Whitchurch Road, Denbigh, LL16 4ER
Plas Clough: Denbigh, LL16 5TL
Bach-y-graig: Tremeirchion, Saint Asaph, LL17 0UH

In the area of Tremeirchion, the name of Richard Clough (1530–1570) was synonymous with otherworldly riches and diabolical pacts. Born in Denbigh to a humble family, Clough's extraordinary singing voice brought him fame and led him to London and then to Jerusalem, where he became a Knight of the Holy Sepulchre.

After making his fortune as a merchant in Antwerp, he returned to Wales in 1565 to build two houses, Bach-y-graig and Plas Clough, both in Flemish style. Their magnificence led locals to believe they were the work of the Devil, to whom Clough had sold his soul. A room at the top of Bach-y-graig was rumoured to be the temple where Clough summoned his dark master, but it was likely his observatory, as he was a keen astronomer. Clough died in Hamburg, but his heart was buried in a silver urn in St Marcella's Parish Church, Denbigh. Both of his houses are privately owned, though Bach-y-graig has been converted into farmhouse accommodation and can be rented.

Sir Richard Clough

Plas Clough

X. Scotland

Lowlands, 242
Highlands, 258
Islands, 264

X. SCOTLAND

- WITCHES AND CUNNING FOLK
- THE OLD GODS
- MAGIC, RITUALS, AND THE OCCULT
- ANCIENT MEGALITHS
- PORTALS TO THE OTHERWORLD
- DEMONS AND THE DEVIL
- CURSES AND PORTENTS
- FILM AND TV LOCATIONS
- LITERARY LOCATIONS

ROUSAY
EYNHALLOW
SKARA BRAE
ORKNEY
SKAILL HOUSE
THE RING OF BRODGAR
STENNESS
MAESHOWE
CALANAIS STANDING STONES
ISLE OF LEWIS
HIGHLANDS
MACBETH'S HILLOCK
NAIRN - INSHOCH CASTLE
SUENO'S STONE
AULDEARN
CLAVA CAIRNS
FYVIE CASTLE
BOLESKINE HOUSE
LOCH GARTEN
CALEDONIAN FOREST
SKENE
BEN MACDUI
MARY'S CHAPEL
GLAMIS CASTLE
THE GRAND LODGE OF SCOTLAND
FINGAL'S CAVE, STAFFA
NATIONAL MUSEUM OF SCOTLAND
THE WITCHES' WELL
IONA
EDINBURGH
ABERFOYLE
ST ANDREW'S OLD KIRK
THE DEVIL'S PULPIT
GOBLIN HA' YESTER CASTLE
HOUSE OF THE BINNS
ROSSLYN CHAPEL
STOBO KIRK
EARLSTON
DRUMELZIER
MELROSE ABBEY
ALLOWAY
LOWLANDS
HARTFELL SPA
CULZEAN CASTLE
HERMITAGE CASTLE
NINESTANE RIG
GLENLUCE ABBEY
CREETOWN
ANWOTH OLD KIRK
CASTLE KENNEDY GARDENS
KIRKCUDBRIGHT
LOGAN BOTANIC GARDEN
BURROW HEAD
ST NINIAN'S CAVE

Lowlands

Searching for Summerisle

Robin Hardy's *The Wicker Man* (1973), the cinematic totem of folk horror, is largely defined by its setting, the fictional Summerisle. Led by a silver-tongued aristocrat whose grandfather reintroduced the old gods as a tool of social control, the island is inhabited by a community of pagans who worship the fertility of the land. With its idyllic rural setting, Summerisle—a composite of several locations in the southwest of Scotland—remains one of the most memorable locations in film history.

ANWOTH OLD KIRK

Castle Douglas, DG7 2EF

The roofless remains of this 17th-century kirk provided the backdrop to the deconsecrated churchyard that supposedly housed Rowan Morrison's grave. Outside the gates, a maypole was installed for the youngsters to dance around. The old school house opposite the kirk served as Summerisle school.

KIRKCUDBRIGHT

DG6 4DU

Sitting on the banks of the river Dee, the town of Kirkcudbright lent many of its corners to Summerisle. Sergeant Howie prays at Greyfriars church, and May Morrison's shop stood on 84 High Street, now a contemporary art and craft gallery.

CREETOWN

Newton Stewart, DG8 7JQ

The interiors of The Green Man were shot at the Ellangowan Hotel, a former coaching inn in Creetown, while the pub's façade was borrowed from a terraced house on 11 Ann Street in Gatehouse of Fleet, a few miles to the east. Plans to turn the Ellangowan into a Wicker Man sanctuary recently fell through, but the Heritage Museum boasts a small section dedicated to the folk horror classic.

LOGAN BOTANIC GARDEN, PORT LOGAN

Nr. Stranraer, DG9 9ND / £

"He brought you up to be a pagan!"
"A heathen, conceivably, but not, I hope, an unenlightened one."
—THE WICKER MAN

Among the exotic palm trees and tree ferns that grow in this subtropical haven, Lord Summerisle tells Sergeant Howie of his grandfather's farming experiments and of the pagan past of the island. Logan dates back to 1869, and since 1969 it has been part of Edinburgh's Royal Botanic Garden.

CULZEAN CASTLE

Maybole, KA19 8LE / £

Lord Summerisle's on-screen abode is an imposing 18th-century fortress perched on the Ayrshire cliffs. The castle is the setting of an old ballad that tells of the kidnapping of the heiress of Culzean by an evil knight called Sir John (in earlier versions of the story the villain is the supernatural Elf-Knight), who had drowned his previous seven wives. It has a happy ending: the plucky heiress pushes her nemesis off Games Loup Rock into the sea before he can do away with her.

Seven ghosts reputedly haunt the castle grounds, of which the most famous is a ghostly bagpiper, whose music has been heard at Piper's Brae, a tree-lined walk near the castle. Legend has it that the piper and his dog were sent into the caves below to prove they weren't haunted, but neither of them returned. The castle is open to the public during the warmer months.

CASTLE KENNEDY GARDENS
Stranraer, DG9 8SJ / £
Castle Kennedy was ravaged by fire in the 17th century, but this didn't stop the 2nd Earl of Stair laying out gardens around his ruined home. The gardens were restored in the 19th century, when Lochinch Castle was also built. For the film, Lochinch's foyer was used as Lord Summerisle's drawing room; while below the ruins of Castle Kennedy, on a mound at the bottom of a paddock, a stone circle was erected. Fans might want to cut some capers on the path through the gardens, where the May Day procession was held. Sadly, Lochinch Castle isn't open to the public, so Lord Summerisle's drawing room remains out of bounds.

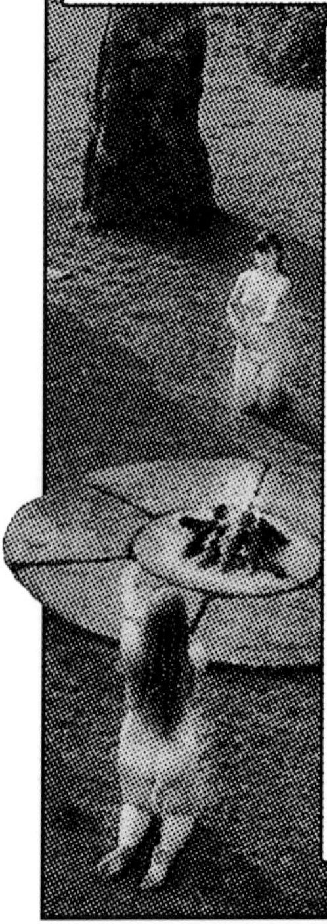

BURROWHEAD
Burrowhead Holiday Village, Stewart, DG8 8JB
Many will feel irresistibly drawn to start singing "Summer is i-cumen in" as they approach Burrow Head. The wicker man was erected on a spot two miles southwest of St Ninian's Cave. After its removal, two stumps remained, but they've been gradually eroded by souvenir hunters.

ST NINIAN'S CAVE
Physgill Lodge, Whithorn, Newton Stewart, DG8 8JU
A place of pilgrimage since the Middle Ages, this small sea cave is believed to have been a retreat of St Ninian's, Scotland's first saint. It is here where Rowan Morrison reappears, seemingly ready for her appointment with the Wicker Man; and it is also on this beach that Lord Summerisle rolls his beer barrels to place an offering to the water gods.

The Sorcerer from the North

Glenluce Abbey: Glenluce, Newton Stewart, DG8 0AF / £
Melrose Abbey: Abbey St, Melrose, TD6 9LG / £

ASTRONOMER, astrologer, translator, mathematician and alchemist, the polymathic talents of Borders-born Michael Scot (c. 1175–c. 1235) earned him the position of court astrologer to Emperor Frederick II of Sicily, a reputation as a powerful wizard, and the dubious honour of being the only Scot sentenced to eternal torment in Dante's *Inferno*. Travelling widely over the course of his career and generating numerous legends after his death, he is associated with several locations around Scotland. One of them is the area around Glenluce Abbey, which he reportedly visited in the 13th century. Some stories say he set his familiars to work spinning ropes by the sea at nearby Ringdoo Point; others have him imprisoning the plague there by locking it in a dungeon. According to *The Lay of the Last Minstrel*, Michael Scot was buried at Melrose Abbey, with a monk recalling how he "buried him on St. Michael's nigh" in holy ground to "scare the fiends from the Wizard's grave".

Michael Scot in Bodleian "De physionomiae".

Hermitage Castle

Face peering down

Hallways through the Hermitage Castle dungeon

HERMITAGE CASTLE

Newcastleton, Hawick, Roxburghshire, TD9 0LU / £

Old Redcap Sly

Standing on the edge of the Liddesdale moors in the historically turbulent Scottish Borders, this imposing, semi-ruined castle has been associated with the de Soulis family since its first incarnation as a 13th-century motte-and-bailey castle. In 1320, during the Wars of Scottish Independence, Hermitage Castle was owned by William de Soulis, who took part in a failed plot to kill Robert the Bruce and was imprisoned for treason in Dumbarton Castle, where he died in mysterious circumstances. The Borders ballad "Lord Soulis", recorded in the 18th century by folklorist John Leyden, tells a different story, describing William as a tyrant trained in black magic by the legendary magician Michael Scot. William's familiar was a redcap—a type of murderous goblin said to haunt ruined castles along the borders, killing travellers to dye their hats with their victims' blood—known as "Old Redcap sly", whom he summoned by tapping three times on an iron chest. With him at his side, the laird kidnapped a young woman, terrorised the countryside and remained impossible to kill, until he was finally boiled in molten lead by his neighbours at the nearby Neolithic stone circle of Ninestane Rig.

William de Soulis' redcap is said to still haunt Hermitage Castle, opening the door of the chamber in the dungeons—where his master supposedly summoned evil forces—every seven years.

NINESTANE RIG

B6399, TD9 0LZ · NY517973

As well as being the site of the legendary boiling of William de Soulis, this Late Neolithic stone circle is said to have a treasure buried beneath the stones, though any attempts to find it have been unsuccessful.

Ninestane Rig stone circle

ALLOWAY

Robert Burns' cottage: 16 Alloway, Ayr, KA7 4PY / £
Auld Kirk: 40 Alloway, Ayr, KA7 4PQ
Brig o'Doon: Ayr, KA7 4PJ

The birthplace of the National Bard, the poet Robert Burns (1759 – 1796), the village of Alloway was also the setting for his narrative poem Tam O' Shanter. As Burns tells it, witches and warlocks dance at the Auld Kirk to the tune of the Devil's bagpipes, but they can't chase Tam over the Brig o'Doon—the pattern on the cobbles of the medieval bridge stopped all supernatural creatures from crossing to the other side. The Auld Kirk is regularly lit in green for added eeriness as a tribute to these scenes.

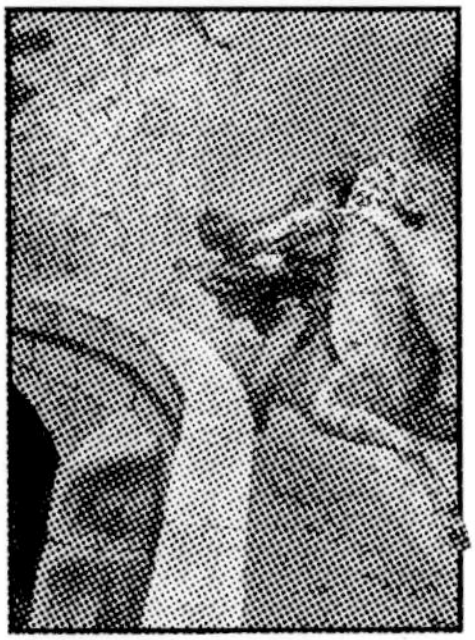

Tam O'Shanter on Alloway Brig

Alloway's "Haunted Kirk"

Robert Burns at Alloway

The Trail of the Scottish Merlin

THE MAGICIAN MERLIN, advisor to King Arthur, is drawn from various legendary Romano-British and Celtic characters, and is linked with Scottish locations in several Arthurian tales.

CALEDONIAN FOREST

Glenmore Forest Park:

Aviemore, PH22 1QU

According to the Middle Welsh accounts of Myrddin Wyllt ("Myrddin the Wild"), the mad, defeated Merlin roamed the Caledonian Forest following the Battle of Arfderyd—hence his epithet in later texts, Merlinus Caledonensis. This ancient temperate rainforest, which once covered much of the Highlands, now survives only in 35 small remnants, but they're still a magical place to explore—try taking the Ryvoan Trail through Glenmore Forest Park for a beautiful walk through pine and birch forest.

HARTFELL SPA

Moffat, DG10 9LT

Some stories say that Merlin spent his final years by this natural spring in the hills of the Scottish Borders near Moffat. An overhanging rock nearby forms a natural cave-like shelter—could Merlin have sheltered here?

STOBO KIRK

B712, Peebles, EH45 8NU

Close by Drumelzier is Stobo Kirk, a site of worship since the 6th century, where St Kentigern is said to have converted Merlin to Christianity. This scene is depicted in one of the kirk's stained glass windows.

DRUMELZIER

B712, ML12 6JD

Legend has it that Merlin is buried on the banks of the Drumelzier Burn (or Powsail Burn), a tributary of the Tweed, near the village of Drumelzier. This led to Thomas the Rhymer's prophecy that "when Tweed and Powsail meet at Merlin's grave, Scotland and England shall one monarch have"—which was supposedly fulfilled in 1603, when the Tweed is said to have burst its banks and spilled into the Powsail on the day James VI of Scotland was crowned James I of England.

The Prophecies of Thomas The Rhymer

THE 13TH-CENTURY Scottish laird Thomas Learmont from Earlston is best remembered in legend as Thomas the Rhymer. An old ballad tells how he acquired the gift of prophecy from the Queen of Elfland, who dragged him to the fairy realm, where he was to remain for seven years before he returned to this world as a seer, authoring several prophetic verses.

EARLSTON
Rhymer's Stone: Melrose, TD6 9HA
Eildon Hill: Melrose, TD6 9HS · NT549324
Rhymer's Tower: Melrose Rd, TD4 6DL

The ruined 16th-century tower known as Rhymer's Tower stands on the site of Thomas Learmont's original house, and the Rhymer's Stone marks the spot where Thomas met the Queen of Fairyland, according to the legend. Further along the path to the Eildon Hill is Bogle Burn, a stream named after the goblins supposedly lurking there. The triple peak of the hill is said to have been created by Michael Scot's speaking "words that cleft Eildon hills in three", in the words of Walter Scott.

FYVIE CASTLE
Fyvie, Turriff, AB53, 8JS / £

This magnificent fortress has changed ownership many times since it was built in the 13th century, allegedly the result of a curse placed by Thomas the Rhymer when he was denied shelter there on a stormy night. To reverse the curse and allow the estate to be inherited in direct line, the three so-called Weeping Stones—which were sourced from a demolished chapel and used to build the castle—must be brought together. One of the stones is in the castle's charter room, the second is said to have been built into the foundations, but the third stone has never been recovered. One of the window ledges is inscribed with the words "D. Lillias Drummond", purportedly carved by the Green Lady that haunts the house. When her husband, Lord Seton, shunned her, Lillias starved to death in one of the rooms—though some say he poisoned her. Lord Seton remarried shortly after her tragic demise. After a night of anguished moans coming from outside the newly-weds' bedroom window, the etching was discovered, upside down and some 15 metres from the ground below.

Green Man, Rosslyn Chapel

Rosslyn crypts

ROSSLYN CHAPEL

Chapel Loan, Roslin, Midlothian, EH25 9PU / £

A few miles outside Edinburgh stands an ornately carved 15th-century chapel, the subject of much speculation over the years for its rumoured connections to the Knights Templar, the Holy Grail and Freemasonry. Founded in 1446 by Sir William St Clair, the chapel's activities were brought to a halt by the Reformation. During the Civil War, Oliver Cromwell stabled his horses there, but, after Queen Victoria's personal appeal for Rosslyn Chapel to be "preserved for the country", restoration work enabled services to be held there again for the first time in over 200 years.

The St Clair family has had long-standing links with Freemasonry, beginning with Sir William Sinclair becoming the first Grand Master of the Scottish Masons in 1630. This connection has fuelled numerous theories about the hidden symbolism within the chapel's carvings, which exploded into mainstream pop culture after the publication of

Dan Brown's 2003 blockbuster *The Da Vinci Code*. Brown's dubious revisionism has been debunked by historians, but visitors to Rosslyn can explore its elaborate gothic architecture and stunningly intricate carvings of plants, Biblical and rural scenes, and over 100 green men in and around the chapel, reflecting overlaps between medieval Christianity and folk beliefs surrounding life, death and renewal.

Ceiling of Lady Chapel

GOBLIN HA', YESTER CASTLE

Gifford, East Lothian, EH41 4PG · NT556668

> "Dread artisans of hell…
> laboured under Hugo's spell"
> (Walter Scott, *Marmion*, 1808)

Beneath the ruins of the 13th-century Yester Castle lies a mysterious vaulted chamber rumoured to have been built by demonic forces—the subterranean Goblin Ha'. The stone keep was erected by one of the guardians of Alexander III of Scotland, Hugo de Giffard, whose reputation as a necromancer earned him the sobriquet "the Wizard of Yester". Hugo's astonishing underground hall was the proof of his devilish dealings: since such a place couldn't have been carved out of stone by human hands, it must have been "wrought by witchcraft"—or so said the old tales mentioned by Walter Bower in his 15th-century *Scotichronicon*.

Yester Tower

In the 16th century, Hugo's descendants moved into a new tower house on the site of the present-day Yester House, and the castle gradually fell into disrepair. Today, it is almost hidden by woodland, but Goblin Ha' remains intact and can be found via a small entrance behind the castle. A narrow passageway suddenly opens into a grand, cathedral-like structure with a vaulted gothic ceiling. In one corner is a flight of steps descending even deeper, walled up at the end—is this to block off a well, or (as some stories would have it) a gateway to hell?

Windows of Goblin Ha'

EDINBURGH

THE CAPITAL CITY of Scotland is guarded by Arthur's Seat, an impressive hill formed by an ancient volcano, said to be a slumbering dragon who once tormented the area and who might wake again to impose his reign of terror. The hillfort at its summit was the seat of power of a Celtic warrior tribe, the Votadini. Its folk name, however, reflects its association with the kingdom of Camelot.

THE WITCHES' WELL

EH1 2NQ

This memorial drinking fountain attached to a wall at the Castle Esplanade was commissioned in 1894 as a tribute to the witches burned at the stake nearby between 1479 and 1722. Decorated with foxgloves, the evil eye, healing hands, and snakes, the fountain also bears an inscription that assumes all victims had magical powers—hence the calls for a new, more historically accurate memorial.

FREEMASONS' HALL

Mary's Chapel: 19 Hill St, EH2 3JP

The Grand Lodge of Scotland: 96 George St, EH2 3DH

The oldest Masonic lodge still in existence, Mary's Chapel has records dating back to 1599, long before what many consider the birth of modern Freemasonry—the society originated in Scotland before becoming a national network. Just around the corner is the Grand Lodge of Scotland, whose museum presents intriguing Masonic regalia to curious visitors.

NATIONAL MUSEUM OF SCOTLAND

Chambers St, EH1 1JF

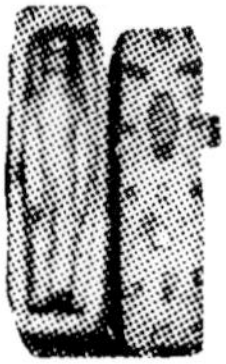

The museum's collection includes the eight surviving miniature coffins of Arthur's Seat, discovered in a cave on the hill in 1836. The intriguing 17 coffins were filled with tiny wooden figures, meticulously carved and dressed in custom-made clothes. Though several theories have been suggested for their existence (including that they represented the 17 bodies dug up by Burke and Hare, who notoriously supplied corpses to Edinburgh's medical school), their ultimate purpose remains a mystery.

The witches of North Berwick

St Andrew's Old Kirk: Kirk Ports, North Berwick, EH39 4HH

FROM St Andrew's Kirk, in the stretch of coastline that runs between Tantallon Castle and North Berwick, witches summoned the elements to sink the royal fleet of King James VI and Queen Anne of Denmark in 1589—or so the monarch believed. In August, the couple had married by proxy in Kronborg Castle, but the meeting between bride and groom was repeatedly thwarted by violent storms. The king

finally managed to reach Denmark in October, and when the couple returned to Scotland after the winter, he embarked on his sanguinary crusade: the North Berwick witch trials, in which around seventy individuals, mostly women, were tortured and killed, accused of high treason by means of black magic. In 1656, half of St Andrew's Kirk collapsed during a storm, which was regarded as divine punishment.

HOUSE OF THE BINNS

Binns View, Linlithgow, West Lothian, EH49 7NA / £

The most infamous resident of this 17th-century house was the feared Scottish Royalist general Sir Thomas Dalyell (1615–1685), known as "Bluidy Tam" for his treatment of dissidents following the Restoration of Charles II and as "the Muscovite De'il" for introducing torture techniques he learnt from his time in the Russian military. Tam's bloodthirsty reputation made people believe he was capable of anything, including dealing with Old Nick himself. He was said to have cheated the Devil during a game of cards at the house, hiding a mirror behind the table in order to read his opponent's cards. Furious at his tricks, the Devil threw the table at Tam, which narrowly missed him and ended up in Sergeant's Pond outside.

Sir Thomas Dalyell

House of the Binns Tower

Over two hundred years later, a drought during the hot summer of 1878 caused the pond to dry up—and a marble-topped table emerged. It was carried back into the house, where it stands in the entrance hall to this day. On one corner of the table is a distinct semi-circular mark—the imprint of the Devil's hoof, seared into the marble.

Today, the House of the Binns is owned by the National Trust for Scotland, and is surrounded by beautifully landscaped grounds and woodlands, including the now refilled Sergeant's Pond.

THE DEVIL'S PULPIT

Finnich Glen, Stirlingshire, G63 9QJ · NS496850

The Devil's Pulpit

Deep in the moss-covered gorge of Finnich Glen, anyone who makes their way down to the rushing red waters of Carnock Burn will discover a mushroom-shaped rock formation with sinister associations. Some say the rock is where the Devil stood to address his followers, the burn turning blood-red where his feet touched the water. Other stories tell of secret druid rituals being performed there, while suspected witches are said to have been executed at this site. The large rocky outcrop at the nearby Kilpatrick Hills, known as the Whangie ("slice"), has a deep gash down the middle, said to have been caused by the Devil flicking his tail as he flew past.

Whangie, Kilpatrick Hills

The water's crimson colour actually comes from the stream's sandstone bed, flowing brightest after heavy rainfall. The Devil's Pulpit can be reached via a steep stone staircase, known both as Jacob's Ladder and the Devil's Steps. The steps can be slippery, so hiking boots are recommended.

ABERFOYLE

Doon Hill: FK8 3UX · NN525002

Old Kirk Graveyard: Manse Road, FK8 3XA

Known for *The Secret Commonwealth of Elves, Fauns, and Fairies*, a popular treatise also covering witchcraft and second sight, Reverend Robert Kirk (1644 –1692) was buried in the old kirkyard at Aberfoyle, though local lore states the tomb is empty, as the fairies took away his body due to his prying too deeply into their secrets.

Kirk believed there was a gateway to the Secret Commonwealth at the local Doon Hill, the destination of his daily walks. The story goes that the Unseelie Court had warned him not to go there, but he was irresistibly drawn to it. One night, during one of his visits, he collapsed and died. His cousin Graham of Duchray claimed Kirk's ghost had visited him in the night, explaining he was trapped in the realm of the fairies, and asking for help to be released. In order to do so, Duchray would have to throw an iron knife at his spectre when Kirk reappeared next. The occasion was the baptism of Duchray's child. Sadly, Duchray failed to react, and Kirk's spirit vanished forever. Some say it remains trapped in the largest pine tree at the top of Doon Hill, waiting to be released.

On Nocturnal Dances of Faeries. Olaus Magnus, 1555

Grave of Robert Kirk

Offering to fairies on Doon Hill

Encounter with visitation

GLAMIS CASTLE

Forfar, DD8 1RJ / £

Although in Shakespeare's play the Weird Sisters call him Thane of Glamis, the real Macbeth had no connection to Glamis Castle. However, this 15th-century keep—the Queen Mother's childhood home and the birthplace of Princess Margaret—is rife with tales of curses, secret rooms, and solemn initiations.

Among the crowd of ghosts said to roam the castle's corridors are the 16th-century Lady of Glamis, accused of witchcraft against King James and burned at the stake, and the wicked Earl Beardie, said to have lost his soul to the Devil after gambling with him on a sabbat. Outside, the River Dean is said to take a human life each year, and it is known as the Dowie Dean, meaning "doleful" or "sinister".

The Horror of Glamis

AFTER visiting Glamis Castle in 1790, Walter Scott wrote of how its atmosphere made him feel "too far from the living and somewhat too near to the dead." He was one of the many visitors who tried to unravel its mystery—a mystery said to be locked away in a secret chamber. Scott didn't say what the chamber supposedly hid, but half a century after his visit, a legend appeared fully formed: the secret room was to keep a captive deemed a monster, the product of the curse that supposedly befell the Earls of Strathmore and that came to be known as "The Horror of Glamis".

Some sources point at a tragic story behind the legend. In 1821, Thomas and Charlotte Bowes-Lyon's first child, Thomas, was recorded as having died at birth. Rumours circulated that the boy had been born with severe birth defects and immediately locked away in a secret chamber. The family secret, it was said, was kept for generations, revealed to every new heir in a solemn ritual only when they reached the age of 21. They were then taken to the chamber where the rightful heir lived in seclusion, cared for by some trusted servants.

The secret room—if there is one—has never been found. However, the mystery is kept alive by a quote reportedly from Claude Bowes-Lyon, the grandfather of the Queen Mother and heir to the Earldom in 1865: "If you could even guess the nature of this castle's secret, you would get down on your knees and thank God it was not yours."

Claude Bowes-Lyon

Loch Skene

SKENE

Kirkton of Skene Churchyard: Westhill, AB32 6XE
Skene House: Westhill, AB32, 7BQ

Kirkton of Skene churchyard

The 17th-century laird Alexander Skene from Skene House was rumoured to have studied necromancy at Padua University, where he sold his soul to the Devil. Always escorted by a conspiracy of ravens, Skene was said to be able to bend anyone's will to his own, bewitching a local ceilidh he disliked so they danced until their feet bled, and *reesting* his enemies so they would remain glued to the floor for as long as he wished. One night, as he was on his coach traversing the frozen Loch of Skene accompanied by the Devil, his coachman glanced at the passenger's seat and caught Old Nick's eye, which made him lose control of the vehicle. They all sank to the bottom of the loch. The sorcerer is buried at the kirkyard, and it is said he will raise from the dead if anyone walks 100 times around his grave.

Skene House's name and history might have inspired the ancestral house of black magician Oliver Haddo in W. Somerset Maugham's *The Magician* (1908). The Skene from the novel, however, is located in Staffordshire.

Highlands

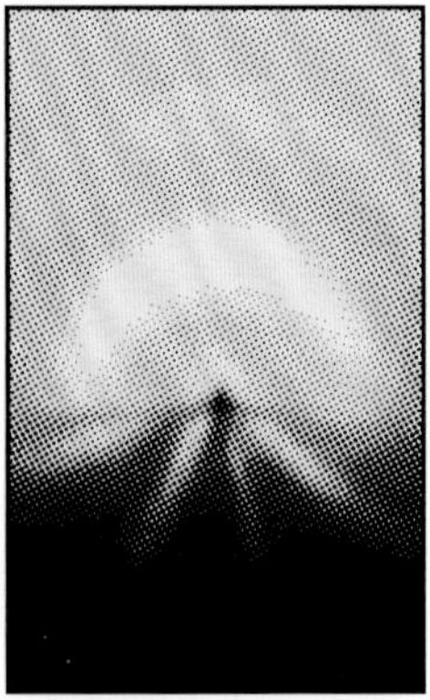

A Brocken spectre

Loch Garten

BEN MACDUI

Ballater, PH22 1RB · NN988989

The summit of Ben Macdui, the second highest mountain in the UK, is said to be haunted by a strange presence known as the Am Fear Liath Mòr—the Big Grey Man. Rarely seen but often felt or heard, the creature is described as being over ten feet tall. Theories about its nature range from it being a form of the Brocken spectre—an optical illusion common in mountain environments—, a hallucination caused by exhaustion and isolation, a type of cryptid, or, more enticingly, a genius loci, the embodiment of the spirit of the Cairngorms. The Big Grey Man is often seen (or rather, felt) at the cliffs of Lurchers Crag, over the northern entrance to the Larig Ghru Pass. To the west of the latter stands Bod an Deamhain (literally, the Penis of the Demon), known as the Devil's Point in English, a euphemistic translation first given to Queen Victoria by a local ghillie when she was visiting the area.

LOCH GARTEN

Abernethy National Nature Reserve, Nethy Bridge, PH25 3EF

This Highland freshwater loch and the neighbouring Loch Mallachie (the Loch of the Curse) were said to be frequented by a spirit known as The Old Man of Garten, which appeared as a glowing white cloud emitting high-pitched screams to warn of an impending death.

BOLESKINE HOUSE

Loch Ness, Inverness, IV2 6XT

This 18th-century manor by the side of Loch Ness has a long history of occult connections. Built in an area with a reputation for strange happenings, it has burned down twice, contains a secret passage from the house to the graveyard, and for many years was the home of famed occultist Aleister Crowley.

In the 17th century, before the house was built, the grounds were occupied by Boleskine Kirk and kirkyard. The minister, Thomas Houston, purportedly had to tackle a case of necromancy and lay animated corpses back to rest after a powerful local wizard, An Cruinair Friseal, had raised them from the dead. According to legend, the kirk itself later caught fire during a service, killing everyone inside.

Boleskine House was built on the same site in the 1760s by Colonel Archibald Fraser, originally as a hunting lodge. Aleister Crowley purchased it in 1899, deeming it ideal to develop his occult practice. He embarked on a lengthy ritual he

Aleister Crowley

Boleskine cemetery

Boleskine House

Lucifer Rising (Kenneth Anger, 1972)

The Boleskine House FOUNDATION

called the Operation of the Sacred Magick, which involved summoning the lords of Hell, but was called away to Paris during this time—before, it's said, he could safely banish them. He left Boleskine in 1913. The house passed briefly through the hands of experimental filmmaker and occultist Kenneth Anger, before being bought by Led Zeppelin's Jimmy Page in 1970. Weird occurrences were reported by numerous occupants of the house; in 2000, a BBC film crew making a documentary about Crowley called in an exorcist after camera equipment repeatedly malfunctioned and they were plagued by an infestation of beetles.

In 2019, the house was acquired by the Boleskine House Foundation, with the aim of restoring it to its former Georgian and Jacobean glory and reflecting its occult past, opening it to the public once the work is completed.

Entrance to Clava Cairns

CLAVA CAIRNS

Near Inverness, IV2 5EU

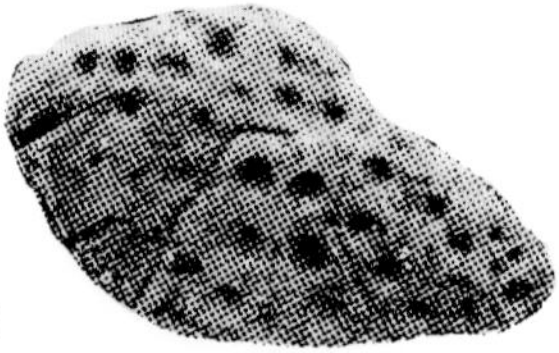

Standing in woodland not far from the river Nairn, the 4,000-year-old Clava Cairns are all that remains of a much larger Bronze Age burial ground. Each of the three cairns is surrounded by a stone circle, and many of the stones used to create the cairns have cup marks on them. Later burials have also taken place at the site, suggesting that it remained a place of spiritual significance for centuries.

In 2000, a tourist posted a 1kg stone back to Clava Cairns that he had taken as a souvenir, asking tourism staff to replace it in order to end the run of terrible luck his family had experienced since.

Standing stone

The Confessions of Isobel Gowdie

ONE OF THE most intriguing figures in the history of witchcraft in Scotland, Isobel Gowdie was a 17th-century cottar who claimed to be a member of a devil-worshipping coven. Her vivid confessions describe sexual intercourse with the Devil, shapeshifting, spells, and nocturnal escapades with the Queen of the Fairies. Because her incredibly detailed testimony wasn't prompted by torture, scholars have described the material as extraordinary, either the product of a talented narrator or the consequence of a bout of ergotism. Gowdie's stories formed the basis of Margaret Murray's Witch-Cult hypothesis, and have inspired countless books, songs, and plays.

AULDEARN

Kirk: 12 Church Rd, Nairn, IV12 5TS

Lochloy House: Off Lochloy Road, Nairn, IV12 5LE · NH925577

Gowdie lived in a cottage in the area of Auldearn, and claimed the Devil sucked blood from the mark he carved on her shoulder at the kirk of Auldearn. It's been suggested that the earliest part of Lochloy House might have been Gowdie's cottage.

NAIRN

Inshoch Castle: Nairn, IV12 5LE · NH936567

The fields around Nairn are speckled with fairy mounds, one of which was Downie Hill, where Gowdie said the Queen and King of Fairies held their court. Nearby also stands Macbeth's Hillock, where the Scottish general purportedly met the three witches. Gowdie said she copulated with the Devil "in the new wards of Inshoch", a "very huge, black, rough man, very cold". The castle, which stands beside farm buildings on private land, is now ruined.

Macbeth and the Witches

Macbeth's Hillock: Brodie, Forres, IV36 2TD · NH959568
Sueno's Stone: Findhorn Rd, Forres, IV36 3WX

WRITTEN shortly after King James sat on the English throne, *Macbeth's* atmosphere of supernatural dread is driven by the Weird Sisters, the three witches and prophetesses who embodied the fears of 17th-century spectators fuelled by the reigning monarch's obsession with black magic. Shakespeare was mainly influenced by Holinshed's *Chronicles* (1587), where Macbeth and Banquo encounter "three women in strange and wild apparel, resembling creatures of elder world", a meeting that has become part of the folklore of the Scottish landscape. A small hill near the 16th-century Brodie castle is one of the contenders for the legendary meeting point; the other is a former crossroads marked by the 6.5-metre tall Pictish stone known as Sueno's Stone, where the Weird Sisters are said to be imprisoned.

Islands

Iona Abbey

Sìthean Mòr

St Oran's Chapel

IONA

Tomb of St Columba: Iona Abbey and Nunnery, PA76 6SQ
Dùn I: PA76 6SW · NM284252
Sìthean Mòr: PA76 6SJ· NM272237
St Oran's cemetery: St Oran's Chapel, PA76 6SL

The birthplace of Celtic Christianity in Scotland, the grassy landscape and turquoise seas of this tiny island are filled with myths, enchantment and sacred spaces. Near the tomb of St Columba, the founder of Iona Abbey in 563, once stood the Black Stones, named not for their colour, but for the dark fate befalling anyone who dared break an oath sworn upon them. Legend says the Stone of Scone—the traditional Scottish Coronation Stone—was once among their number. Somewhere at St Oran's cemetery lies the grave of the real Macbeth, and just below the summit of Dùn I ("the hill of Iona"), the Well of Eternal Youth, said to have been blessed by St Brigid while visiting the island on the Summer Solstice, purportedly brings healing to all searching for renewal.

Iona's most intriguing landscape feature might be Sìthean Mòr ("large fairy hill"), also known as the Hill of the Angels. Here, St Columba spoke to the divine messengers; other stories mark it as a gateway to the land of the fairies. Perhaps for the best, the hill now stands on private land.

The Mystery of Netta Fornario

ON the afternoon of 19th November 1929, the body of a woman was found near Sìthean Mòr, naked except for a blackened silver chain around her neck, holding a knife that she'd used to cut a large cross in the turf where her body was lying. She was identified as Netta Fornario, a 32-year-old member of the Hermetic Order of the Golden Dawn who had travelled to Iona from London three months earlier. Much has been speculated about the strange circumstances of her death.

Fornario was an Italian-British writer drawn to Iona after reading the work of fellow Golden Dawn member William Sharp (using the pen name Fiona MacLeod), who had written about the island at length and described a fairy portal in the area around Loch Staonaig. She spent much of her time walking around the island and going into trances which could last for days. According to Francis King's *Ritual Magic in England* (1970), she had expressed fears to her landlady that "certain people" were affecting her telepathically, and had decided to leave the island. Instead, she disappeared.

Netta's official cause of death was "exposure from the elements" or "heart failure", but her interest in fairies led to more fanciful theories that supernatural forces may have been at work. F. Marian McNeill's *An Iona Anthology* (1952) suggests Netta "apparently slipped out one night to the fairy hill naked carrying only a knife with which to open the hill" and ultimately "fell victim to the fairies". More recent discussions of the case have suggested that her blackened silver jewellery could have been due to high body acidity caused by untreated diabetes, which in turn could have caused mental confusion. Present-day Golden Dawn member Demedia Harding has hypothesised that Netta's death could have been a murder covered up by the islanders, although there is no evidence of foul play.

Netta Fornario is buried in a simple grave in St Oran's Chapel Cemetery, marked with her initials. While we will probably never know exactly what happened, her story deserves to be told.

William Sharp

IONA MYSTERY

LONDON WOMAN FOUND DEAD

MYSTERIOUS CIRCUMSTANCES

News was received yesterday of the death of Miss Nora Emily Fornario, of Mortlake Road, Kew. She was found dead on Tuesday of last week in a sheltered spot in the island of Iona, and she was buried by the islanders on Friday. The cause of her death is at present unknown, but it is presumed to be from exposure.

STAFFA

FINGAL'S CAVE

Isle of Staffa · NM324350

Fingal's Cave

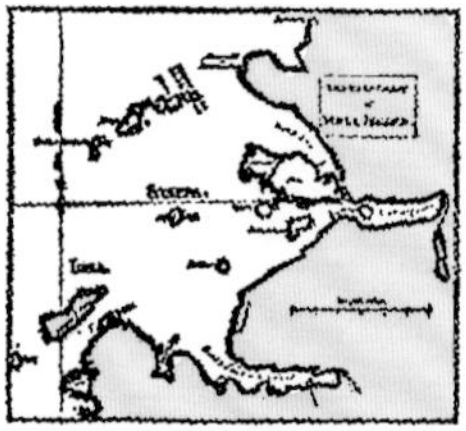

Location of Fingal's cave

The joined hexagonal columns of basalt that form this cave on the uninhabited island of Staffa give it exceptional acoustics, leading it to become known as the Cave of Melody. In the 19th century, Felix Mendelssohn named his overture to *The Hebrides* after the cave, following a trip to the island. Its popularity turned the cave into a tourist destination, visited by the likes of Jules Verne, Robert Louis Stevenson, Keats, Turner, Walter Scott, and Queen Victoria and Prince Albert. Legend says both this cave and the Giant's Causeway in Northern Ireland were the end parts of a bridge built by Irish giant Fionn MacCumhaill, allowing him to cross over from Ireland to Scotland to fight his nemesis, the giant Benandonner. Geology tells us that both features were created by the same ancient lava flow some 60 million years ago, when both sites might have been joined. Other tales claim that Hell lies just below the island and that it can be entered through the cave.

Closeup of hexagonal rock formations

The Blue Men of the Minch

THE STRAIT between the Isle of Lewis and the Shiant Isles is said to be the dwelling place of the Blue Men of the Minch, bearded mermen who conjured storms, preyed on sailors, and could only be defeated by those who had the last word in a rhyming duel.

ISLE OF LEWIS

CALANAIS STANDING STONES

A859, Isle of Lewis, Outer Hebrides, HS2 9DY · NB212330

Erected 5000 years ago in the shape of a cross with a circle at its centre, these 12-foot tall stones may have been used as a kind of astronomical observatory—perhaps, as archaeologist Patrick Ashmore suggested, to mark a heavenly event that took place every 18.6 years and that saw the moon skim especially low over the southern hills.

According to folklore, the stones were once giants who refused to build a church for St Keiran and were petrified as a punishment. Their name in Gaelic is Fir Chreig, which means "False Men". Another story tells how early on Midsummer, the "Shining One"—often interpreted as a sun-god figure—walks the length of the stones, heralded by the cuckoo.

Calanais stones

Calanais stones

ORKNEY

Around 70 islands, 20 of which are currently inhabited, conform the archipelago of Orkney. Its ancient, mystical landscape is formed of green fields and rugged cliffs, megaliths and tumuli, all of them steeped in folklore and magic.

THE MAINLAND

The Ring of Brodgar

B9055, Stromness, KW16 3JZ · HY294133

The third largest stone circle in Britain stands on a plateau on the Ness of Brodgar, a thin strip of land that separates two lochs. 27 of the original stones—erected around 2500 BCE—remain. Folklore regards them as dancing giants petrified by the first rays of morning sunlight, with the so-called Comet Stone (also known as the Oily Stane) fiddling for them. In 1774, the Rev. George Low recorded the belief that the Ring of Brodgar was a temple of the sun and the standing stones of Stennes were a temple of the moon. Couples would swear their vows here, the man kneeling down and praying to Woden in the Temple of the Sun, and the woman doing the same in the Temple of the Moon. They would then hold hands through the hole of the Odin Stone. Both temples still remain, but the holed stone was destroyed in 1814.

Stenness

Stromness, KW16 3JY

Arranged in an elliptical shape in around 3100 BCE, the standing stones of Stenness might be the earliest stone circle in Britain. The Watch Stone, an outlier to the north west of the circle, is said to walk to the Stenness Loch at Hogmanay for a refreshment.

Maeshowe

Stoneyhill Rd, Stromness, KW16 3HQ

This chambered tomb was built so its entrance passage would align with the midwinter sun. In the 12th century, Norse crusaders carved runes into the rocks that form it. Local tradition believed it inhabited by a Haugbui or Hogboy, a supernatural mound-dweller who required regular libations to be appeased.

Skaill House

Sandwick, Stromness, KW16 3LR

The south wing of this 17th-century manor house overlooking the Neolithic settlement of Skara Brae was built on a pre-Viking burial ground, which might be connected with the reports of unseen presences.

EYNHALLOW

KW17 2PJ · HY360290
Between Orkney mainland and Rousay lies this abandoned isle whose name translates as the Holy Island. Before a church was built here in the 12th century, it was thought to be the summer home of the mysterious Finfolk, notorious for kidnapping humans to make them their spouses. A farmer known as the Goodman of Thorodale arrived at the island to rescue his wife from the Finman who had kidnapped her. Even though the Finfolk had protected the island with curses and magic, the farmer succeeded in defeating them, winning back his wife and performing a ritual to expel the Finfolk forever. Soon afterwards, the church was erected and the island inhabited by a small community.

ROUSAY

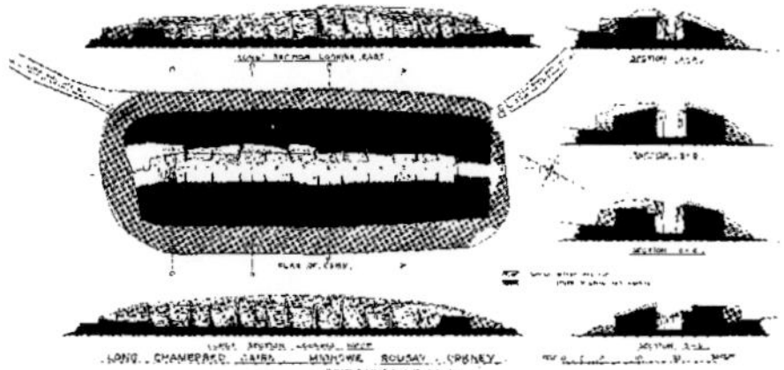

KW17 2PR · HY417298
Known as the Egypt of the North for its concentration of ancient ruins, the island of Rousay is home to the one-mile-long Westness Heritage Walk, the most important archaeological mile in Scotland. The Midhowe Cairn, known as the Great Ship of Death, is one of its most fascinating treasures.

XI. Northern Ireland

Fermanagh, 274
Armagh, 278
Down, 282
Tyrone, 284
Derry, 286
Antrim, 288

XI. NORTHERN IRELAND

RATHLIN ISLAND
THE GIANT'S CAUSEWAY
BALLYCASTLE
BONAMARGY FRIARY
ANTRIM
GIANT'S GRAVE
DUNDERMOT MOUND
GALGORM CASTLE
THE GOBBINS
THE WITCH'S STONE
SHANE CASTLE
CARRICKFERGUS
CAVE HILL
C. S. LEWIS'S SQUARE
THE GIANT'S RING
GREY ABBEY
LURGAN
THE NAVAN COMPLEX
DOWN
BALLYNOE STONE CIRCLE
ARMAGH
SLIEVE DONARD
SLIEVE GULLION

Fermanagh

Church of the Sacred Heart

Stained glass window in the interior of the church

Cup and ring markings on the Reyfad Stones

BOHO

Church of the Sacred Heart: Enniskillen, BT74 8BF
Reyfad Stones: BT74 8BF · NV218121

The Church of the Sacred Heart was built in 1832 on the site of an early nunnery founded by St Faber, who is depicted in one of the stained glass windows along with her pet deer. A local tradition tells that a spoonful of clay from the grave of Father James McGirr, a 19th-century parish priest buried in the churchyard, can cure infection when it's wrapped in a cotton pouch and placed under the pillow. The clay, however, must be returned within four days to avoid users being struck by bad luck. When microbiologists analysed the soil in 2018 they found a unique strain of an antibiotic-producing microorganism, lending credence to the folk cure, which likely predated McGirr.

500 meters to the rear of the church stand the Neolithic Reyfad stones, the most-densely packed examples of rock art in Ireland, with cup and ring marks similar to those at Newgrange, the prehistoric monument in Co. Meath.

The Curse of St Faber

St Faber's Well: BT74 8BF · NV207137

ST FABER, the virgin of Boho, first attempted to build a church by the holy well in Killydrum, but an invisible being destroyed the foundations overnight. A deer led her to the site where she would eventually build her nunnery, and carried her sacred books on its antlers. But while they were passing the banks of the Sillees river, the river's genius loci, opposed to the spread of Christianity in the region, made the deer slip and the books fall off. St Faber cursed the Sillees to run backwards to Lough Erne, rather than to the sea, and made it bad for fishing and good for drowning.

Killydrum's holy well is named after the saint, and the water collected in its associated bullaun—a rock with a depression—was long believed to cure male infertility.

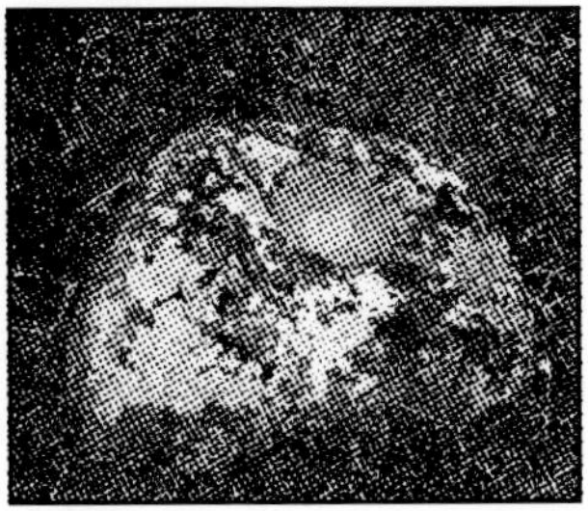

St Faber's bullán

LOUGH ERNE

THE MAJESTIC Lough Erne, formed by two interconnected lakes, remains a magical destination in Ulster, with parts of its islands remaining untouched for centuries. Its name might derive from Erne, a lady-in-waiting of the mythical Queen Méabh or Maeve at Cruachan. According to the legend, Erne drowned when fleeing from a giant, and her body dissolved to form the lake. The best known of the islands is probably Devenish, whose monastic ruins tell the story of one of the earliest communities in Ireland.

WHITE ISLAND

Enniskillen BT94 1PP · NV287256

The eight carvings in the wall of the early church on White Island demonstrate the light hand with which Christianity first visited the area. In the 1970s, Helen Hickey, Curator of the Fermanagh Museum, identified the first carving as a Sheela-na-Gig, and the fifth and sixth as "Christ with Griffins" and "Christ the warrior with sword and shield", in the fashion of the Ulster warrior hero Cú Chulainn.

BOA ISLAND
Caldragh Cemetery:
Enniskillen, BT93 8AA · NV202281

The 4th-century Caldragh Graveyard was built around the bilateral Boa Island figure, one of the most remarkable idols in Ireland. The two-faced idol depicts an unknown deity squatting in the Celtic manner. The heads of the conjoined bodies are separated by a deep socket that supposedly vibrates when touched by the right person and that is regularly used to leave small offerings.

The smaller figure standing next to it was transplanted to Boa in 1939. Known as the Lusty Man after its original home on nearby Lustymore Island, it actually presents the war goddess Badb or Badhbh, the Divine Hag, recognisable by her blinded left eye—an appropriate relocation, as it is from this goddess that Boa derives its name.

The two-faced deity

Offerings to the deities

Armagh

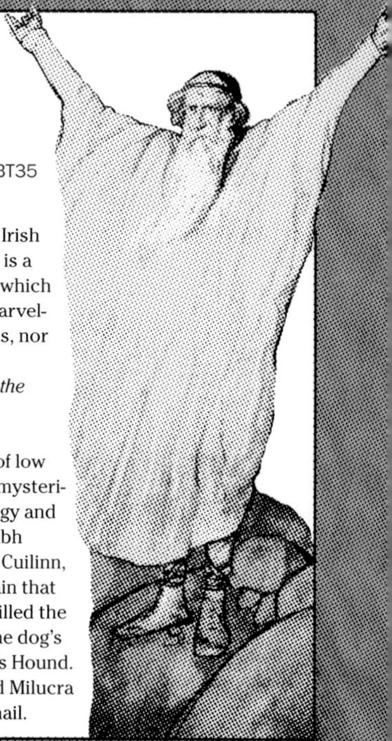

SLIEVE GULLION

Slieve Gullion Forest Park, 89 Drumintee Rd, Newry, BT35 8SW · SB106786

"Slieve Gullion is perhaps the most mystic of our Irish mountains... On the mountain somewhere, there is a well of wisdom and magic meather [mead], from which if we only knew the recipe, we could go to that marvellous ale that once tasted—'age could not touch us, nor sickness, nor death'."
– T.G.F Paterson, *Country Cracks—Old Tales from the County of Armagh*, 1939.

AT THE HEART of the Ring of Gullion, a ring of low hills formed by volcanic activity, stands this mysterious mountain, deeply embedded in Ulster mythology and local superstition. Its name derives either from Sliabh gCuillinn, the hill of the steep slope, or from Sliabh Cuilinn, Culann's Mountain. It was at the foot of the mountain that Sétanta, the hero of the Ulster cycle, accidentally killed the guard-dog of Culann, the smith, and vowed to do the dog's job himself, taking the name Cú Chulainn—Culann's Hound. The mountain is also associated with a witch called Milucra and with the legendary hero-giant Fionn Mac Cumhail.

BALLYKEEL DOLMEN
Ballykeel Rd, Newry, BT35 9UA

The Neolithic portal tomb at the foot of the western side of Slieve Gullion is known locally as Cathaoir na Caillí, the Hag's Chair. Excavations unearthed sherds of Neolithic pottery and flint tools.

SLIEVE GULLION PASSAGE TOMB

SB103786

In 1789, locals endeavoured to find Milucra and stormed into her house on the southern end of the summit, but found only human bones there. The witch's home was a passage tomb likely erected between c.3500–2900 BCE, the highest intact of its type in Ireland and England. On the Winter Solstice, the rays of the December sun enter the tomb's passageway and focus on a recess at the back of the chamber.

The site's folk name hints at the true identity of the witch Milucra: the Cailleach Bhéara or Hag of Beare is known across Ireland, Scotland, and the Isle of Man as the Queen of Winter, the opposite of Brighde and the personification of the darker season. Oral folklore tells the Cailleach Bhéara guards an elixir against sickness, old age, and death.

Visible from the summit of Slieve Gullion is another mountain with several megalithic features and associated with similar folklore: Sliabh na Caillíghe, the Mountain of the Old Woman in Loughcrew, in the Republic of Ireland.

HAG'S LOUGH

SB101793

Close to the summit is the Hag's Lake or Lough, where Milucra is said to have tricked Fionn Mac Cumhail, luring him into its waters. He came out withered and aged, and although his followers forced the witch to lift the curse from Fionn, his hair stayed white—a fate that may yet befall anyone who bathes in the lake.

Flanked by two burial cairns, the Hag's Lough is believed to have been a votive site and a portal to the Otherworld. Local belief imagines the lough continues underground, coming out at the nearby votive site known as the King's Stables.

Across the Ring of Gullion are several megaliths of interest: Annaghmare, also known as the Black Castle (BT35 9JL · SA982772), a court tomb with a small standing stone in the forecourt ; the unusual Clonlum, with its closed rectangular chamber (BT35 8LQ · SB125787); the court tomb of Clontygora, known locally as the King's Ring (BT35 8NX · SB177771); and the Neolithic court tomb of Ballymacfermot (BT35 8QA · SB147820).

THE NAVAN COMPLEX

Legends tell that the hilltop enclosure of Eamhain Mhacha—anglicised as Navan Fort—was formed when Macha, the ancient goddess of fertility and war, traced the outline of this sacred stronghold with her brooch pin. The seat of the kingdom of Ulaidh, from which Ulster gets its name, and the home of the legendary heroes Cú Chulainn and Conchobar mac Nessa, Navan Fort is the centre of an important complex of ceremonial sites that offer a glimpse at ancient beliefs.

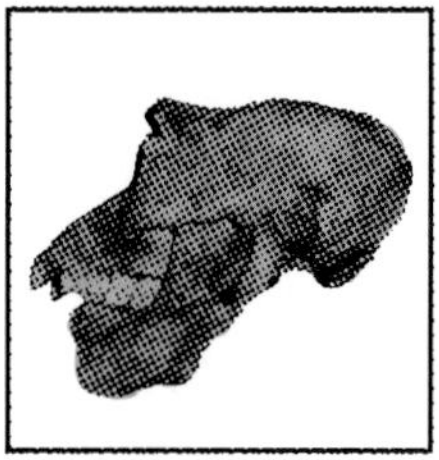

NAVAN FORT
81 Killylea Road, BT60 4LD / £
Archaeologists have uncovered the remains of several buildings at Navan Fort, the most intriguing of which is a circular temple constructed c. 95BCE. The structure was filled with thousands of stones and burned down, its embers smothered with soil brought from across the county before the site was turned into a mound. This process was repeated several times over the centuries, with new structures being built and burned, leading to various hypotheses about its sacrificial role. Some theories suggest the hill was a portal to the Otherworld, the home of gods and ancestors, used in the coronations of kings and other ceremonies.

The *Annals of the Four Masters*, a 17th-century compilation of earlier chronicles of Irish history, record the site's abandonment in 331AD, after it was burned down by the sons of Eochaid, but recent archaeological research shows evidence of continuous activity through to the medieval period. Excavations also unearthed the remains of a Barbary macaque, unique to North Africa and Gibraltar and thought to have been brought to Ireland as an exotic present for someone of royal status.

THE KING'S STABLES
Navan, BT60 4PS · NV940053 / £
The name does little to paint the history and significance of the structure, a man-made pool cut into the earth in the first millennium BCE, now completely overgrown. Excavations revealed that precious items were thrown into the pool as offerings to the gods. Archaeologists also unearthed the segment of a human face carefully removed from the rest of the skull, and unusually

Reconstruction of an Iron Age roundhouse

high numbers of canine bones, suggesting dogs were used as part of the sacrifice.

Legend says the pool is one end of a water tunnel that comes out again 30 km away at Hag's Lough on top of Slieve Gullion. However, this has never been verified, as most attempts to interfere with the pool are cut short by supernatural forces, including a dragon.

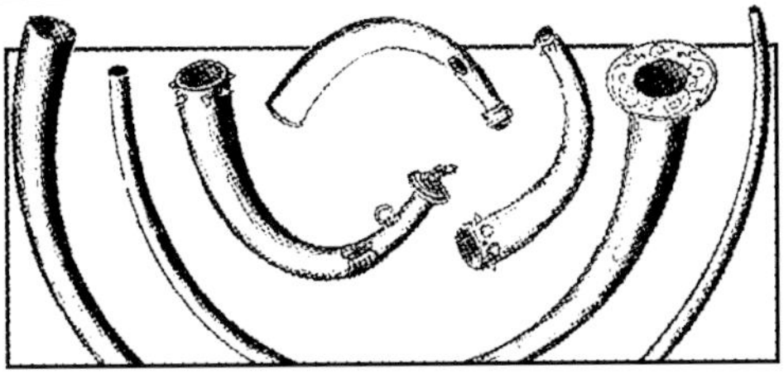

Bronze horns in the collection of the Irish Museum

LOUGHNASHADE

BT60 4BG · NV953051

In 1794, a votive deposit of four bronze horns, human skulls and other bones was found at a bog near Navan Fort, formerly the ancient lake of Loughnashade. The only surviving horn, dating from the Iron Age, now lives at the National Museum of Ireland.

The Celtic Mysticism of Æ

Armagh County Museum: The Mall, Armagh, BT61 9BE, **Lurgan Town Hall:** 2-4 Union St, BT66 8DY, **Æ's natal house:** 12 William Street, Lurgan, BT67 9AQ, **Brownlow House:** Windsor Avenue, Lurgan, BT67 9BJ

THE AUTHOR, artist, and mystic George W. Russell (1865 – 1935) was born at the inland linen town of Lurgan, in a house now adorned with an Ulster Historical plaque on 12 William Street. His family then moved to a cottage on the grounds of the town's estate house, Brownlow. It is likely that the youthful visions recounted in his memoirs took place in this countryside.

Russell moved to Dublin, where he studied art, and took up the mystical pseudonym Æ, through which he sought to share his knowledge of the World of Spirit. Alongside Yeats he was a prominent member of the Theosophical Society, but he formed his own group, the Hermetic Society, in 1898. Although he was "grateful to Providence for the mercy shown to me in removing me from Ulster", he is well-remembered in the province with a handsome bust in Lurgan Town Hall, and his mystic paintings and palette are on display in the Armagh County Museum.

Down

Slieve Donard

Trig point on top of the summit of Slieve Donard

Ballynoe stone circle

SLIEVE DONARD

Newcastle, BT33 0GR · SB441832

The two cairns at the summit of this mountain are the highest-placed in Ireland, some 2789 feet above sea level. The Lesser Cairn dates back to the Bronze Age, whereas the Greater Cairn is Neolithic, and traditionally believed to be a portal to the Otherworld.

Slieve Donard translates as "Donard's mountain", after a Christian missionary said to have been a follower of St Patrick. In the most popular story about its origin, Donard is blessed by St Patrick while in her mother's womb so he would never die, but live inside the mountain, becoming its perpetual watcher. According to tradition, St. Donard made his hermitage at the summit, using the Greater Cairn as his cell and the Lesser Cairn as an oratory in which to say the Easter Tuesday mass. Even centuries after his death in 507AD, the saint is rumoured to say mass there and warn ramblers of the slope's dangers.

Up until the early 19th century, the summit was the destination of a pilgrimage held on the last Sunday of July, possibly a Lughnasadh ritual that marked the beginning of the harvest season and that later became Christianised.

BALLYNOE STONE CIRCLE

Downpatrick, BT30 8ET · SB576947

The position of this Neolithic stone circle, built at the same latitude as the Swinside stone circle in Cumbria, hints at influence from the Beaker people in northern Britain. 1930s excavations revealed cremated bones in its interior. In the winter solstice, the movements of the sun seem to align with the stones and with the peak of Slieve Donard in the background.

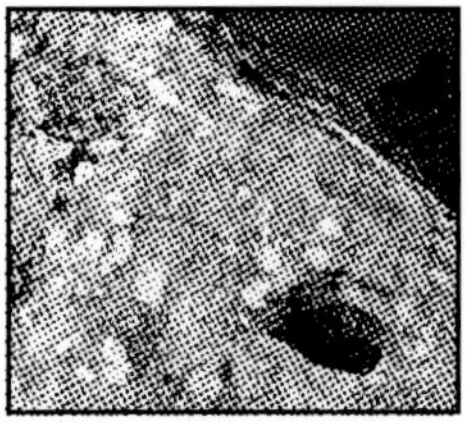

Cup-marked stone

THE GIANT'S RING

Belfast, BT8 8LE · NW446233

Four miles from Belfast city centre, on the bank of the River Lagan, lies this remarkable henge measuring 200m in diameter. Built in the late Neolithic or Early Bronze Age, it was a large ceremonial site with a complex of structures and three rings of timber posts. Only the central passage grave, likely the focus of all rituals, remains.

Farming activity in the 19th century uncovered large quantities of bones, and further analysis revealed they'd been subjected to different burial customs, including cremation and excarnation—where the bodies would have been exposed to the elements in a mortuary enclosure before being buried—, which suggests the tomb was used for a long period of time.

Giant's Ring

In the 18th century the space was used as a racecourse, which 19th-century antiquarian William C. Borlase, influenced by contemporary theories of pagan survivals, interpreted as the remnants of ancient "funeral games, in which racing bore the principal part".

William C. Borlase

GREY ABBEY

129 Main St, Greyabbey, BT22 2NQ

Although a remarkable example of Anglo-Norman Cistercian architecture in its own right, Grey Abbey is of interest to the curious for its corbel-table of unusual carvings, most notably a man without a head splaying his buttocks to reveal his anus, his large scrotum dangling beneath. The Sean-Na-Gig is joined by a pig's head, a cow with long ears, and various humans with almond-shaped eyes.

Grey Abbey

Tyrone

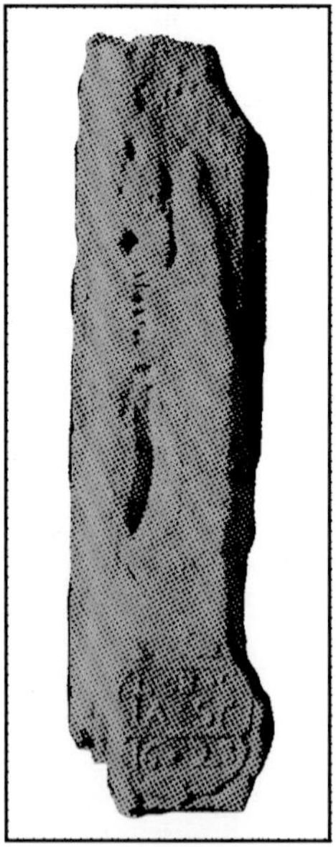

Cloch-Oir

ST MACARTAN'S CATHEDRAL

74 Main St, Clogher, BT76 0AA

Housed in the porch of this 18th-century cathedral is an ancient stone thought to be the oracular Cloch-Oir, or the Stone of Gold. The entity speaking through it went by the name Cermand Cestach, described by competing sources as a god, a giant, or a demon. The oracle famously prophetised that the hero of antiquity Conchobar Mac Nessa would become king of Ulster and establish his kingdom at Emania (now Navan Fort, near Armagh).

The area of Clogher was once a prominent seat of pagan scholarship, nurturing aspirant druids and bards in the shadow of the Cloch-Oir, from which the town got its name. St. Patrick is reputed to have banished Cermand Cestach, founding the diocese of Clogher and leaving it in the hands of his disciple Macartan, its first presiding bishop. The Cloch-Oir was given to Macartan by the last remaining pagan noble of Clogher, which would explain the stone's presence in the cathedral—disappointingly, however, some scholars argue it's a door lintel from an 8th or 9th-century church.

Aynia's Cove

AYNIA'S COVE

Knockmany Forest, Augher, BT77 0DL · NV657181

The Neolithic passage grave at the summit of the fairy hill of Knockmany was known as Aynia's Cove, after the Fairy Queen of Tyrone, originally a lunar deity connected with psychic ability, healing, and herbalism—but also with madness. Some of the sites associated with her are said to exert a magical magnetism that can prove dangerous: the stone known as Aynia's Chair or Madman's Chair near Dunany Point in Louth, in the Republic of Ireland, was believed to lure people and animals into the sea, her domain.

Knockmany Hill was also the home of the legendary hero-giant Fionn Mac Cumhaill and his wife. The cairn and earth mound that once crowned Aynia's Cove have long gone, but in 1959 a concrete chamber was built around it. The remaining stones, three of them carved with spirals and other symbols, can be seen from the entrance, and full access can be arranged with the Historic Environment Division.

Fairy Queen of Tyrone

BEAGHMORE

64-62 Blackrock Rd, BT80 9PA

Discovered in the 1930s during peat-cutting and first excavated in the 1940s, this complex of early Bronze Age megalithic alignments, circles, and cairns in the Sperrin Mountains presents a mystery. The name of the site, Beaghmore (from an Bheitheach Mhór, meaning "big place of birch trees"), suggests the area was a woodland before being cleared of trees, and pollen analysis proved the land was farmed from around 3500 BCE. Why then would Bronze Age farmers convert cultivated land into a place of rocky ritual? One of the theories is that the site was erected in response to the encroachment of peat and failing soil fertility.

Dragon's Teeth

Six of the circles in the site are paired, and each of the pairs has a small cairn between the two stone circles. A seventh circle, unpaired, is filled with 800 smaller stones known as the Dragon's Teeth. Some, but not all of the alignments match up with the movement of the sun and the moon. Self-taught archaeologist and folklorist George Barnett (1876 – 1965), who discovered the site, believed it to be a lunar observatory—whatever its purpose was, Beaghmore remains among Northern Ireland's "darkest skies", which makes it a perfect spot for stargazing.

Stone rows at Beaghmore

Derry

View through west door

Banagher Old Church

St Murrough's mortuary house

BANAGHER

Feeny picnic site: Feeny Road, BT47 4TW · NV799672
Owenreagh River Pool: Banagher Glen forest park, 98 Maghera-more Rd, BT47 · NV822655
Banagher Old Church: Carnabane Road, Dungiven, BT47 4SR
Lough Foyle: F93 DK84

Under a bridge near the source of the Owenreagh River is a pool said to have been the domain of a monstrous, fire-breathing monster—Lig-na-paiste, "the last of the serpents", which St Patrick missed when he banished all the serpents from Ireland.

Desperate, the locals turned to Murrough O'Heany, a holy man who lived on the site of Banagher Old Church. He approached the monster with three rods made from river reeds, and the beast, amused, thought the locals had sent him a human sacrifice. But when Murrough placed the reeds upon it, they changed to steel, imprisoning Lig-na-paistie. Since then, the serpent lives in its cage in Lough Foyle, and some say its writhing is responsible for the unusual currents of the lake.

The remains of St Murrough, the founder of Banagher church in the 5th century, are kept in a mortuary house at the churchyard. The oldest part of the church ruins dates from the 12th century.

To reach the pool of Lig-na-Paiste, start at the Banagher Glen forest car park, follow the path up the hill and take the left hand fork. The pool is to the right of the bridge. A sculpture depicting Lig-na-paistie, its body tied up in Celtic knots, accompanies picnickers at a site in Feeny.

DUNGIVEN PRIORY

4 Bleach Green, Dungiven, BT47 4UH

The evocative ruins of the 12th-century Dungiven Priory, built on the site of a 7th-century church, are associated with a banshee named Grainne Rua, whose piercing wails warned the O'Cahan clan that their princess Finvola, the Gem of the Roe, had died and been buried in Islay, Scotland, far from her homeland. Only when Finvola's body was brought back to Dungiven the banshee's lament stopped. Although Finvola is said to be buried in the churchyard, the most famous grave on the site is a canopy tomb in the church's chancel that commemorates Cooey-na-Gall, an O'Cahan chief who died in 1385.

Visitors might also follow the sign that leads to the wart well, a bullaun among thorn trees said to cure verrucas—the wet rags used to rub the skin must be hung from one of the trees; as they rot, so will the wart.

GIANT'S GRAVE, SLAGHTAVERTY

Coleraine, BT51 5BX · NV977731

Despite its common nickname, the Slaghtaverty dolmen isn't associated with a giant, but with a diminutive, tyrannical chieftain and magician named Abhartach. After perpetrating great cruelties on the local community, he was slain by a neighbouring chieftain—sometimes identified with Fionn Mac Cumhail—and buried standing upright to prevent his return from the dead. But the dwarf came back and terrorised the townland. He was slain a second time, and returned once again, more vengeful than ever, feasting on the blood of the peasants. Finally, Abhartach's adversary consulted a druid who told him to bury the dwarf with his head facing downward in order to subdue his magical powers. When the dwarf was slain the third time, he was buried properly, and a laght or sepulture was placed upon his remains. A hawthorn—a fairy tree—grows over the grave, and attempts to cut it back have resulted in accidents and injuries.

The first accounts of Abhartach appeared in Geoffrey Keating's *Foras Feasa ar Éirinn* in 1631, then again in English in 1875 in Patrick Weston Joyce's *The Origin and History of Irish Place Names*. A Dublin civil servant called Bram Stoker was known to have read Joyce's work. Around the time Stoker was working on *Dracula*, Keating's original manuscripts were on display in the National Museum of Ireland. However, Stoker didn't read Irish, so was unlikely to know that droch-fhoula, the Irish for "bad blood", is pronounced droc'ola.

Flowers of the fairy thorn

Antrim

BELFAST

THE HILLS surrounding the capital city of Northern Ireland are peppered with Iron Age hill forts, but Belfast wasn't established until 1613, and it was only granted city status in 1888. The area is associated with several tales of witchcraft and magic, with the imposing Cave Hill as the epicentre of local folklore.

CAVE HILL, BT36 7WH

THE ancient seat of the distinguished O'Neill dynasty, the Cave Hill, looms over Belfast, its dark outline suggesting a dead or sleeping giant. Author and cleric Jonathan Swift (1667–1745), serving in the nearby parish of Kilroot, was inspired by the landscape to imagine Lemuel Gulliver pegged to the ground by Lilliputians.

Named for the five caves found in its cliffs—possibly early iron mines—, this rocky hill contains the remains of several early settlements. On the highest point is McArt's Fort, an Iron Age ráth or hill fort. To the north west of the fort stands Ballyaghagan Cairn, and beneath it lies a crater known as the Devil's Punch Bowl, the rumoured site of hidden treasure.

Naturalist Robert Lloyd Praeger correctly noted that, in the Ulster accent, the name of the Cave Hill can sound like "The Key of Hell" and the hill has long been an attractor of strange occurrences. Irish republican revolutionary, suffragette and actress Maud Gonne (1866 – 1953) had a vision there, when she visited with the illustrious poet and dramatist W. B. Yeats in 1899, and a mysterious airship descended on the hill multiple times through 1909. Up until the 19th century, the summit was the scene of the annual Humours of the Cave Hill, a debauched revel of drinking, dancing, and fighting.

Maud Gonne

C. S. LEWIS'S SQUARE
402 Newtownards Road, BT4 1HH

Statue of the benevolent lion Aslan

SEVEN statues inspired by characters from the fantasy classic *The Lion, the Witch, and the Wardrobe*—including the faun Tumnus and Jadis, the White Witch, tempting visitors with her Turkish delight—stand in this public space honouring Belfast-born author C. S. Lewis (1898 – 1963) and his magical creations.

Belfast's Satanic Panic

Between 1972 and 1974, Belfast was gripped by Satanic Panic. From black masses and secret covens to ritual murders and animal sacrifice, the press portrayed a region whose every corner seemed to hide a black candle or an inverted crucifix. Sociologist Richard Jenkins investigated these black magic fears and recorded the testimony of Captain Colin Wallace, the head of the British Army's "black operations" in Northern Ireland at the time, who admitted this was part of a secret propaganda campaign during the Troubles. By exploiting the public fear of Satanism, the army aimed to link in the public's mind the rise of paramilitary groups with the threat of supernatural evil.

SUNDAY WORLD

Be-Leagured!

BLACK MAGIC FEAR IN TWO BORDER TOWNS

He's a little brick!

SHANE CASTLE

Antrim, BT41 4NB

The family seat of the O'Neills of Clanaboy was ravaged by fire in 1816, an outcome attributed to the fury of a banshee. Centuries before then, one of the men of the family cut a branch of a thorn tree—sacred to the fairies—to release a trapped cow. When he returned home, he found his daughter had been carried off by the Little People to the bottom of Lough Neagh. From then onwards, her shrieks were heard every time that disaster was about to befall a member of the family. An empty room was kept for the spirit, but after it was used during a busy house party, the castle was engulfed by flames.

Today, the castle ruins—possibly dating from the 16th century—are open to visitors during the spring and summer months by appointment only. The adjoining graveyard houses an intriguing burial chamber, built in 1722 for one of the O'Neill chiefs in a triangular shape. On the east face of the tower near the lake is the Black Head of the O'Neills, a female figurehead thought to predate the rest of the castle. Tradition states that if it falls, the family will come to an end.

The Cry of the Banshee

IN IRISH folklore, a banshee (from *bean sí,* "woman of the fairy mound" or "fairy woman") is a female spirit who foretells the death of a family member by shrieking or wailing. She is usually depicted as an old woman washing blood-stained clothes in the river, or sitting in the wedge-shaped rocks known as banshee's chairs. Sometimes she appears as a young and beautiful member of the family who died prematurely and was subsequently tasked with the role of harbinger of death. The O'Brien's Irish-English Dictionary states that "no families which are not of an ancient and noble stock are believed to be honoured with this fairy privilege", and all the most noteworthy families of Ireland were said to have their own. Banshees stayed with the family until all of their members passed away and were safely buried.

Banshee, "woman of the fairy mound"

THE WITCH'S STONE

Antrim Round Tower, 14 Steeple Rd, Antrim, BT41 1BL

The indented stone beside the 10th-century Round Tower in Antrim is said to have been made by a witch who, aggrieved by the construction of the Christian settlement by St. Aedh, threw herself from the top and left her impression on the rock below. The tower was erected as protection against raiders, but its associated monastic site was burnt in 1147.

Round Tower in Antrim

The Islandmagee Witches

The Stocks: Highstreet/Joymount, Carrickfergus, BT38 7DQ
The Gobbins: Islandmagee, BT40 3TB

ONLY FOUR trials took place under the 1586 Irish Witchcraft Act, a dearth that can be ascribed to local legal practices and to the distinct relationship the majority Gaelic Catholic population had to witches in comparison to their Protestant neighbours. Tellingly, two of these trials were conducted in Carrickfergus, the heartland of the Ulster-Scots Presbyterian settler community, the last of which, in 1711, was the only mass witch trial on the island.

The events started at Knowehead House in Islandmagee, with the death of the elderly widow of a Presbyterian minister, Ann Haltridge, said to have been bedevilled by a demonic child with a relish for smashing windows and for tearing bedsheets to shape them like a corpse. The 18-year-old Mary Dunbar, staying at Knowehead House for the wake, displayed signs of demonic possession and identified eight local women—four of them from Islandmagee—as her spectral tormentors. The eight women were found guilty and sentenced to a year in prison and to public humiliation at the pillory. They would become known as the Islandmagee witches.

A replica of the stocks now stands in the same spot as the original, but the commemorative plaque planned for the Gobbins coastal walk, close to Knowehead Brae, was blocked by a local counsellor who feared it would become a pilgrimage site for pagans.

A pact with the Devil

GALGORM CASTLE

BT42 1HL

This 17th-century Jacobean castle was built by Sir Faithful Fortescue, best known as Sir Faithless after having defected from the Parlamentarians to the Cavaliers during the Civil War. He sold it to the Anglican divine Dr. Alexander Colville (c. 1597 – 1679), whose vast fortune, according to his Presbyterian neighbours, was the result of a pact with the Devil. His infernal library was said to include copies of *The Book of Black Earth* and *The Red Book of Appin*, and a servant girl confessed to having learnt the Black Arts when she was in his employment. Colville succeeded in tricking the Archfiend twice, and it was only twenty years later, when the debt was finally due, that the Devil got his revenge.

Galgorm Castle

Some say the doctor was whisked to Hell in a puff of sulphur; others have him driven to an early grave, clutching his Bible to his chest. Irish writer Joseph Sheridan Le Fanu (1814–1873), who based his much-anthologised story "Sir Dominick's Bargain" on the doctor's tale, went with the former.

Both the grounds of the estate and the castle have been used as a set for the gothic thriller *The Frankenstein Chronicles*. The grounds, now Galgorm Parks, are open to the public, but the castle is part of the Galgorm Spa and Golf Resort. It is said to be haunted by the restless ghost of Alexander Colville, who roams the grounds seeking the treasure he buried there. His portrait, hanging from one of its walls, is forbidden to leave the premises, or disaster will fall.

Sheridan Le Fanu

DUNDERMOT MOUND

Station Road, Glarryford, BT44 9RA · NW219708

Dr. Alexander Colville

Whispers of strange lights, sacrifices, and black magic persist around this raised copse, an accepted "Gateway to Hell" that has been known to open up and devour travellers. In 1798, the coachman Thomas McCarg was on an urgent mission from Belfast to Derry. A storm forced his passage through the Dundermot Mound and he was never seen again. Black Tom's coach, however, is occasionally released from the Otherworld to career through the local roads, but be warned: anyone who speaks to the driver will die within a year.

THE GIANT'S CAUSEWAY

Bushmills, BT57 8SU / £

The 40,000 interlocking hexagonal basalt columns that comprise The Giant's Causeway are known as "the stepping stones of the Fomhóraigh", the mythological race of dark deities that challenged the island's first settlers, the Tuatha Dé Danann. During the war, the Fomorians were thrown into the sea. Later, the victorious Danann were forced underground by the next settlers, the Milesians. The various Sidhe—the fairy people of Irish folklore—, some living in water, some in mounds under the earth, are said to be remnants of these ancient races.

The Causeway's English name relates to later myths of the giant Fionn Mac Cumhaill, said to have used it as a path to Scotland. Identical columns are found at Fingal's Cave on the isle of Staffa, the end part of his bridge.

Although the Causeway is a natural feature and seems to have no spiritual significance for the people, it has long been a focus of fascination, most obviously fulfilling its magical potential on the sleeve of Led Zeppelin's Houses of the Holy. Currently maintained by the National Trust, ticket prices cover use of the car park. Despite the signage, it is possible to access the Causeway for free without going through the visitor's centre.

The Children of Lir

Ballycastle: BT54 6BN

Oweynagolman Cave, Rathlin Island: BT54 6TF · NR354082

A sculpture at the seafront of Ballycastle remembers the Children of Lir, who, in Irish mythology, were turned into swans by their jealous stepmother, the witch Aoife. They spent 300 years in Lake Derravaragh, 300 more on the Straits of Moyle, and their final 300 on the Isle of Inishglora, where they returned to their human forms. The picturesque Rathlin Island on the Sea of Moyle is also associated with the legend: the rock bar that during low tide grants access to Oweynagolman Cave—known locally as Avaragh Cave—was said to have been put there by a wise woman to protect the children.

BONAMARGY FRIARY

43 Cushendall Rd, Ballycastle, BT54 6QR

The 17th-century prophetess Julia McQuillan, The Black Nun, was known for her visions of Ballycastle's future, including accidental deaths and changes in local landmarks. A perforated cross marks the spot in the ruined nave of this 15th-century Franciscan friary where she was asked to be buried, so that mass-goers would walk over her penitent body as they entered and left services.

Bonamargy friary

RATHLIN ISLAND

Cooraghy Bay: BT54 6SB · NR287075
Bruce's cave: BT54 6TF · NR354084

Every seven years, a ghostly island between Rathlin and the mainland is said to rise out of the sea—it is known as the Enchanted Island. But Rathlin, the most northerly of Ireland's inhabited islands, is also embedded in legend. Folklore attributes its creation to Muireann Muncháem, mother of the giant Fionn Mac Cumhaill, when she spilled soil from her apron as she was crossing the causeway to supply her son with Scotch whiskey.

Scotland's national hero Robert the Bruce (1274 – 1329) famously took refuge in one of the many caves in Rathlin, following a defeat by Edward I's army. Bruce was inspired to return and reclaim his kingdom by a resilient spider who worked hard to spin its web. In another cave, at the western bay of Cooraghy, the Devil's ghostly hand seized a mug of tea that some visitors had placed on a flat-topped boulder.

Stacks by Rathlin Island

"Bruce's Cave" on Rathlin Island

Image Sources

Every effort has been made to ensure that the images included do not infringe copyright. Low-res film stills, posters, and book covers have been used as part of the critical commentary. All images have been edited and colorised, and in no case does their use in this book have a negative impact on the potential market for the original.

I. THE SOUTH WEST

CORNWALL. The Pipers: Jim Champion, CC BY-SA 2.0. The Hurlers and Trethevy Quoit: Richard Scott-Robinson, CC BY-SA 3.0. Rillaton Barrow: stone-circles.org.uk. British Library, "The Circle or Historical Survey of Sixty Parishes and Towns in Cornwall [With ten engraved plates.]", British Library, PD. Mên-An-Tol: Unknown author, CC BY-SA 2.5. British Library digitised image, "Churches of west Cornwall; with notes of antiquities of the district, British Library, PD. The Merry Maidens: photoeverywhere, CC BY 3.0. Boscawen-Un: Waterborough, CC BY-SA 3.0. Tregeseal East: Jim Champion, CC BY-SA 3.0. Plan of the Fougou: from *Churches of West Cornwall*, by JT Blight, 1885. Head, by Ithell Colquhoun: Spjholland, CC BY-SA 3.0. Museum of Witchcraft: JuweL, CC BY-SA 3.0. Porthcurno Cove: Nic Trott. Merlin's Cave: Anthony Harrison, CC BY-SA 2.0. King Arthur Statue: Unknown author. Bant's Carn Burial Chamber: David Purchase, CC BY-SA 2.0. Lanyon Cromlech. St Mary's: old engraving, Day and Sons, 1850. Zennor Quoit: R. T. Pentreath, *Archaeologia Cambrensis* (1857), PD. **DEVON.** Great Storm: Unknown artist, PD. Lych Way: Derek Harper, CC BY-SA 2.0. Vixen Tor: A. B. Collier, from *A Book of the West* Public by Sabine Baring-Gould (1899), PD. Arthur Conan Doyle: from Current History of the War v.I (1914-1915), New York: New York Times Company, PD. Wistmans Wood: Herby, CC BY-SA 4.0. The Hound of the Baskervilles: Sidney Paget, 1901, PD. Lewtrenchard Manor: from *Early Reminiscences*, by Sabine Baring-Gould (1923), PD. Sabine Baring-Gould: Strand Magazine (1869), PD. Shebbear: unknown author, visitdevon.co.uk. *The Shout and Other Stories* by Robert Graves: Penguin Books Ltd, 1978. *The Shout* (1978), by Jerzy Skolimowski (dir.), The Rank Organisation. Sir Francis Drake: Jodocus Hondius, PD. Portrait of John Pinney: Thomas Maynard. Screaming skull: Unknown author. St. Mary's Church: Chris Downer, CC BY-SA 2.0. Knowlton Henge: Ethan Doyle White, CC BY-SA 4.0. Plaque to Gerald Gardner: Centre For Pagan Studies, CC BY-SA 3.0. Gerald Gardner: illustration by Nathaniel Hébert. Arched Doorway: Ethan Doyle White, CC BY-SA 4.0. Badbury Rings: Heywood Sumner (1914), PD. Chewton Mill House: Kim Dent-Brown, PD. Cerne Abbas Giant's phallus: SiGarb, PD. Cerne Abbas Giant: The Gentleman's magazine, Vol 34 (August 1764), PD. Cerne Abbas Giant: Ordnance Survey, 1891, PD. Dorset Ooser: Pasicles, CC0 1.0. Dorset Ooser: J.W.Chaffins and Sons, Yeovil, PD. **SOMERSET.** Frederick Bligh Bond (1921): Unknown author, PD. "Distant view of Glastonbury Tor": from The BL King's Topographical Collection, British Library, PD. Dion Fortune: Unknown author, PD. Wookey Hole: Leonora (Ellie) Enking, CC BY-SA 2.0. A view at Stanton Drew: William Stukeley, PD. Stanton Drew: Rosalind Mitchell, CC BY-SA 2.0. John Aubrey: Unknown author, PD.

Assembly Rooms and The Circus from a balloon: Roger Beale. CC BY-SA 2.0. Frieze details at The Circus: MichaelMaggs, CC BY-SA 2.5. Roman Baths and Abbey: Snapshots Of The Past, CC BY-SA 2.0. Gorgon's Head: Joyofmuseums, CC BY-SA 4.0. Higher Farm, Chilton Cantelo: Mike Searle, CC BY-SA 2.0. **GLOUCESTERSHIRE.** Rococo Gardens, Painswick: Mark Holland, CC BY-SA 2.0. Statue of Pan: Maria J Pérez Cuervo. The Great God Pan: Arthur Machen, 1894. Roman Temple: jeff collins, CC BY-SA 2.0. Curse upon Senicianus: Roman Inscriptions of Britain. J. R. R. Tolkien: Unknown author, PD. Bellas Knap: Pahazzard, CC BY-SA 4.0. Snowshill Manor: Rodw. CC BY-SA 4.0. Snowshill Manor samurai suit: Celuici, CC BY-SA 1.0. Charles Paget Wade: Unknown author. Tintern Abbey from the Devil's Pulpit: Philip Halling, CC BY-SA 2.0. **WILTSHIRE.** Avebury: William Stukeley, PD. Snake Temple painting, originally by Les Matthews, from *Children of the Stones* (1976), Peter Graham Scott (Dir.), HTV West. Ground plan of Avebury: John Aubrey. West Kennet Avenue: Ethan Doyle White, CC BY-SA 3.0. The Sanctuary: Martin Stewart, CC BY-SA 2.0. Overton Hill Barrows: Chris Collyer, stone-circles. org.uk. Alexander Keiller: Unknown author, PD. Stonehenge (Restored) and Approach to Stonehenge from the East: John Cassell, PD. Drawing of Stonehenge: Description of Great Britain and Ireland, BL, PD.

II. THE SOUTH EAST

HAMPSHIRE. Charcoal-burners finding the body of Rufus: Morris Meredith Williams, PD. Glasshayes: Anonymous, PD.Brusher Mills: Brian Pike, CC BY-SA 3.0. Beaulieu, Palace House: Graham Horn, CC BY-SA 2.0. Bignell Wood and The Naked Man: Jim Champion, CC BY-SA 2.0. *The Complete Art of Witchcraft* by Sybil Leek (1975), Leslie Frewin of London. **BERKSHIRE.** Wayland's Smithy: cisko66, CC BY-SA 3.0. Wayland the Smith: Poetic Edda (1893), PD. St Mary's Church: Philip Hind, CC BY-SA 2.0. Oakley Court: George Grinsted, CC BY-SA 2.0. **BUCKINGHAMSHIRE.** Francis Dashwood: Nathaniel Dance-Holland, PD. Hellfire Caves: unknown author, PD. Hellfire Caves: Stefan Wolmarans, CC BY-SA 4.0. *Night of the Eagle* (1962): Sidney Hayers (dir.), Independent Artists. Taplow Court: Troxx, CC BY-SA 3.0. St Mary the Virgin, Hambleden: Eymery, CC BY-SA 4.0. **OXFORDSHIRE.** Bodleian Library: Diliff, CC BY-SA 3.0. Balliol College: A. D. White Architectural Photographs, PD. John Speed's map of Oxford, 1605, PD. Portrait of John Dee: scan from site of National Maritime Museum, Greenwich, PD. History of Science Museum: History of Science Museum, CC BY-SA 4.0. Pitt Rivers Museum Totem pole: Adam Hopkinson, CC BY-SA 2.0. Rollright Stones: malcwest, Pixabay License. The Rollright Stones: William Camden's Britannia (1695), PD. St James's, Bix Brand: Andrew Smith, CC BY-SA 2.0. Uffington White Horse: W C Plenderleath, PD. Epona bas relief: Owen Cook, CC BY-SA 4.0. Icknield Way: David Hawgood, CC BY-SA 2.0. **ISLE OF WIGHT.** The Needles: Simon Burchell, CC BY-SA 4.0. The Longstone: Mypix, CC BY-SA 4.0. Jacquetta Hawkes: Unknown author. **SURREY.** Mother Ludlam's Cave: S. Hooper (1785), PD. Horsley Towers entrance: AndyScott, CC BY-SA 4.0. Horsley Towers from the lake: AndyScott. CC BY-SA 4.0. *The Stone Tape* (1972) Peter Sasdy (dir.), BBC. Ada Lovelace portrait: Science Museum Group, PD. **SUSSEX.** Neolithic Dew-ponds and Cattle-ways (1907): Arthur John Hubbard & George Hubbard, PD. Doreen Valiente: illustration by Nathaniel Hébert. John Fuller's Tomb: T. Croft, PD. **KENT.** Kit's Coty House: William Stukeley, 1722, Bodleian Library, Gough Gen, Top. 57, Plate 32, PD. Long Man of Wilmington: Cupcakekid, CC BY-SA 3.0. Derek Jarman's garden: Jasper33, PD. Goodwin Sands: Unknown author, PD. South Foreland Lighthouse: Michael Garlick, CC BY-SA 3.0. Goodwin Sands: George Cruikshank, PD.

III. LONDON

Tower of London: Engraving of a Plan of the Tower Liberties, 1597, William Hayward & John Gascoyne, PD. Police constable and the London Stone: Leonard Bentley, CC BY-SA 2.0. London Stone: diamond geezer, CC BY-SA 2.0. Unlucky Mummy: Pearson's Magazine, PD. Grand Temple: Unknown author, openhouselondon.open-city.org.uk. Aleister Crowley: Unknown author, PD. Treadwell's Books: secretlondon123, CC BY-SA 2.0. Atlantis Bookshop: Unknown author. St George's Church: Tony Hisgett, CC BY-SA 2.0. Senate House: Paul the Archivist, CC BY-SA 4.0. John Dee: from *Old England: A Pictorial Museum*, Charles Knight (1845), PD. Edward Kelly: Thomas Pennant, PD. Elliott O'Donnell: Unknown author, PD. John Dee's crystal: Unknown author, CC BY-SA 4.0. Watkins books: Unknown author. Mithras: Ethan Doyle White, CC BY-SA 4.0. Head of Mithras in Phrygian cap (CIMRM 815), from Walbrook Mithraeum in Londinium, AD 180-220, Museum of London, Britain (14007708809): Carole Raddato, CC BY-SA 2.0. Temple Church: Diliff, CC BY-SA 3.0. Tradescant tomb: Unknown author, PD. Newton: William Blake. PD. St George, Bloomsbury: amandabhslater, CC BY-SA 2.0. St George's: John Coney. Christ Church: Steve Cadman, CC BY-SA 2.0. St. Alphege: R. H. Best and Josiah Neele, PD. St Mary Woolnoth: Unknown author. Limehouse Pyramid: Unknown author. William Blake: W. C. Edwards, PD. The Ancient of Days (detail): William Blake, PD. St Paul's Cathedral: MrsEllacott, CC BY-SA 4.0. St Paul's Cathedral Nave: Diliff. CC BY-SA 3.0. Highgate Cemetery: MrsEllacott, CC BY-SA 4.0. Highgate Cemetery: HeritageDaily, CC BY-SA 4.0. 1970 Newspaper Story: Evening Standard, August 1970.

IV. EAST ANGLIA

ESSEX. Matthew Hopkins: from The discovery of witches, PD. Old woman draught at Ratcliffe Highway: Unknown author, PD. George Pickingill: illustration by Nathaniel Hébert. English witch and her familiar: from "The Wonderful Discoverie of the Witches of Margaret and Phillip Flower", 1619, P.D. Colchester Castle: Unknown author, from BL Flickr, PD. **BEDFORDSHIRE.** Five Knolls: Mikestuchbery, CC BY-SA 3.0. St Mary the Virgin, Clophill: Unknown author. Grave stones: Dennis Simpson, CC BY-SA 2.0. **HERTFORDSHIRE.** Poster from *The Devil Rides Out* (1968), Terence Fisher (dir), Hammer Films. Bricket Wood: Sunblade1500, CC BY-SA 3.0. Royston Cave: J Beldam, 1884, PD. **CAMBRIDGESHIRE.** Gogmagog: "More about unknown London" (1921), by Walter George Bell, PD. King's College: Photochrom Print Collection, PD. Plan of King's Hall: William Douglas Caröe, 1909, PD. Flag Fen: Midnightblueowl, CC BY-SA 3.0. Stone Lion outside the Fitzwilliam Museum: Ethan Doyle White, CC BY-SA 4.0. **SUFFOLK**. M.R. James: Unknown author, 1900, PD. St Peter Great Livermere: Keith Evans, CC BY-SA 2.0. Greyfriars: JohnArmagh, CC BY-SA 4.0. Dunwich Church: John Preston Neale, PD. Demon Dog: Abraham Fleming, PD. Holy Trinity Church: Robert Cutts, CC BY-SA 2.0. St Botolph's church in Iken: Evelyn Simak, CC BY-SA 2.0. Orford Castle, Suffolk: Richard Bernard Godfrey, PD. Kentwell Hall: John Preston Neale, 1824, PD. Familiar, "The discovery of witches", Matthew Hopkins, PD. Matthew Hopkins, Witch-finder: Wellcome L0000812, Wellcome Collection gallery, CC-BY-4.0. **NORFOLK**. Neolithic flint implements: William George, 1908, PD. Church of St Peter and St Paul: Evelyn Simak, CC-BY-2.0.

V. WEST MIDLANDS

HEREFORDSHIRE. St Michael's church: John Salmon, CC BY-SA 2.0. Dextra Dei: Bob Embleton, CC BY-SA 2.0. Grotesque: Poliphilo, CC BY-SA 1.0. Hergest court: Andy Dolman, CC BY-SA 2.0. Ellen Gethin: Philip Halling, CC BY-SA 2.0. **WORCESTERSHIRE**. The Fleece: Dave

Bushell, CC BY-SA 2.0. Parsons Folly: Philip Halling, CC BY-SA 2.0. Penda's Fen (1974), Alan Clarke (Dir.), BBC. The King and Queen Stones, Bredon Hill: Philip Halling, CC BY-SA 2.0. St Andrew's, Dowles: Unknown author, c. 1905. Margaret Murray interviewed by the BBC: UCL Institute of Archaeology, CC BY-SA 4.0. "Who put Bella in the witch elm": Mat Fascione, CC BY-SA 2.0. Graffiti: David Buttery, PD. **WARWICKSHIRE.** St Augustine: Unknown artist, PD. St Peter and Paul Lych Gate: JiriMatejicek, CC BY-SA 3.0. East Meon: Chris Gunns, CC BY-SA 2.0. Black Dog: Yellow Fairy Book, H. J. Ford, 1894. PD. *The Casebook of Sherlock Holmes: The Last Vampyre* (1992), Tim Sullivan (Dir.), Granada Television. **STAFFORDSHIRE.** Abbots Bromley: John Benjamin Stone, c. 1900 Stone, PD. St. John's Church: Author unknown, c.1840. St John's Church: AtticTapestry, CC BY-SA 4.0. James Bateman: Unknown author, PD. Biddulph Grange: EDempsey, CC BY-SA 3.0. The Winking Man: Richard Law, CC BY-SA 2.0. Doxey Pool: Bill Boaden, CC BY-SA 2.0. Gawain: Howard Pyle, PD. Lud's Church: Bob Jones, CC BY-SA 2.0. Thor's Cave: Graham Hogg, CC BY-SA 2.0. **SHROPSHIRE.** Stokesay: BL digitised image, p. 45 of "The Castles and Old Mansions of Shropshire, by F. Stackhouse Acton, PD. Stokesay Castle: Unknown author, from an antique print. Mitchell's Fold: Dave Croker, CC BY-SA 2.0. Wodan's Wilde Jagd: F. W. Heine, PD. Stiperstones: Dave Croker, CC BY-SA 2.0. Grave of the last sin-eater: Unknown author. Merlin Cocai with two of his characters eating macaroni: Unknown author, CC BY 4.0. Caynton Caves: Michael Scott, PD. Moreton Corbet Castle Chimera and wyvern: Sjwells53, CC BY-SA 3.0. Moreton Corbet: Alan Livesey, CC BY-SA 3.0. Moreton Corbet Castle windows: Kinder Knott, CC BY-SA 4.0.

VI. EAST MIDLANDS

NORTHAMPTONSHIRE. Canons Ashby: Gardens Old and New Vol 2 and 3, Charles Latham, PD. Jacobean Decoration: David Merrett, CC BY 2.0. Guilsborough village sign and tapestry: M.Woolley, PD. Braunston goddess: Unknown author, PD. Church of All Saints: Tim Heaton, CC BY-SA 2.0. **LEICESTERSHIRE AND RUTLAND.** Tomb of Sir Roger Smith: J.Hannan-Briggs, CC BY-SA 2.0. Humber Stone excavation, 1878: Unknown author, PD. Humber Stone: Ashley Dace, CC BY-SA 2.0. Maze at Wing: Henry Ernest Dudeney, PD. The Old Maze: Unknown author, PD. Belvoir witches: 17th century illustration, PD. St Mary's Church: Julian P Guffogg, CC BY-SA 2.0. **LINCOLNSHIRE.** Woolsthorpe Manor: Internet Archive Book Images, PD. Isaac Newton: Unknown author, PD. *Moondial* (1988), BBC. Belton House: Richard Croft, CC BY-SA 2.0. Lincoln imp: Hongking, PD. Woodwose: Jost Amman, 1589, PD. St Andrew's church: Richard Croft, CC BY-SA 2.0. Church of St Botolph: Dave Hitchborne, CC BY-SA 2.0. *Lost Hearts* (1973), Lawrence Gordon Clark (Dir.), BBC. Mausoleum: Stephen Richards, CC BY-SA 2.0. Thornton Abbey: Godfrey Bingley, PD. Thornton Abbey: Tanya Dedyukhina, CC BY-SA 2.0. **NOTTINGHAMSHIRE.** Hemlock Stone, 1910 postcard: Unknown author. George Oliver: Unknown author, PD. Rock Cemetery: Alan Murray-Rust, CC BY-SA 2.0. Robin Hood: Louis Rhead, PD. Newstead Abbey: from llustrated Notes on English Church History, by Rev. C. Arthur Lane, 1891. Newstead Abbey: Tony Grist, PD. Faun: Lee Haywood, CC BY-SA 2.0. Blidworth Druid Stone, 1911: Unknown author, PD. The Druid Stone: Unknown author, PD. Southwell Minster: Mattan, PD. Ironstone Implement, Robin Hood Cave: William Boyd Dawkins, PD. Creswell Crags: Alan Heardman, CC BY-SA 2.0. Bones: From Quarterly Journal of the Geological Society of London, vol. 31 no. 51, John Magens Mello, PD. **DERBYSHIRE.** Arbor Low: Beep boop beep, CC BY-SA 4.0. Gib Hill: MichaelMaggs, CC BY-SA 4.0. Nine Stone Close: Mark Kelly, CC BY-SA 2.0. Rowtor Rocks: Richard Bird, CC BY-SA 2.0. Rowtor Rocks: Unknown author, PD. Rude Stone: James Fergusson, PD. Nine Ladies: Beep boop beep, CC

BY-SA 4.0. Stanton Moor: Alunsalt, CC BY-SA 3.0. Doll Tor: Unknown author, CC BY-SA 3.0. Mam Tor: Bill Boaden, CC BY-SA 2.0. Path to Mam Tor: Andrew Hill, CC BY-SA 2.0.

VII. THE NORTH WEST

CHESHIRE. *The Weirdstone of Brisingamen*: Alan Garner, Ace, 1978. Alderley Edge: Unknown author. The Devil's Grave: Mike Pennington, by CC BY-SA 2.0. The Holy Well: Raymond Knapman, CC BY-SA 2.0. Wizard's Well: John Reppion. Druid's Circle: Andrew Huggett, CC BY-SA 2.0. Merlin: Gustave Dore, PD. Alex and Maxine Sanders: Unknown author, PD. Minerva's Shrine: Unknown author. PD. Wardley Hall, 1890: Ardfern, CC BY-SA 4.0. Plans of Wardley Hall, 1884: Unknown author, PD. Ambrose Barlow: John Payne, PD. Chethams Library: Michael D Beckwith, CC0 1.0. John Dee: Unknown author, PD. The Green Man: Acaller, PD. John Rylands Library: Mdbeckwith, CC BY-SA 3.0. **MERSEYSIDE.** Sun Goddess: David Nulty, CC BY-SA 2.0. Cotton Mather: Unknown author, PD. Toxteth: Rodhullandemu, CC BY-SA 4.0 & GFDL. Prince Rupert of the Rhine: Unknown author, PD. Boy: Attributed to Louise Hollandine of the Palatinate, PD. Simpson's "Stone 1": Sir James Simpson, PD. Carvings on Stone A (after Forde-Johnson): Unknown author, PD. Crank Caverns: Andy Gibson, CC BY-SA 2.0. **LANCASHIRE.** Witches flying: from Mathers' Wonders of the Invisible World, 1689, PD. Witchcraft: Woodcut, 1720, Unknown author, PD. Pendle Church: Tomw37, CC BY-SA 4.0. Witchcraft: Woodcut, 1720, Unknown author, PD. Alice Nutter Statue: Graham Demaline, CC BY-SA 3.0. Necromancy: coloured aquatint, unknown author, PD. Edward Kelly: Thomas Pennant, PD. The Written Stone: from an old postcard, unknown author. **CUMBRIA.** Fairy Steps: from an old postcard, unknown author. The Devil's Bridge, 1898, unknown author. Birkrigg: Yohan euan o4, CC BY-SA 3.0. Swinside: Andrew Hill, CC BY-SA 2.0. Castlerigg: NickW, CC BY-SA 3.0. Fairies dancing: from a 17th-century chapbook, PD. Long Meg: Paul Farmer, CC BY-SA 2.0. Levenshall: Unknown author, PD. Levens Hall, 1907, PD. Screaming Skulls of Calgarth Hall, 1925, PD. The Witch of Eagle's Crag: John Heywood, 1895, PD. Lady Sybil at the Eagle Crag: Unknown author, PD. **ISLE OF MAN.** Witches' Mill, Castletown: unknown author. Peel Castle Garrison Hall: Manx_James, CC0 1.0. St Trinian's: Harvey Milligan, CC BY-SA 4.0. The Phynodderree, and other legends of the Isle of Man (1882): Edward Watson Callow, PD.

VIII. THE NORTH EAST

YORKSHIRE. Swastika stone: Alexander P Kapp, CC BY-SA 2.0. Rombald: Unknown author. Rombalds Moor: Andrew Whale, CC BY-SA 2.0. Mother Shipton: Jooniur, CC BY-SA 4.0. Resemblance of Mother Shipton to Mister Punch of Fleet St: Unknown author, PD. Title page from 1870's "The Strange and Wonderful History of Mother Shipton", PD. Wishing Stone and Pulpit, 1914: Unknown author, PD. Druid's Temple: Gordon Hatton, CC BY-SA 2.0. Burton Agnes Hall: jo-h, CC BY-SA 2.0. Burton Agnes: From English Homes, Vol 1, by Charles Latham, PD. Monolith: Godfrey Bingley, PD. St. Andrew's cross: Lee Hadden, CC BY-SA 3.0. Ryedale Folk Museum: Humphrey Bolton, CC BY-SA 2.0. Title page of *Daemonologie, in forme of a dialogue*, by James I, PD. St Mary, Lastingham: Amanda Slater, CC BY-SA 2.0. Whitby Abbey: Michael D Beckwith, CC0 1.0. Whitby Abbey arches: Lewek-rafek, CC BY-SA 4.0. Die eingemauerte Nonne: Vinzenz Katzler, PD. Whitby's 99 steps: Derek Dye, CC BY-SA 2.0. Bram Stoker, 1906: Unknown author, PD. La Main de Gloire: Albertus Parvus Lucius, PD. Hob Holes: Stephen McCulloch, CC BY-SA 2.0. Gisborough Priory: Godfrey Bingley, PD. Gisborough Priory: Unknown author. **COUNTY DURHAM.** Sockburn: Ataffo, CC BY-SA 4.0. Jabberwocky: John Tenniel, PD. St. Edmund's Church: Mike Quinn, CC BY-SA 2.0. St. Edmund's Church: Unknown author, PD.

TYNE AND WEAR. Penshaw Monument: Mark Healey, CC BY-SA 4.0. Illustration from More English Fairy Tales, by John Dickson Batten, PD. **NORTHUMBERLAND.** Mithras altar: Carole Raddato, CC BY-SA 2.0. Thomas Plantagenet: Enluminure, PD. Bamburgh Castle, 1814: from an old engraving by J Greig. Laidly Worm: from English Fairy Tales, Joseph Jacobs, 1895, PD. *Robin of Sherwood* (1984-1986), ITV. Lindisfarne Castle: Robert Eyers, CC BY-SA 4.0. Duddo Stones: Brendandh, CC BY-SA 3.0.

IX. WALES

GWENT. Arthur Machen: Unknown author, PD. Twmbarlwm: Gareth James, CC BY-SA 2.0. Nodens: Folklore society, PD. Plans: Unknown author, PD. Caerwent: from "Transactions of the Bristol and Gloucestershire Archaeological Society", 1903, PD. Evan Morgan: unknown source. Tredegar House: WelshDave, CC BY-SA 4.0. Harold's Stones: Philip Halling, CC BY-SA 2.0. St Nicholas' Church cross: Unknown author, PD. **GLAMORGAN.** Views of upper Palaeolithic and a Mesolithic site, Glamorgan. Wellcome M0016517, Wellcome Images, CC-BY-4.0. Goat's Hole: Unknown author, PD. Arthur's stone: RobinLeicester, CC BY-SA 3.0. Arthur's stone: Gastineau, Henry G, PD. Swansea Devil: Nicky Thomas, CC BY-SA 4.0. Ogmore castle: Samuel Hooper, CC0 1.0. Tinkinswood: Nilfanion, CC BY-SA 4.0. John Crichton-Stuart: Unknown author, PD. Castell Coch: Nilfanion, CC BY-SA 4.0. **DYFED.** Pentre Ifan: Daniel Phillips, CC BY-SA 4.0. Roman anthropomorphic handle: The Portable Antiquities Scheme, Mark Lodwick, CC BY-SA 2.0. Caio Church: Philip Halling, CC BY-SA 2.0. Compendium Maleficarum engraving: Derek Smootz, PD. Book of incantations by John Harries: CC0 1.0. POWYS. *Sleep no More. Twelve Stories of the Supernatural* (1948): L.T.C. Rolt, Constable, London. PolyGram Pictures and The Guber-Peters Company. Abergavenny: Unknown author, PD. St Martin's Church: Dara Jasumani, CC BY-SA 2.0. Christ: KJP1, CC BY-SA 4.0. Wall painting: ceridwen, CC BY-SA 2.0. **GWYNEDD.** Cadair Idris: Thomas Pennant, PD. View of Cader Idris: Pugh, R. and Clark, W, PD. Old Courthouse: Peter Broster, CC BY-SA 2-0. *The Owl Service* (1969-1970): ITV (Granada Television), book cover by Penguin, 1969. Oak: 1889 litograph, PD. Engraving: Richard Colt Hoare, CC0 1.0. Bardsey Island: Stray Croc, CC BY-SA 2.0 Bala Lake: George Samuel, PD. Doctor Faustus: late edition, Iohn Wright, PD. Huw Lwyd's Pulpit: Andrew Wilson, PD. Dinas Emrys: Richard Colt Hoare, PD. Merlin: illustration from middle ages, PD. The Red Dragon periodical cover page, February 1882, edited by Charles Wilkins, PD. Dinas Emrys Tower: James Frankcom, CC BY-SA 3.0. Penmaenmawr Meini Hirion a Tal-y-Fan: Anatiomaros, PD. Meini Hirion: Eric Jones, CC BY-SA 2.0. *The Wicker Man*: Thomas Pennant, PD. Bryn Celli Ddu: Wolfgang Sauber, BY-SA 3.0. BrynCelliDdu3: Rhion Pritchard, PD. **CLWYD.** Gogmagog: F W Fairholt, PD. Dinas Bran castle: James Basire, PD. St. Dugain Church: Dot Potter. CC BY-SA 2.0. Sir Richard Clough, by Moses Griffith: Thomas Pennant, PD. Plas Clough, from The Life and Times of Sir Thomas Gresham, PD.

X. SCOTLAND

LOWLANDS. The Wicker Man (1973). Robin Hardy (Dir.), British Lion Films. Anwoth Old Kirk: Fox on the trot, CC BY-SA 4.0. Kirkcudbright, Greyfriars: Dr Neil Clifton, CC BY-SA 2.0. 'The Wicker Man' Filming Locations: The Ellangowan Hotel, Creetown: James T M Towill, CC BY-SA 2.0. Logan Botanic Gardens: Tom Parnell, CC BY-SA 4.0. Culzean Castle, South Ayrshire, 1834: D.O.Hill, PD. Castle Kennedy Gardens: S. Rae, CC BY-SA 2.0. St Ninian's Cave: Otter, CC BY-SA 3.0. Michael Scot: Unknown author, PD. Glenluce Abbey: David Baird, CC BY-SA 2.0. Melrose Abbey: Steve Collis, CC BY-SA 2.0. Hermitage Castle: Tom Parnell, CC BY-SA 2.0. Nine Stones

Stone Circle: Walter Baxter, CC BY-SA 2.0. Tam O'Shanter on Alloway Brig: George Cruikshank, PD. Alloway Kirk Ayr: Miscellaneous Items in High Demand, PPOC, Library of Congress. PD. Robert Burns at Alloway: John McGready. PD. Merlin: Aubrey Beardsley, PD. Caledonian Forest Walk: Stuart Meek, CC BY-SA 2.0. Merlin and St Kentigern, Stobo Kirk: Rosser1954, PD. Drumelzier Burn: Jim Barton, CC BY-SA 2.0. Thomas the Rhymer: Unknown author, PD. Rhymer's Stone: Unknown author. Rosslyn Chapel green men: Johanne McInnis, CC BY-SA 3.0. Rosslyn crypt: Andreas Faessler, CC BY-SA 4.0. Rosslyn Chapel: Tallulahbang, CC BY-SA 4.0. Rosslyn Chapel ceiling: Cornell University Library, PD. Yester Tower, 1814: L. Connell, PD. Goblin Ha: M J Richardson, CC BY-SA 2.0. Arthur's Seat and Edinburgh Castle: Ad Meskens, CC BY-SA 3.0. Mary's Chapel: Kim Traynor, CC BY-SA 2.0. Coffin: Kim Traynor, CC BY-SA 2-0. Witches: from Daemonologie, 1597, PD. St Andrew's Church: wfmillar, CC BY-SA 2.0. Thomas Dalyell: Unknown author, PD. House of the Binns: PaulT (Gunther Tschuch), CC BY-SA 4.0. The Whangie: dave souza, CC BY-SA 3.0. On Nocturnal Dance of Fairies: Olaus Magnus, PD. Robert Kirk's Grave: Faye Donnelley, CC BY-SA 4.0. Offerings to the fairies of Doon Hill: James Allan, CC BY-SA 2.0. Claude Bowes- Lyon: Philip de László, PD. Loch of Skene: Peter Ward, CC BY-SA 2.0. Skene churchyard: Lizzie, CC BY-SA 2.0. *The Magician* (1967), by W. Somerset Maugham, Penguin. **HIGHLANDS.** A Brocken spectre within a glory's rings: Brocken Inaglory, CC BY-SA 3.0. Loch Garten: Lee Carson, CC BY-SA 2.0. Aleister Crowley, 1929: Unknown author, PD. Boleskine cemetery: Martyn Gorman, CC BY-SA 2.0. Boleskine House: Aleister Crowley, PD. *Lucifer Rising* (1972), Kenneth Anger (Dir.), Puck Film Productions. Logo for The Boleskine House Foundation: The Boleskine House Foundation. Clava Cairns: Bubobubo2, CC BY-SA 3.0. Standing stones at Clava: Steven Brown, CC BY-SA 2.0. Clava Cairns: Elliott Simpson, CC BY-SA 2.0. The Witches' Sabbath: Hans Baldung, PD. Inshoch Castle: Anne Burgess, CC BY-SA 2.0. Weird Sisters: Alexandre-Gabriel Decamps, PD. Macbeth's Hillock: Alan Hodgson, CC BY-SA 2.0. Sueno's Stone: Pasicles, CC0 1.0. **ISLANDS.** Iona: Donatella Tronca, CC BY-SA 3.0. St. Oran's Chapel: Keith Laverack, CC BY-SA 2.0. William Sharp, 1894: Frederick Hollyer, PD. Netta Fornario newspaper: from Glasgow Herald, 1929. Fingal's Cave: Luk~commonswiki, CC BY-SA 4.0. Triton: Sebastian Münster, c. 1600, PD. Calanais: Tom Parnell, CC BY-SA 2.0. Calanais: Otter, CC BY-SA 3.0. Skara Brae: Antony Sleg, CC BY-SA 2.0. Ring of Brodgar: Mikenorton, CC BY-SA 3.0. The Watch Stone: William Craig. Sjøtrollet, 1887: Theodor Kittelsen, PD. Long chambered burial cairn, Midhowe, Rousay, Orkney: Wellcome M0011784, Wellcome Images, CC BY-SA 4.0.

XII. NORTHERN IRELAND

FERMANAGH. Sacred Heart Church: Youngbohemian, PD. Interior: Eric Jones, CC BY-SA 2.0. Reyfad: Youngbohemian, CC BY-SA 3.0. Stained Glass Window: Unknown author, CC BY-SA 3.0. St Faber's bullán: Youngbohemian, PD. White Island figures: Rosemary Nelson, CC BY-SA 2.0. Janus: Jon Sullivan, PD. Offerings: Kenneth Allen, CC-BY-SA2.0. **ARMAGH.** Ballykeel Dolmen: Ron Murray, CC BY-SA 2.0. Chambered Grave and Hag's Lough: Ross, CC BY-SA 2.0. Macha: Stephen Reid, PD. Roundhouse: Notafly. CC BY-SA 3.0. Bronze Age Irish horn: Patrick W. Joyce, PD. George W. Russell: Unknown author, PD. DOWN. Slieve Donard: Ross, CC BY-SA 2.0. Summit: Colin Park, CC BY-SA 2.0. Ballynoe: Ardfern, CC BY-SA 3.0. Borlase: Unknown author, PD. Grey Abbey: Kognos, CC BY-SA 4.0. **TYRONE.** Clogh-Oir: Kenneth Allen, CC BY-SA 2.0. Knockmany: R0025693, CC BY-SA 4.0. The Legend of Tyrone. Fairy Queen: James A.S. Torrance, CC. Beaghmore: Mervyn Greer, CC BY-SA 2.0. Stone Row: Alun Salt, CC BY-SA 2.0. DERRY. Banagher: from "Journal of the Royal Society of Antiquaries of Ireland", 1849, unknown author, PD. Old Church: Phil Champion, CC BY-SA 2.0. **ANTRIM.** Cave Hill: Donna, CC BY-SA 2.0. Maude Gonne: Bain News Service, PD. C.S. Lewis Square: Paul Bowman, CC BY-SA 2.0. Statue of C.S. Lewis: CC BY-SA 2.0. “Black Magic Fear”: from Sunday World, October 28th 1973. Shane’s Castle: Kenneth Allen, CC BY-SA 2.0. Banshee: W.H. Brooke, PD. Round Tower: William Mervyn Lawrence, PD. Child levitation: from Saducismus Triumphatus, William Faithorne, PD. Pillory: Albert Bridge, CC BY-SA 2.0. Calgorm Castle: Mainlymazza, CC BY-SA 4.0. Sheridan Le Fanu: Unknown author, PD. Rev. Dr. Alexander Colville: Unknown author, PD. *Houses of the Holy* (1973): Led Zeppelin, Atlantic. Swans: Harold Robert Millar, PD. Bonamargy Friary: Jo Turner, CC BY-SA 2.0. Stacks by Rathlin Island: Laurent Bélanger, CC BY-SA 4.0. Bruce’s Cave: Henry George Hine. PD. Robert the Bruce plaque: Ross, CC BY-SA 2.0.

Film, TV, and Literary References

FILM AND TV REFERENCES

An American Werewolf in London (John Landis, 1981), 226
Children of the Stones (HTV/ITV, 1977), 48, 49
Count Dracula (BBC, 1977)
Doctor Who,
"The Stones of Blood" (BBC, 1978), 20
Dracula (Terence Fisher, 1958), 63
Interview with a Vampire (Neil Jordan, 1994), 92
Lost Hearts (BBC, 1973), 153
Macbeth (Roman Polanski, 1971), 210
Moondial (BBC, 1988), 151
Night of the Demon (Jacques Tourneur, 1957), 86
Night of the Eagle (Sidney Hayers, 1962), 64
Penda's Fen (BBC, 1974), 125
Robin of Sherwood (HTV/ITV, 1984-86), 210
Sherlock Holmes (Granada/ITV):
"The Priory School" (1986), 171
"The Last Vampyre" (1993), 131
The Blood on Satan's Claw (Piers Haggard, 1971), 69
The Devil Rides Out (Terence Fisher, 1968), 106
The Devils (Ken Russell, 1971), 210
The Frankenstein Chronicles (ITV, 2015-2017), 293
The Plague of the Zombies (John Gilling, 1966), 63
The Reptile (John Gilling, 1966), 63
The Rocky Horror Picture Show (Jim Sharman, 1975), 63
The Shout (Jerzy Skolimowski, 1978), 31
The Stone Tape (Peter Sasdy, 1972), 73
The Third Day (HBO, 2020), 103
The Tractate Middoth (BBC, 2013), 171
The Owl Service (Granada TV, 1969), 229
The Wicker Man (Robin Hardy, 1973), 242, 243, 244
The Witches (Cyril Frankel, 1967), 65
The Woman in Black (ITV, 1989), 103
The Woman in Black (James Watkins, 2012), 103
Witchfinder General (Michael Reeves, 1968), 116
Whistle and I'll Come To You (BBC, 1968), 112

LITERARY REFERENCES

Ackroyd, Peter:
Hawksmoor, 92
Beowulf, 62
Burns, Robert:
"Tam O'Shanter", 247
Carroll, Lewis:
"Jabberwocky", 204
Colquhoun, Ithell:
The Living Stones, 21, 24
Conan Doyle, Arthur:
The Hound of the Baskervilles, 28, 29
Garner, Alan:
The Weirdstone of Brisingamen, 166, 167
The Moon of Gomrath, 166, 167
The Owl Service, 229
James, M. R.:
"A Vignette", 111
"The Ash Tree", 111
"A Warning to the Curious", 110
"Oh, Whistle, and I'll Come To You, My Lad", 111, 112
Kirk, Robert:
The Secret Commonwealth of Elves, Fauns, and Fairies, 255
Le Fanu, Joseph Sheridan:
"Sir Dominick's Bargain", 293
Machen, Arthur:
"The Great God Pan", 44, 217
"The Hill of Dreams", 216
Moore, Alan, and Campbell, Eddie:
From Hell, 92
Rolt, L. T. C.:
"Cwm Garon", 226
"The House of Vengeance", 226
Shakespeare, William:
Macbeth, 256, 262, 263
Sir Gawain and the Green Knight, 136, 137
Somerset Maugham, William:
The Magician, 257
Stoker, Bram:
Dracula, 199, 201, 287
The Lair of the White Worm, 206
Tolkien, J. R. R.:
The Lord of the Rings, 45

Index

A

Abbey Gardens (Tresco), 23
Aberfoyle Old Kirk Graveyard, 255
Aberfoyle, 255
Abhartach, 287
Ackroyd, Peter, 85, 92
Æ's Natal House, 281
Alderley Edge, 166
Aldworth, 62
All Saint's Church (Braunston), 147
All Saint's Church (Sockburn), 204
Alloway Auld Kirk, 247
Alloway, 247
Ancient Chapel of Toxteth, The, 174
Ancient Market Cross, The (Castletown), 188
Anger, Kenneth, 260
Anglesey, 233
Annaghmare, 279
Antrim, 288
Anwoth Old Kirk, 242
Aoife, 294
Arbor Low Stone Circle, 159
Archer Stone, The (Liverpool), 176
Armada Beacon, The (Alderley Edge), 167
Armagh County Museum, 281
Armagh, 278
Arthur, King, 18, 22, 23, 35, 38, 209, 221, 232, 248, 252
Arthur's Stone, 221
Ashmole, Elias, 67, 91
Ashmolean Museum (Oxford), 67
Atlantis Bookshop, The, 87
Aubrey, John, 40, 41
Auldearn Kirk, 261
Auldearn, 261
Avebury Stone Circles, 48
Avebury, 48
Aynia, 284, 285
Aynia's Cove, 284

B

Bach, Ifor, 223
Bach-Y-Graig, 237
Badbury Rings (Knowlton), 35
Bala Lake, 230
Balliol College (Oxford), 66
Ballycastle, 294
Ballykeel Dolmen, 278
Ballymacfermot, 279
Ballynoe Stone Circle, 282
Bamburgh Castle, 209
Bamburgh, 209
Bambury Stone (Bredon Hill), 125
Banagher Old Church, 286
Banagher, 286
Bants Carn Burial Chamber, 23
Barclodiad Y Gawres, 235
Bardsey Island, 230
Baring-Gould, Sabine, 30
Bartlett, John Allan, 38
Bateman, James and Maria, 134
Bath, 41
Bawdstone, 135
Beacon House (Painswick), 43
Beaghmore, 285
Beaulieu, 60
Bedfordshire, 105
Beetham Fairy Steps, 182
Belas Knap Long Barrow, 46
Belfast, 288
Belton House, 151
Belvoir Castle, 150
Ben Macdui, 258
Berkshire, 62
Bettiscombe, 33
Biddulph Grange, 134
Bidston Hill, 173
Birkrigg Stone Circle, 184
Black Annis, 148
Black Castle, The (Ring of Guillion), 279
Black Mountains, The, 226
Blake, William, 77, 85, 94
Blavatsky, Helena, 86, 89
Bligh Bond, Frederick, 38
Bloomsbury, 86
Boa Island, 277
Bodleian Library (Oxford), 66
Bodmin Moor, 16
Boho, 274
Boleigh Fougou, 21
Boleskine House, 259
Bomere Pool, 139
Bonamargy Friary, 295

Boscawen-Un, 20
Bowes-Lyon, Claude, 256
Bram Stoker's Bench, 201
Brân the Blessed, 85, 236
Bredon Hill, 124
Bricket Wood, 106
Brig O'Doon, 247
Brimham Rocks, 196
British Museum, The, 86, 88
Brockenhurst, 59, 61
Brown, Agnes, 146
Brownlow House, 281
Bruce's Cave, 295
Bryn Celli Ddu, 235
Buckinghamshire, 64
Buckland Abbey, 32
Bunhill Fields, 94
Burley, 61
Burns, Robert, 247
Burrowhead, 244
Burton Agnes Hall, 197
Byron, George Gordon, Lord, 73, 156, 157

C

C. S. Lewis's Square, 289
Cabell, Sir Richard, 28, 29
Cadair Idris, 228
Caerwent, 217
Caesar, Julius, 74
Cage, The (St Osyth), 104
Cailleach Bhéara, 279
Caio Parish Church, 225
Calanais Standing Stones, 267
Calderstones, The, 176
Caldragh Cemetery, 277
Caledonian Forest, 248
Calgarth Hall, 186
Cambridgeshire, 108
Canewdon, 103
Canons Ashby, 146
Carn Cottage, 24
Carn Kenidjack, 20
Carrawburgh Mithras Temple, 208
Carroll, Lewis, 204
Castell Coch, 222
Castle Kennedy Gardens, 244
Castlerigg Stone Circle, 185
Cave Hill (Belfast), 288
Caynton Caves, 140
Cerne Abbas, 36
Chaceley, 125
Chalice Well Gardens, 38
Chanctonbury Ring, 74
Cheshire, 166
Chetham's Library, 171
Chilton Cantelo, 42
Christ Church (Spitalfields), 92
Church Cemetery (Nottingham), 155
Church of St Andrew's (Stainfield), 152
Church of St Botolph (Iken), 114
Church of St Issui, 227
Church of St Pancras (Widecombe-In-The-Moor), 26
Church of St Peter and St Paul (Long Compton), 129
Church of St Trinians, 188
Church of The Sacred Heart (Boho), 274
Churchyard of St Andrew's (Dowles), 126
Cibber, Caius Gabriel, 151
Circus, The (Bath), 41
Clava Cairns, 260
Cleopatra's Needle, 88
Clonlum, 279
Clontygora, 279
Clophill Church, 105
Clough, Richard, 237
Clutterbuck, Dorothy, 36
Clwyd, 236
Coffin Stone, 27
Colchester Castle, 104
Colman-Smith, Pamela, 87
Colquhoun, Ithell, 21, 24
Colville, Alexander, 292
Conan Doyle, Arthur, 28, 29, 58, 59, 60
Conchobar Mac Nessa, 280, 284
Conyers, John, 204
Cooraghy Bay, 295
Cornwall, 16
County Durham, 204
Cox, Katharine Laird, 24
Crank Caverns, 177
Creetown, 243
Cresswell, Helen, 151
Creswell Crags, 158
Crowley, Aleister, 24, 25, 74, 86, 90, 131, 218, 259, 260
Crowley's Natal House, 131
Cú Chulainn, 276, 278, 280
Culpeper, Nicholas, 89
Culzean Castle, 243
Cumbria, 182
Cwrt-Y-Cadno, 225
Cynfal-Fawr, 231

D

Dafo, 106
Dalyell, Thomas, "Bluidy Tam", 253
Danby, William, 196
Dartmoor, 26
Dashwood, Francis, 64, 65
de Beverley, Constance, 220
De Giffard, Hugo, 251
De Richleau, Duke, 106
de Soulis, William, 246, 247
Dee, John, 67, 77, 86, 88, 171, 180, 181, 231
Derbyshire, 159
Derek Jarman's Prospect Cottage, 77
Derry, 286
Devil's Bridge (Carnforth), 183
Devil's Dyke (Sussex), 75
Devil's Point (Plymouth), 32

Devil's Pulpit, The (Chepstow), 47
Devil's Pulpit, The (Finnich Glen), 254
Devil's Stone, The (Shebbear), 30
Devon, 26
Devorguilla of Galloway, 66
Diana, 95
Dinas Bran, 236
Dinas Emrys, 232
Doll Tor Stone Circle, 160
Doon Hill (Aberfoyle), 255
Dorset County Museum, 37
Dorset Cursus (Knowlton), 35
Dorset Ooser, The, 37
Dorset, 33
Down, 282
Doxey Pool, 135
Dozmary Pool, 18
Dracula, 63, 199, 201, 202, 287
Dracula's Steps, 201
Drake, Francis, 32
Druid Stone (Blidworth), 157
Druid's Circle, The (Alderley Edge), 167
Druid's Temple (Swinton Estate), 196
Druids' Circle, The (Anglesey), 234
Drumelzier, 248
Duddo Five Stones, 211
Dùn I, 264
Dunbar, Mary, 291
Dundermot Mound, 293
Dungeness, 77
Dungiven Priory, 287
Dunstanburgh Castle, 208
Dunwich, 112
Durham Cathedral, 204
Dyfed, 224
Dynas Mawddwy, 229

E

Eadric the Wild, 139
Eagle Crag, 187
Earlston, 249
East Anglia, 99
East Midlands, 143
Edgwarebury House (Elstree), 106
Edinburgh, 252
Edmondthorpe, 148
Edward Rowlands' Stone of Gronw, 229
Eildon Hill, 249
Elva Hill Stone Circle, 185
Epona, 69
Essex, 102
Eynhallow, 269
Eyre, Thomas, 160

F

Farrant, David, 97
Faugh's Quarry, 179
Feeny Picnic Site, 286
Felixstowe, 111
Fermanagh, 274
Ferny Knapp, 61
Fingal's Cave, 266
Fitzwilliam Museum, 109
Five Knolls, 105
Flag Fen, 109
Fleece Inn, The (Bretforton), 124
Flower, Joan, Margaret and Philippa, 150
Forman, Simon, 91
Fornario, Netta, 265
Fortune, Dion, 39, 86
Four Stones (Hagley Estate), 127
Fox Tor, 28
Frazer, James, 155
Freemasons' Hall (Edinburgh), 252
Freemasons' Hall (London), 86
Frensham, 72
Fuller, John "Mad Jack", 75
Fyvie Castle, 249

G

Galgorm Castle, 292
Gardner, Gerald, 22, 35, 36, 58, 61, 86, 87, 106, 130, 188
Garner, Alan, 166, 167, 229
Gawain, 136, 137
Giant's Causeway, The, 294
Giant's Grave (Slaghtaverty), 287
Giant's Ring, The (Belfast), 283
Giantess' Apron, The, 235
Gisborough Priory, 203
Glamis Castle, 256
Glamorgan, 220
Glasshayes House, 59
Glastonbury Abbey, 38
Glastonbury Tor, 38
Glastonbury, 38
Glenluce Abbey, 245
Glenmore Forest Park, 248
Gloucestershire, 43
Goat's Hole, 220
Gobbins, The, 291
Goblin Ha' (Yester Castle), 251
Gogmagog, 108, 236
Golden Idol of Trewern, The, 224
Gonne, Maud, 288
Goodwin Sands, 78
Gowdie, Isobel, 261
Grand Lodge of Scotland, The, 252
Graves, Robert, 31
Great Livermere, 111
Greater Manchester, 170
Green Chapel, The, 136
Gretham, Thomas, 154
Grey Abbey, 283
Griffith, Katherine "Anne", 197

Grimes Graves, 117
Grimnir, 117
Guilsborough, 146
Guy's Cliffe House, 131
Gwent, 216
Gwyn ap Nudd, 38, 236
Gwynedd, 228

H

Haddo, Oliver, 257
Hag's Lough, 279
Hagley Estate, 127
Hambleden, 65
Hampshire, 58
Hand of Glory, The (Whitby Museum), 202
Hardy, Robin, 242
Harries, John and Henry, 225
Hartfell Spa, 248
Hawkes, Jacquetta, 34, 71
Hawksmoor, Nicholas, 87, 92, 93, 95
Hellfire Caves, The, 64
Hemlock Stone (Bramcote), 155
Herefordshire, 122
Hergest Court, 123
Hermitage Castle, 246
Hertfordshire, 106
Highcliffe-On-Sea, 35
Highgate Cemetery, 96
Highlands, 258
History of Science Museum (Oxford), 67
Hob Holes (Runswick Bay), 203
Hollins Cross, 161
Holmes, Sherlock, 28, 29, 59, 131, 161
Holmyard, Paul, 141
Holy Trinity Church (Blythburgh), 114
Holy Trinity Church (Buckfastleigh), 29
Holy Well, The (Alderley Edge), 166
Hopkins, Matthew, 102, 103, 104, 110, 116
Horse Carving (Bidston Hill), 173
Horsley Towers, 73
House of The Binns, 253
Humber Stone, The, 149
Hurlers, The, 16
Huw Lwyd's Pulpit, 231
Hyett, Benjamin, 43

I

Icknield Way, The, 69
Ine Qane, Margaret, 188
Inshoch Castle, 261
Iona, 264
Ipplepen, 29
Islandmagee, 291
Islands, 264
Isle of Lewis, 267
Isle of Man, 188
Isle of Wight, 70

J

Jack o' Kent, 219, 227
James VI of Scotland and I of Britain, King, 198, 248, 262
James, M. R., 108, 110, 111, 112, 153, 161
Jarman, Derek, 77
John Ryland's Library, 172
Joseph of Arimathea, 38

K

Keiller, Alexander, 51
Kelley, Edward, 88, 89, 180, 181
Kemp, Ursula, 104
Kent, 76
Kentwell Hall, 116
King And Queen Stones, The (Bredon Hill), 125
King Stone, The (Stanton Moor), 161
King's College (Cambridge), 108
King's Stables, The (Navan), 280
King's Ring, The (Ring of Guillion), 279
Kirk, Robert, 255
Kirkcudbright, 242
Kirkton of Skene Churchyard, 257
Kit's Coty House, 76
Kneale, Nigel, 65, 73
Knowlton Church and Rings, 34

L

Laidley Worm's Trough, 209
Lambton, John, 206
Lamorna, 21
Lancashire Witches Walk, The, 179
Lancashire, 178
Lancelot, Sir, 209
Lanyon Quoit, 19
Lavenham, 116
Le Fanu, Joseph Sheridan, 293
Lee, Elizabeth, 205
Leek, Sybil, 61, 133
Leicester Castle, 148
Leicestershire And Rutland, 148
Leigh, Molly, 133
Levens Hall, 186
Lewis, C. S., 289
Lewtrenchard, 30
Lilly, William, 67
Lincoln Cathedral, 152
Lincolnshire, 151
Lindisfarne, 210
Llyn Tegid, 231
Loch Garten, 258
Lochloy House, 261
Logan Botanic Garden (Port Logan), 243
London Stone, The, 85
London, 81

Long Compton, 128
Long Man of Wilmington, The, 76
Long Meg and Her Daughters, 185
Lough Erne, 276
Lough Foyle, 286
Loughnashade, 281
Lovelace, Ada, 73
Lowlands (Scotland), 242
Lud's Church, 137
Lurgan Town Hall, 281
Lwyd, Huw, 231
Lych Way, The, 27
Lydney Park Estate, 44

M

Mac Cumhaill, Fionn, 266, 278, 279, 295
Macbeth, 210, 256, 262, 264
Macbeth's Hillock, 262
Machen, Arthur, 44, 90, 216, 217
Maen Ceti, 221
Maeshowe, 268
Malew Church, 188
Mam Tor, 161
Manchester, Sean, 97
Martello Tower, 110
Mary's Chapel (Edinburgh), 252
Mather, Richard, Katherine, Increase, and Cotton, 174
McGirr, James, 274
McLeod, Fiona, aka William Sharp, 265
McQuillan, Julia, 295
Méabh or Maeve, Queen, 276
Mead, G. R. S., 90
Melrose Abbey, 245
Men Scryfa, 19
Mên-An-Tol, 19
Meon Hill, 130
Merlin, 22, 52, 230, 232, 248
Merlin's Cave, 22
Merry Maidens of Boleigh, 20
Merseyside, 173
Mick Mills' Race, 75
Mill House (Highcliffe-On-Sea), 35
Mills, Brusher, 59
Milucra, 278, 279
Minerva, 42, 169
Minerva's Shrine (Chester), 169
Minterne, John, 34
Mitchell's Fold, 138
Mithras, 74, 90, 208
Moore, Alan, 92
Moreton Corbet Castle, 141
Morgan, Evan, 218
Mother Ludlam, 72
Mother Ludlam's Cave (Frensham), 72
Mother Shipton, aka Ursula Sontheil, 195
Mother Shipton's Cave, 195
Mottistone Longstone, 71
Mound In Dark Grove, The, 235
Munslow, Richard, 140
Murray, Margaret, 51, 67, 86, 127, 130, 261
Museum of Witchcraft and Magic, 22

N

Nairn, 261
Naked Man, The, 61
Nannau Park, 228
National Library of Wales, 225
National Museum of Scotland, 252
Navan Complex, The, 280
Navan Fort, 280
Needles, The (Isle of Wight), 70
Neuburg, Victor, 74
New Forest, The, 58
Newchurch (Burnley), 179
Newstead Abbey, 156
Newton, Isaac, 151
Nine Ladies Stone Circle, 160
Nine Maidens of Boskednan, 19
Nine Stone Close Stone Circle, 159
Ninestane Rig, 247
Nodens, 44, 45, 217
Norfolk, 117
North Berwick, 253
North East, The, 191
North West, The, 163
Northamptonshire, 146
Northern Ireland, 271
Northumberland, 208
Nottinghamshire, 155
Nutter, Alice, 179

O

O'Donnell, Elliott, 89
Oakley Court, 63
Odin, 117, 268
Ogmore Castle, 222
O'Heany, Murrough, 286
Old Courthouse (Dolgellau), 228
Orford Castle, 116
Orkney, 268
Osea Island's Causeway, 103
Other Place, The (Isle of Wight), 70
Owenreagh River Pool, 286
Oweynagolman Cave (Rathlin Island), 294
Oxford, 66
Oxfordshire, 66

P

Page, Jimmy, 260
Painswick Church, 43
Painswick, 43
Palace House (Beaulieu), 60
Pan, 43, 44, 51, 131, 157, 217

Pantcoy, 225
Pearson, Margaret, 178
Peel Castle, 188
Pelham Mausoleum, 153
Penda, 125
Pendle Heritage Centre, 178
Pendle Hill, 178
Pendle, 178
Penshaw Hill, 206
Pentre Ifan, 224
Pickingill, George, 103
Pilsdon Pen (Bettiscombe), 33
Pinvin, 125
Pipers, The, 16
Pitt Rivers Museum (Oxford), 67
Plas Clough, 237
Porthcurno Cove, 22
Powys, 226
Pratt, Elizabeth, 105
Price, Harry, 87
Price, Vincent, 116
Prospect Cottage, 77

R

Rathlin Island, 295
Red Castle, The, 222
Reyfad Stones, 274
Rhymer's Stone, 249
Rhymer's Tower, 249
Rillaton Barrow, 17
Ring of Brodgar, The, 268
Ring of Gullion, 279
Roaches, The, 135
Roades, Mother, 147
Robert Burns' Cottage, 247
Robert the Bruce, 246, 295
Robin Hood, 156, 176, 210
Robinson, Fletcher, 29
Roche Rock, 18
Rococo Gardens (Painswick), 43
Rohmer, Sax, 93
Rollright Stones, The, 68
Rolt, L T C, 226
Roman Baths (Bath), 42
Rombald, 194
Rombalds Moor, 194
Rosslyn Chapel, 250
Roughlee, 179
Rousay, 269
Rowtor Rocks, 160
Royal Crescent (Bath), 41
Royston's Templar Cave, 107
Rudston Monolith, 197
Rupert of the Rhine, 175
Russell, George W. (Æ), 281
Russell, Ken, 137, 210
Ryedale Folk Museum, 198

S

Sanctuary, The (Avebury), 50
Sanders, Maxine and Alex, 169
Saunton Sands, 31
Science Museum, The (London), 89
Scilly (Isles of), 23
Scot, Michael, 185, 245
Scotland, 239
Scott, Walter, 249, 251, 256, 266
Seddon, W. H., 43
Sele, Hywel, 228, 229
Senate House, 87
Serpent Temple, The (Avebury), 49
Seven Barrows, The (Avebury), 50
Shaffer, Anthony, 206
Shakespeare, William, 85, 256, 262
Shane Castle, 290
Shropshire, 138
Silbury Hill (Avebury), 51
Sinclair, William, 250
Singing Barrows, The, 33
Sìthean Mòr (Iona), 264
Skaill House, 268
Skene House, 257
Skene, 257
Skene, Alexander, 257
Skirrid, The, 227
Slieve Donard, 282
Slieve Gullion Passage Tomb, 279
Slieve Gullion, 278
Smith, Lady Ann, 148
Snowshill Manor, 46
Sockburn, 204
Somerset Maugham, William, 257
Somerset, 38
South East, 55
South Foreland Lighthouse, 78
South West, 13
Southerns, Elizabeth "Mother Demdike", 178
Southridge (Highcliffe-On-Sea), 35
Southwell Minster, 158
Spindlestone, 209
St Alfege (Greenwich), 93
St Ambrose Barlow, 170
St Andrew's Church (Ipplepen), 29
St Andrew's Old Kirk (North Berwick), 253
St Anne (Limehouse), 93
St Augustine of Canterbury, 128
St Botolph, 114
St Botolph's Church (Skidbrooke), 153
St Clair, William, 250
St Columba, 264
St Cuthbert, 210
St Digain's Church, 236
St Edmund's Church (Castleton), 161
St Edmund's Church (Edmundbyers), 205
St Faber, 274, 275
St Faber's Well, 275

St George (Bloomsbury), 92
St George In The East (Wapping), 92
St George's Church (Bloomsbury), 87
St Hilda, 199
St James' Old Church (Bix Bottom), 69
St James's Church and Higher Farm (Chilton Cantelo), 42
St John The Baptist Church (Glastonbury), 38
St John The Baptist's Church (Burslem), 133
St Leonard's Churchyard, 180
St Macartan's Cathedral, 284
St Marcella's Parish Church, 237
St Margaret's Churchyard (Ratlinghope), 140
St Martin's Church (Cwmyoy), 227
St Mary At Lambeth (London), 91
St Mary The Virgin Church (Frensham), 72
St Mary The Virgin Church (Mortlake), 89
St Mary The Virgin's Church (Bottesford), 150
St Mary Woolnoth (The City), 93
St Mary's Church (Aldworth), 62
St Mary's Church (Batcombe), 34
St Mary's Church (Kington), 123
St Mary's Church (Lastingham), 198
St Michael's Church (Garway), 123
St Nicholas' Church (Abbot's Bromley), 132
St Nicholas' Church (Abergavenny), 219
St Nicholas' Churchyard (Brockenhurst), 59
St Ninian's Cave, 244
St Oran's Cemetery, 264
St Patrick, 284, 286
St Paul's Cathedral, 95
St Peter's Church (Great Livermere), 111
Staffa, 266
Staffordshire, 132
Stanton Drew, 40
Stanton Moor, 160
Stenness, 268
Stiperstones, 139
Stobo Kirk, 248
Stocks, The (Islandmagee), 291
Stoker, Bram, 137, 199, 201, 202, 206, 287
Stokesay Castle, 138
Stonehenge, 52
Stormy Point (Alderley Edge), 166
Stuart, John Patrick Crichton, 223
Stukeley, William, 49, 51, 68, 154, 198
Sueno's Stone, 262
Suffolk, 110
Summerisle, Lord, 242, 243, 244
Sun Goddess and Moon Goddess (Bidston Hill), 173
Surrey, 72
Sussex, 74
Swansea Devil, The, 221
Swansea Museum, 221
Swift, Jonathan, 288
Swinside Stone Circle, 184

T

Tacitus, 233
Taplow Court, 65
Tate Britain, 94
Temple Church (London), 90
Temple of Mithras (London), 90
Temple of Theseus (Hagley Estate), 127
Tennant, Ann, 129, 130
Thomas the Rhymer, 248, 249
Thornton Abbey, 154
Thoth, 134
Tikinswood, 222
Tolkien, J.R.R., 45
Tomb of "Mad Jack", The, 75
Tomb of St Columba, 264
Tower of London, The, 84
Treadwell's Bookshop, 87
Tredegar House, 218
Tregeagle, Jan, 18
Tregeseal, 20
Trelleck, 219
Tremeirchion, 237
Trethevy Quoit, 17
Trewern Hall, 224
Tristan, 23
Tunstall, 117
Twmbarlwm, 216
Tyne And Wear, 206
Tyrone, 284

U

Uffington White Horse, The, 69
Uriel, 89

V

Valiente, Doreen, 74
Vaughan, Joan, 146
Vaughan, Thomas, 123
Venus, 64
Victoria And Albert Museum, 94
Vixana, 27
Vixen Tor, 27
Vortigern, 232